Is Paris Lost?

The English Occupation
1422–1436

IS PARIS LOST?

THE ENGLISH OCCUPATION
1422–1436

by

Raymond Reagan Butler

Is Paris lost? Is Rouen yielded up?
If Henry were recall'd to life again,
These news would cause him once more yield the ghost.

Shakespeare, *King Henry the Sixth, Part 1*, Act One, Scene 1

SPELLMOUNT
Staplehurst

British Library Cataloguing in Publication Data:
A catalogue record for this book is available
from the British Library

Copyright © Raymond Reagan Butler 2003
Map copyright © Spellmount Ltd 2003

ISBN 1-86227-215-8

First published in the UK in 2003 by
Spellmount Limited
The Old Rectory
Staplehurst
Kent TN12 0AZ

Tel: 01580 893730
Fax: 01580 893731
E-mail: enquiries@spellmount.com
Website: www.spellmount.com

1 3 5 7 9 8 6 4 2

The right of Raymond Reagan Butler to be identified
as the author of this work has been asserted by him
in accordance with the Copyright, Designs
and Patents Act 1988

Typeset in Palatino by MATS, Southend-on-Sea, Essex
Printed in Great Britain by
T.J.International Ltd
Padstow, Cornwall

Contents

For
David Prosser
'D.G.P.'
1921–2003

Acknowledgements

I am deeply indebted to the late Sir Anthony Glyn, for introducing me to the subject, and to Kenyon Lilley, for helping me to explore medieval Paris. Also on a personal note, I am grateful to Stephen Baum-Webber, Roberto Bellemare, Louis le Coz, Andrew Wilson-Jenner, David and Patricia Knowles and Julian Nixon. For their professional help and advice I am indebted to Charlotte Chipchase at the Royal Armouries, Tamsin Phoenix and Isabel Rambaut, and David Edge (armoury curator at the Wallace Collection). The staff of the Archives Nationales, Bibliothèque Nationale, the British Library and my local library in Leamington Spa have all been of great assistance. I perhaps owe my greatest debt to a man long dead, the anonymous 'Bourgeois de Paris', whose account of these times I have drawn upon heavily – so much so that any quotations not accounted for may fairly be assumed to be his. But above all, I would like to thank my editor, David Grant, not only for his expertise but also his great patience with a tyro historian.

A Note on Currency

The value of money changed very rapidly throughout the period covered by this book, so much so that it is difficult to assess the actual worth. There were two main denominations: the *livre tournois* and the *livre parisis*. The *tournois*, sometimes called the *franc*, was in commonest use. It was sub-divided into twenty *sous*, each *sou* being worth twelve *deniers*.

The *livre parisis* was a more expensive currency, 25% more than the *livre tournois*, and was the preferred coin of the royal treasury. It was little used outside the capital. Both coins, however, were hardly more than monetary gauges, as the government apportioned rates to them according to the prevailing circumstances.

From the point of view of the English visitor – whether soldier or civilian – the exchange rate was most often favourable. Although it often depended on the physical condition of the coins when they were handed over, or even on the disposition of the moneychanger on the day, the *livre tournois* was usually of a lower value than the pound sterling. In the early 1420s the exchange rate was approximately 6.6 *livres tournois* to the English pound.

Throughout, the abbreviations used are: l.t. = *livre tournois*/l.p. = *livre parisis*.

[Source: Doucet, R, 'L.t. et livre sterling pendant l'occupation anglaise sous Charles VI et Charles VII', *Revue numismatique*, 4th series, 1926]

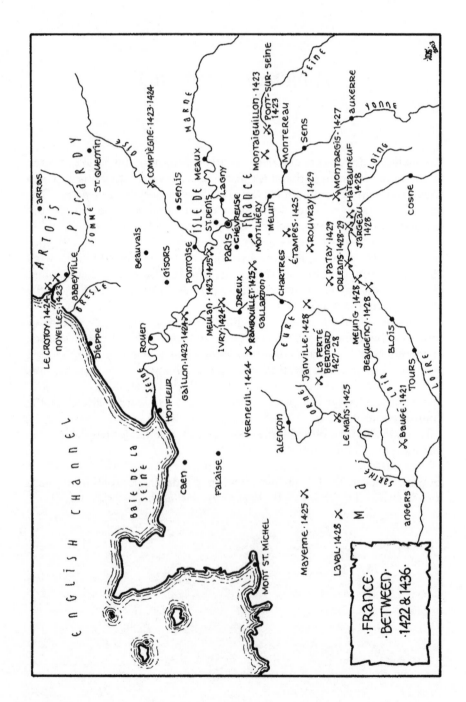

ENGLISH CHANNEL

ARTOIS · PICARDY · ISLE DE MEAUX · FRANCE

arras
ST. QUENTIN
SOMME
BRESLE
OISE
COMPIÈGNE · 1423·1424
SENLIS
MARNE
MONTAIGUILLON · 1423
PONT-SUR-SEINE 1423
MONTEREAU
SENS
SEINE
AUXERRE
YONNE

LE CROTOY · 1424
NOYELLES · 1423
ABBEVILLE
beauvais
GISORS
PONTOISE
ST. DENIS
LAGNY
PARIS
CHEVREUSE
MONTLHÉRY
MELUN
ÉTAMPES · 1425
ROUVRAY · 1429
MONTARGIS · 1427
CHÂTEAUNEUF 1428
JARGEAU 1428
LOING
COSNE

Dieppe
Rouen
SEINE
GAILLON · 1423·1424
MEULAN · 1423·1425
IVRY · 1424
DREUX
GALLARDON
RAMBOUILLET · 1425
CHARTRES
EURE
PATAY · 1429
ORLEANS · 1428-29
MEUNG · 1428
BEAUGENCY · 1428
BLOIS
LOIRE

HONFLEUR
BAIE DE LA SEINE
CAEN
FALAISE
VERNEUIL · 1424
ALENÇON
ORNE
JANVILLE · 1428
LA FERTÉ BERNARD 1427-28
Le MANS · 1425
LOIR
TOURS
BAUGÉ · 1421
SARTHE
ANGERS

MONT ST. MICHEL

MAYENNE · 1425

LAVAL · 1428

MAINE

·FRANCE·
·BETWEEN·
·1422 & 1436·

X

Prologue

At the beginning of the fifteenth century France was ripe for a fresh invasion by the English, since the country was already in a state of civil war. The royal houses of Orléans and Burgundy contended with each other, both vying for domination over the elderly King Charles VI, who had been mad for most of his long reign. Each party's strength was based on the feudal control of different regions in France, but their main objective was always to command the king and, through him, Paris. For it was thought that whoever held the capital controlled the kingdom. The two great houses had been at each other's throats for decades, and a relentless hatred existed between them. From 1407 the Count of Armagnac, who possessed the finest private army in France, had been intent on avenging the murder of his overlord, Prince Louis of Orléans, knifed by the bravoes of John the Fearless, Duke of Burgundy, and left to bleed to death in a Parisian gutter.[1] The Orléans' faction was renamed the 'Armagnacs' by the Parisians, referring to the lack of discipline shown by the troops.

The French, then, were split into two factions, ranged behind the Armagnac or the Burgundian 'cause'. But their dilemma was that both sides were equally matched, so that each prevailed in turn, and both parties were as pitiless as they were shameless, unstintingly robbing the kingdom and pillaging the countryside during their periods of dominance. Between them, they were strangling the Valois dynasty, and destroying the security of France, which could only come from clear leadership.

Into this political chaos King Henry V of England rode his newly trained army, intent upon conquest, although, at first, he seemed to present no great threat. Two years before he landed in France, in 1415, the Duke of Bourbon had marched into English-held Aquitaine, and had cut to pieces the Anglo–Gascon force at Soubise. Although this defeat was seen as a humiliation, it actually suited Henry, for he had long planned to make war upon France, and this gave him the excuse that he needed. He could now pose as the victim of French aggression, and he at once prepared for an invasion, to take by force what he believed to be his by right, the duchy of Normandy,[2] lost to England in 1204, conquered by Philippe-Auguste. After first forging an alliance with the Burgundians, who promised to remain neutral, the English set sail from England on 11 August 1415.

The port of Harfleur had fallen to Henry by the middle of September, and the battle of Agincourt was a stupendous victory against tremendous odds. Vastly outnumbered by a much better equipped army, it was a triumph for English ingenuity (and for their longbowmen), and it made Henry's reputation as a warrior king. After Agincourt came the successful sieges of Caen and Rouen, where once again superior English tactics overcame enormous odds. And once these vital cities were secured, the rest of Normandy could be absorbed. But to make the duchy secure from the east, it was also necessary to reduce the Île de France and to capture the greatest prize of all: Paris, the largest and most beautiful city in northern Europe.

But in 1418 Paris was in the hands of Henry's lukewarm allies, the Burgundians. For in that year an ironmonger's son had stolen the keys to a gate from his father, and had let in the besieging army of John the Fearless, Duke of Burgundy. John's Parisian partisans, led by a master-butcher and the Chief Hangman, then roamed the streets, slaughtering the citizens who remained loyal to the Armagnacs by the hundreds, until, after two months of carnage, Burgundy had ridden into the devastated city to claim it as his own.

He had arrived in the company of the French Queen Isabeau, his keenest supporter. Having quarrelled with her son, the dauphin Charles, she had then been held prisoner by him and his allies the Armagnacs, from which she had been rescued by Duke John. She was thereafter inseparable from his cause, reconciled with the murderer of Louis of Orléans, who had once been her lover. The duke and the queen were both ecstatically greeted by the Parisians, who firmly believed a Burgundian alliance to be always in their best interests.

Isabeau's husband, Charles VI, became Burgundy's puppet, and the dauphin Charles fled to his lands in the south, seized, it was said, by an Armagnac captain, to be used as a pawn. The dauphin's protector, Bertrand, Count of Armagnac, had been killed in the Burgundian massacre, his naked corpse left for three days in the streets, to be disfigured at will by his jubilant enemies. But much of his army still survived, now commanded by his son, who became the dauphin's major champion. From his 'capital' at Bourges, the dauphin proclaimed himself regent, in defiance of his mother, who also claimed that title. But the capture of Paris had been Burgundy's triumph.

Yet two months after the fall of Rouen, Henry V had extended his conquests as far as Mantes, and when his brother, the bellicose Duke of Clarence,[3] seized Pontoise, the English were almost at the gates of Paris.

Clarence, under Henry's instructions, at once withdrew in good order from beneath its walls, but this unexpected arrival of English troops on their boundaries threatened the security of dauphinist and Burgundian alike, and it could not go unchallenged. The leaders of both French camps saw that they must act together to expel the invader, and a treaty was quickly drawn up. Arrangements were then made for the dauphin and the Duke of Burgundy to meet to implement it, and to plan a concerted attack upon the English.

But, keen as both rivals were to cooperate with each other in this urgent matter, there was too much hatred between them for it ever to succeed. Mutual hatred almost overrode their fear of Henry. When they met, as arranged, on the fortified bridge at Monterau, south-east of Paris, the Duke of Burgundy and his attendants were hacked to death by Armagnac battle-axes. Prince Louis' death must be avenged, and so John the Fearless died with a great hole in his skull, and it was later said that 'the English entered Paris through this hole'.[4]

It was undeniably a colossal political error, for it threw John's heir, Philippe, into the arms of the English, allying the Burgundians more firmly than ever before in the new duke's desire to clear France of the Armagnac murderers. Along with the nominal leader of their party, the dauphin – who may or may not have been implicated in Duke John's death.

John the Fearless had been assassinated on the very day that the English troops withdrew from the walls of Paris, but the situation was changed in Henry's favour from that day on. His territorial demands – already considered exorbitant – greatly increased. Indeed, the only solution now acceptable to him was to be given the crown of France itself, for himself and his Lancastrian heirs, who would also be the heirs of King Charles VI of France, since Henry wished to marry his youngest daughter, Katherine of Valois.

To the astonishment and outrage of ordinary Frenchmen, these demands were taken seriously by the French establishment, and were gradually accepted. But how could they have been rejected? The English king had already proved that he would certainly take what he wanted when it was not freely given, and could anybody stop him from crushing the rest of France and seizing the crown? After the conquest of Normandy, he seemed irresistible. The Princess Katherine had already been pledged to him for some years, her marriage portion even then being enormous, including vast tracts of key territory, and with guaranteed full sovereignty over the lands he had already acquired, but King Henry now wanted *everything*. Nevertheless, the negotiations were complicated and it took over eight months for them to be brought into force, with the Treaty of Troyes.

A new alliance was signed between Burgundy and England on

Christmas Day 1419, whereby Duke Philippe would help the English king to gain the French crown. Then they would both combine to destroy the dauphin Charles, now branded as a murderer and unfit to be his father's heir. To save Philippe from the shame of seeming to depose his liege lord, Henry agreed that Charles VI should continue to reign while he lived. Meanwhile, Henry would bear the title of heir and regent of France.

Financial pressure was brought to bear upon the French queen, in order to bring her to repudiate her son. To do this, the notoriously extravagant Isabeau was deliberately kept short of money, while promises were also made to her that proved eventually as effective. During her arrest by the Armagnacs, she had been stripped of much of her wealth, for which she largely blamed her son Charles. On 17 January 1420, the queen issued letters patent, condemning his acts, and accepting the Anglo–Burgundian alliance.[5] At no time did she ever declare Charles to be a bastard, and therefore ineligible to inherit the crown. This was purely a fabrication of Henry's advisers, to strengthen his claim.

The only people to almost unanimously accept the new changes without raising objections were the Parisians, who were fiercely anti-Armagnac, and who saw the dauphin as their enemy's cat's-paw. (God knew they had suffered enough at the hands of the Armagnacs when Charles had been made Captain of Paris, at the age of 16.) By contrast, Henry V was seen as prudent, wise, and an upholder of justice.[6] After the death of John the Fearless, important men from Paris approached Henry at Gisors, asking him to protect the city. The king sent an embassy to treat with the governors of Paris.

Most persuasively, of course, Henry's army was already on their doorstep, able to cut off their supplies and wreck their trade at will. In fact, King Henry never relaxed his pressure upon the capital, regardless of truces. When, on 8 May, he marched off to Troyes, to set his seal to the new treaty, he made a point of conspicuously parading his troops in close fighting order beneath the walls of the capital. The citizens, massed upon the battlements, cheered until his army was out of sight.

On 21 May Henry walked down the nave of Troyes cathedral, together with Queen Isabeau. Ascending to the high altar, from where the terms of the treaty had been read to the assembled notables, Henry stamped it with the seal that had been used at the last great English triumph, the Treaty of Bretigny in 1360. On the same day, he was formally betrothed to the Princess Katherine. Twelve days of extravagant festivity was followed by a magnificent and colourful wedding, at which the only note of gloom was cast by Philippe of Burgundy, who remained in full mourning for his father.

But after only two days of honeymoon, Henry continued his campaigning Even though he was said to have been genuinely captivated by his beautiful young wife, he knew that he must clear the road to the capital. Although the three sieges of Sens, Monterau and Melun were turned into theatrical events, little more than expanded tournaments, despite the savagery of the fighting. Henry was out to impress the French court, who were taken along as spectators to his triumphs. 'Every day, at sunrise and sunset, eight or ten clarions, and divers other instruments, played most melodiously for an hour before the King of France's tent'.[7]

With the fall of Melun, which resisted strongly, and was severely punished for it, Henry had secured the southern approaches to Paris, and he could now make a ceremonial entrance into the city. He did so in the company of his father-in-law, along with that of his brothers and his finest generals. The two kings, riding side by side, made a dramatic contrast, with Henry at 33, in his magnificent prime, Charles, in his late 50s, barely able to sit astride his horse. Again, Philippe of Burgundy struck the only note of gloom. He followed with his knights, still clad in black. The crowds, lubricated by free-flowing wine, cheered lustily. Priests brought out relics for the two kings to kiss. Te Deums were sung in every church. For many Parisians this unique development seemed to herald the prospect of a real and lasting peace.[8]

On the next day, the two queens arrived, to an even more ecstatic ovation. But this show of mutual trust and solidarity – it was really only that, a show – was quickly brought to an end. Once Henry had manned all the main fortresses of Paris with English troops, and had made his warrior brother, the Duke of Clarence, governor of the city, the ceremonies were terminated and the three main factions parted company. While Henry and Katherine held magnificent court at the Louvre, and her parents retreated to the palace of St Pol, attended by only a few servants, Philippe returned to Burgundy to re-bury the exhumed body of his father in his capital of Dijon.

Henry himself did not stay long in Paris. After resplendent Christmas celebrations, and once he had reorganised the government to his satisfaction, he left for England, after an absence of three years. He took with him his queen and his brother the Duke of Bedford. In London, he received a tumultuous welcome, fittingly so, for he had returned home as the regent and heir to a kingdom three times more populous, and many times richer, than his own.

While Henry was in England, the dauphin's forces won a considerable victory at Baugé, just north of the Loire. The hotheaded Duke of Clarence, always eager to match his brother's prowess, had marched into battle without adequate preparation, and was ambushed by the enemy (although the 'French' forces ranged against him were made up principally of the dauphin's Scottish allies). The result had been a complete rout of Clarence's troops, and his own death, along with that of many of

Henry's best men. Even a successful raid in the summer of 1421 could not restore the loss of prestige that followed on this defeat.[9]

Henry landed at Calais, as soon as he could get away from England, with a well trained army of 4,000 men. But, for the first time since 1415, the English were on the defensive, the French having been greatly heartened by their triumph at Baugé. Within the next year Henry campaigned brilliantly, overturning the French successes one by one. He relieved Chartres, captured Dreux, and drove far enough into the dauphin's territory to raid beneath the walls of Orléans. Afterwards, he marched his troops to Meaux, whose garrison had been raiding Paris to the east. The siege of Meaux was one of Henry's finest military achievements; yet it was also the cause of his ultimate defeat, since it was before its walls that he contracted that scourge of medieval soldiering, the bloody flux.

By July 1422 he was contemplating a major battle with the Armagnacs, who were besieging Cosné, a Burgundian stronghold on the Upper Loire. The dauphin and Duke Philippe had already agreed a date for the battle, and Philippe had asked for help from Henry. Henry, astute as always, had offered not only his archers but also himself as leader, since he considered this to be his best chance yet of meeting the dauphin's army in open battle. But it came to nothing, as he was defeated by his own bodily weakness, even as he set out from Paris. He tried, as was his usual habit with his own troops, to lead the combined Anglo—Burgundian armies in person, but found that he could no longer sit upon a horse. Compromising for the first time in his career, he allowed himself to be carried in a litter. But even this proved to be too much, and he could get no farther than Corbeil, a few miles from the capital. Clearly failing, King Henry was taken to the grim fortress of Vincennes, on the eastern outskirts of the capital.[10]

It took him three weeks to die, yet he remained lucid up to the last few hours, and while on his deathbed he made calm and deliberate arrangements for the management of the two kingdoms, to be safeguarded for his heir, born on 5 December 1421. (The news of the Prince of Wales's birth at Windsor had reached Paris on the Monday before Christmas, when bonfires were lit 'as at St John's Tide'.) Henry at first offered the regency of France to the Duke of Burgundy, but Philippe – who was not present at the deathbed – declined the honour, and so it went to Henry's brother, John of Bedford.[11] All who gathered around the dying king were pledged to continue fighting until the whole of France had accepted the Treaty of Troyes.

Henry's funeral was one of the most magnificent royal processions the Parisians had ever seen, when he was carried in great state to the abbey of St Denis, where a service was held among the tombs of his son's French ancestors. The body was then taken to Rouen, where his widow joined the procession; and from there it was carried to London, to be interred with even greater magnificence in Westminster Abbey. The new regent,

Bedford, who was in charge of the proceedings, was determined that the French should long remember the funeral of Henry the Conqueror. Throughout the day bells tolled continuously, and relays of priests chanted the office of the dead, to create an overlapping service. The chief mourners were Bedford and the Scottish King James the First, then a prisoner of the English. Apart from the dead king's parents-in-law, then residing outside Paris, the other significant figure missing was that of Philippe of Burgundy, who had cannily managed to avoid visiting King Henry on his deathbed, to escape being further compromised. Bedford, in his eulogy, praised his brother as a hero 'too famous to live long'.

Henry's father-in-law, King Charles VI, *had* lived long, and was remarkable only for his madness. But on 30 October, less than two months later, he also died, quietly during the night, passing from life with more dignity than he had lived it.[12] It had been a long reign of forty-two years, and few Parisians could remember a time before his coming to the throne. In some curious way, he personified continuity for them. Even though he had been insane for most of his life, Charles VI had symbolised the *religious* guarantees of kingship.

King Charles lay for two days on his deathbed at the palace of St Pol. His face remained uncovered, to show the people that he had died of natural causes, and a cross stood at the foot of his bed. 'Arrangements proper for such a prince were made at St Pol,' a recorder stated, although there would be a considerable delay in the making of these arrangements. Nothing could be easily settled at such a turbulent time, and the postponement was due largely to the fact that his courtiers were waiting for some great lords of the French royal house to attend him to his entombment. But no such nobles arrived, and his body remained hidden away until 9 November.[13]

Bedford returned to Paris on 5 November, to attend the funeral. But no member of the Valois family was at Notre Dame cathedral for the service, nor when the king was laid to rest at the royal mausoleum of St Denis. '... a thing most piteous to see,' lamented Monstrelet.[14] His estranged son, the dauphin, was not expected, for he would not leave the security of his 'capital' at Bourges. Again, the one great prince who was present at the funeral was Bedford, now Regent of France.

But the ordinary people mourned King Charles sincerely, and many of those watching his funeral cortege did so with trepidation for the future. With both kings dead and the living monarch not yet a year old, it was feared that France would once again be plunged into even greater turmoil.

As with King Henry, a replica of Charles's body was carried above his coffin, but his remains were transported beneath a golden canopy. The small coffin was easily shouldered, but the effigy was so heavy it needed thirty men to carry it. The head was crowned with gold, and a royal sceptre was held in one hand. With the other, the effigy appeared to be offering a last blessing, an invocation those gathered on the streets felt was very necessary, for they had never felt so much in need of divine protection.

After the procession came the solitary figure of the Duke of Bedford, riding alone. He was a fleshy man, high-coloured, with a prominent nose and a well marked chin, very self-possessed, and with an imposing, regal air. Many of those who lined the funeral route recognised that he was now in command, although he was still a relatively unknown quantity, whose actions could be unpredictable.

After the king was laid to rest beside the tombs of his father and mother, a herald cried out that everyone present should pray for his departed soul, and afterwards proclaimed the king's infant grandchild, now the sixth Henry of England, and the second of France. The dead king's servants then turned their maces, staffs and swords upside down, 'as men who no longer hold office'.[15]

The Duke of Bedford realised that few people in the crowds that lined the streets knew who he was. Almost as though he intended to impress his authority upon them from the first, the new regent ordered the late king's sword to be carried unsheathed before him on the way back into the city. This act was perceived as an act of great presumption, for a monarch's naked sword was an emblem of kingly authority, and the onlookers were aghast at this blatant display of assumed sovereignty, although the English duke was already king in all but name, and if his nephew were to die in infancy he would be king in fact.

But the Parisians recognised that, unpalatable though it might be to be ruled by the ancient enemy, this was the best solution for them at a perilous time. They had few friends, and had made many enemies among their countrymen. When the regent rode back into their city with the naked sword carried before him, the English domination of the capital could be said to have commenced in earnest, and a majority of citizens approved of it . . . for the time being. It also seemed significant to many, and even a sign of hope for the future, that the city had been occupied for the first time in its long history without a battle being fought, or a siege raised.

NOTES

1   Autrand, *Charles VII*.
2   Allmand, *English Suits*.
3   Thomas, Duke of Clarence (1387–1421), second son of Henry IV.
4   Newhall, *The English Conquest of Normandy*.
5   Lucie-Smith, *Joan of Arc*.
6   Rymer, *Feodora*.
7   Hutchinson, *Henry V*.

8   Bourgeois de Paris, *Journal*. The Bourgeois was an anonymous chronicler of the period, possibly a minor canon at Notre Dame cathedral.

9   Ibid.

10   The keep of the 14th-century castle is still standing, sombre and magnificent in what is now a suburb, five miles to the east of central Paris.

11   It is unlikely that Bedford's assumption of the regency displeased Philippe. He seems, rather, to have been relieved not to undertake these duties. Bedford, though, was also initially reluctant to assume the role. Rowe, *The Grand Conseil*.

12   Juvenal des Ursins, *Histoire de Charles VII*.

13   Ibid.

14   Enguerrand Monstrelet, a Burgundian 'eye-witness', who published his version of events in his *Chronique* in the early 15th century.

15   Bourgeois de Paris.

CHAPTER I

1422: The Dual Monarchy

Despite being the second choice, the Duke of Bedford was nevertheless superbly qualified for the office of regent, certainly more so than the immature Philippe of Burgundy. Although less brilliant in the arts of war than his brother, Bedford had already shown great administrative qualities, being politically clear sighted and a natural diplomat. Even his French enemies acknowledged his high intelligence, and considered him possessed of a certain '*équité*'. He would always seek conciliation while remaining in resolute pursuit of total mastery.

Throughout the English conquest of northern France, he had proved himself to be both brave and prudent as a soldier. For example, he had easily outfoxed the blockading French at the battle of the Seine, and he had quickly relieved the town of Harfleur in 1416. During what passed for peace in the France of the English conquest, he would go on to show himself to be a more enlightened ruler than those who had preceded him.

But all the same, the Duke of Bedford understood that he had no easy task ahead of him, for he knew the power of King Henry's magnetic appeal to his troops. He had seen how English fortunes ebbed away during Henry's departure for England, and how his absence had improved the morale of the dauphin's war party. The new regent's prospects of success could not be considered hopeful, particularly since orders could no longer be issued to the French in the name of a recognised king, but only in the name of an uncrowned infant.

And the child-king's position in Paris was immediately shown to be insecure, for a plot was almost immediately discovered to hand the city over to the dauphin. Even more serious than the plot itself, perhaps, was the identity of some of those involved in it, since they were men at the highest level of government. Chief among them was Michel de Laillier, Master of the King's Counting House, a man in whom King Charles VI had always shown complete confidence.[1] De Lailler has been described as the sort of man who will survive any political regime, but in this instance he found safety in temporary flight, although a number of his fellow plotters were arrested. The ringleaders were beheaded, while the lesser conspirators were immediately banished. But even though the plot

1

proved a failure, it drew attention to the precarious position of the inadequate English garrison in Paris.

Yet in October 1422 it seemed that there would be no viable alternative to the infant king, for there was a rumour in Paris that the dauphin had fallen to his death in La Rochelle, his only port and his sole outlet to the sea. As he held an assembly in the great hall of the bishop's palace, a floor had collapsed under the weight of the many people who clamoured to attend, with most of them injured; the dauphin among them, it was said.

But, fortunately, Charles had been seated at the farther end of the room, under the protection of an arcade, and although he had fallen, he done so less heavily than his courtiers, being little more than badly bruised. Greatly shaken by this episode, he attributed his escape to a miraculous intervention, seeing it as an omen that God would ultimately favour his cause. Yet the rumour of the dauphin's death persisted among the Parisians for some weeks, and many people remained uncertain of his fate until the following March.[2]

With the Treaty of Troyes, France had received a written constitution, and – under the treaty – the French *parlement* was authorised as the single Supreme Court for the dual monarchy. The bailliffs and other officials of the court, who had traditionally only taken an oath to the *parlement* before assuming office, now also swore to the 'Treaty of the Peace', as it came to be known. 'To keep and enforce by punishment the peace between the two kingdoms of France and England.'

After the old king's death, as if to celebrate the beginning of the dual monarchy, *parlement* began to open the yearly session soon after Martinmas. Presiding at this first assembly, on 19 November, taking advantage of the uncertainty surrounding the untrue report of the dauphin's death, the regent caused the chancellor to deliver an address on the irrefutable right of Henry VI to the throne of his maternal grandfather. This was a show of great daring, for at this same session the patents were registered that styled the Duke of Bedford as the *de facto* ruler of France.

This was carried through before an exceptional assembly that included virtually all the heads of official society in Paris, and most of the senior courtiers of the late king. At this session, the new regent seated himself in the chair of the first President of the new *parlement*, while the chancellor addressed the gathering in his name, Bedford's spoken French apparently not being up to the demands of the occasion.

At this sitting, in a bid to gain their compliance, the regent appeared to go against the dying wishes of his brother by promising that the duchy of Normandy, now held – if somewhat piecemeal – by the English, should be once again united to the crown of France. His reasoning presumably being that since Normandy was now English in all but name, to unite it with greater France might help to make the anglicisation of the as yet unconquered territories easier.

Having won the members of the *parlement* to his side, Bedford then requested that they take an oath of fidelity to the infant king, in which most members complied. As, however disorderly the times, the *parlement* of Paris was the supreme law court of France, staffed by lawyers from all over the country, it was therefore considered to represent the entire kingdom. By asking this hugely disparate group to take the oath, and by his unqualified success, Bedford seemingly performed the miracle of making the greatest state institution in France recognise an Englishman as regent and a half-English child as their king. (Though it was equally possible that this 'forced' oath was, in fact, a precondition the members themselves insisted upon, in order to protect themselves against future reprisals should the Armagnacs regain Paris.)

There were some dissenters, but to say that even they were chafing under a sense of humiliation at this turn of events would be untrue. They were Parisians, after all, and used to making compromises. Many of them were, in fact, willing to compromise with the enemy – which meant *any* enemy. The wealthy burgesses, with much to lose by any continuation of hostilities within the city, were only too pleased that peace had been restored. The merchants were equally delighted to once more trade freely with London.[3]

After all, the infant Henry *was* the son of the marriage that had united England and France, or at least the houses of Lancaster and Valois. Moreover, the church had blessed the union, the crowds had cheered the happy pair, and the *parlement* itself had ratified the treaty. But the most potent argument in favour of this union was that, for over three centuries, the bloodline of the English sovereigns had been more intermixed with that of the French royal house than of any other dynasty in Europe. And was not the child – through *both* his parents – a direct descendant of St Louis, the most revered of all French kings?[4]

The French *parlement*, then, smoothed rather than hindered the succession of the House of Lancaster, but not all of France was in Lancastrian hands, and that fact was always present in the minds of the Parisians. The English ruled only from the Channel to the Loire, and in Guyenne, and their capital cities had always been Rouen and Bordeaux. Yet now that Paris had been added to their suzerainty, the citizens expected to be treated with the same impartiality that these favourite cities had come to enjoy from their English masters. It was, at least, to be hoped for.

Parisians knew that, while governing Bordeaux and Rouen, the English had always been prepared to take a fairly indulgent line with the French governing powers in the lands that bordered theirs, and most Parisians believed their rule in the true capital would be as tolerant. But, even so, a sizeable proportion of the citizens still preferred to recognise only the suzerainty of the young Duke of Burgundy. They accepted the presence of the English reluctantly, and then only because Philippe was their ally and in some way dependent upon the English, though he remained autonomous in his own domain – which also included Flanders, Artois and Champagne, countries that were a permanent threat to their own stability. As both parts of the divided Burgundian dominions straddled the border between France and the Holy Roman Empire, and as Burgundian influence extended to within thirty-five miles of Paris, the citizens were always impressed by the strength of Philippe's military clout. (Philippe had made great acquisitions both through marriage and inheritance, and he would go on to acquire more land throughout the 1420s and early 30s. He was known throughout Europe and beyond as: 'The Great Duke of the Occident, Duke by the Grace of God', and his court was famous for its luxury and refinement).

Outside this union, there was a third force, Brittany, which hesitated between a firm union with the Valois and the Armagnacs, or else with the Lancastrian rulers and the Burgundians. Jean, Duke of Brittany (1389–1442) was praised for the 'prudence and sapience' with which he played the political game, but with hindsight it can be seen that he was simply unsure of his moves, placed as he was between such dangerous partners. The Bretons, therefore, oscillated wildly between the two main choices and, while they were not a direct threat to the people of Paris, should they choose to side with the dauphin, their added strength could swing the outcome in the Valois' favour.

Only central and southern France, a fourth fragment of the kingdom, remained entirely loyal to the dead king's son, yet it was by no means the smallest portion, for its lands stretched from the Loire to the Mediterranean, and within it were contained many rich provinces. There were, too, a number of individual defensible areas that still held out against the English *within* the conquered territory – the conical, rocky islet of Mont St Michel being the major instance. Of this mutilated France, the city of Orléans was the real centre, though the administrative capital was Bourges, in which the dauphin's chancellery and the treasury was situated. The judiciary was at Poitiers, to where the dauphin's government had moved.

All this fourth realm lacked was a king; it had only an heir apparent, the dauphin, the eleventh child of King Charles, himself called Charles, a timid, shifty young man, who was in any case commonly supposed to be a bastard, the son of his uncle, Louis of Orléans. Prince Charles himself was far from certain of his legitimacy, and even he questioned his rightful claim to the throne. But it is significant that the English and Burgundians continued to call him 'dauphin' after his father's death, an illogical title in view of the fact that he was not regarded as such by a considerable portion of the population in the Anglo–Burgundian part of France.

With the English, of course, the use of the style was a matter of derision, but many in his domains continued to regard him as a 'prince-in-waiting', since he was an unconfirmed king. Even those who were nearest to him often treated him with disdain, and Charles could never wholly rely upon his courtiers and functionaries, and his commands were often disobeyed and frequently ignored. His unhappy kingdom was insecurely founded, for the men by whom he was surrounded lacked any discipline, and intrigue thrived in his shabby court. He himself, feeling powerless to change his status, alternated between deep depression and a manic gaiety.[5]

The dauphin's one piece of luck was that he symbolised resistance to the foreigner, for an occupying power, however benign, can never be truly tolerated. The French might have accepted a Lancastrian king, in name at least, but they found it hard to put up with his English garrisons, even though most of them were reduced to skeletal proportions. They also disliked the English attempts at taxing them in order to finance their further campaigns, believing such money should be raised in England, and they grumbled at the necessary English requisitions. Hundreds of peasants refused to collaborate, and islands of resistance were formed in Normandy, the Île-de-France and Champagne. Legitimate or not, unsuitable or not, the dauphin was a passable symbol of opposition to the invader for the more patriotic French.

Yet the dauphin quickly proved himself to be a positive asset for the English, in that he remained generally inert. After receiving the news of his father's death (at which it was said that he 'wept abundantly') he did not assume the title of king until a week had passed. Having worn mourning for only one day, as was the custom with the new King of France, for the state of monarchy continued and he embodied that condition, he took no further steps to make good his title. More importantly, he remained uncrowned, and was still to be anointed with the holy oil that alone could consecrate his rule. Charles, cut off from Rheims, the 'coronation' city, made no arrangements for his crowning, and so many of his own courtiers continued to call him the dauphin.

The other asset the English possessed, of course, was the Duke of Bedford. It was soon clear to all that there was no better person to carry on the task left unfinished by the late King Henry. Lacking his brother's harshness (and his religious fanaticism), John of Bedford possessed to the full King Henry's flair for diplomacy and his strong sense of justice. To these qualities he added a sincere desire to establish enlightened government in France, and a strict fidelity to the terms of the Treaty of Troyes.

On 1 December 1422, only a few weeks after being recognised as regent, the Duke of Bedford was appointed to a presidency of the French *parlement*, there being no election to the court itself. He, in turn, appointed Simon Morhier as the Provost Marshal of Paris during this first visit to the capital as regent, and this was one of his shrewdest decisions, since at that time the English had no real concept of the role the provost marshal should play. (These officers were normally designated and removed by the king. They were entrusted with representing him in the viscounty of Paris, and they had both judicial and fiscal powers. Initially, the provostship had been let out for tender, but Louis IX had given it to a royal officer, who was then paid by the state.)

In his person Morhier fully embodied both the military and judicial sides of the position, and Bedford recognised his unique talents. A member of an ancient family, a true 'noble of the sword', he was also connected to the ranks of the high judiciary, for Morhier had married the daughter of an influential president. He had been Queen Isabeau's chief steward, was both efficient and ruthless, and enthusiastic for the cause of Henry VI. He was highly regarded by both the Parisians and the English, and much respected as a soldier. The post of provost marshal was still used to provide a focus for military control at sensitive times, and the provost was a recognised fighting man. He was also straightforward and uncomplicated. When challenged over his demands for money, levied on the personnel of the Châtelet prison, he bluntly reminded parliament that war made demands on his purse, and that he had to maintain a larger household than in peacetime.

If the military functions of the provost were restored from 1422 onwards and became his most important concern, this was not to be at the expense of his judicial role, although this could not be regarded lightly. The grim fortress of the Châtelet, from which he governed, was the forum for many complex legal cases, and the provost marshal was always the final adjudicator, although he was not expected to rule on every dispute in person. In fact he could not make a judicial ruling without the aid of his legal experts, who were at his side in order to back up an opinion. But this arrangement left him with more time for his military duties.

However, it has to be said that the provost marshal's first effort as the leader of the 'greater number of the people of Paris', the attempt to recapture Compiègne, was a failure. But subsequent undertakings would prove more successful, and during his years in office he would bring considerable ability to the running of the capital.[6]

Bedford was also particularly successful in winning over the leading members of the pro-Burgundians in the capital, to whom he cunningly entrusted those reins of government that did not actually control the horse of state. In a shrewd stroke of diplomacy, he had even appointed an old opponent at the siege of Rouen, Guy de Bouteille, as captain of the city. It would prove to be the rule rather than the exception that the regent could usually rely upon a strong contingent of Franco–Burgundian volunteers, who would prove a useful reinforcement when the army of occupation was at times depleted. He could also generally rely upon the guardians of the University of Paris, whose senior members were always ready to play an active part in events that took place far from the city.

The university quarter had developed in the second half of the twelfth century, when the students – to avoid the detested tutelege of the Bishop of Paris – abandoned the school at Notre Dame, left the Île de la Cité, and settled on Mont Sainte Geneviève. It was still a large and turbulent community, fiercely protective of its own practices, which included the preservation of the dog Latin that was the university's official language, hence the designation of the area as the 'Latin Quarter'. But by the early fifteenth century the university's reputation was international, and it was generally seen as the greatest institute of theology in the western world. Despite the losses from rioting that occurred when the Burgundians invaded the city in 1418, along with the departure of several of its most eminent figures to create a daughter university in the provinces, it remained a cosmopolitan establishment. Even under the English, always keen to promote Parisian interests above those of outsiders, those students born in the capital made up only a small minority of the scholars.

But there was still – and would always be – opposition to the English presence in Paris. About Christmas time in 1422 some of the burghers plotted to deliver the city up to the dauphin. To this end their chief man tried to persuade the regent to mount an attack against some of Charles's party, who were – he alleged – raiding in the neighbourhood and harassing innocent people. Their plan was for an armed group to rise up and take the city while the duke and his men were out of Paris, in pursuit of this imaginary force. But Bedford, already suspicious of the ringleader, had secret inquiries made and the plot was very soon uncovered. As a result, some of the conspirators were beheaded, and a woman was burned. In his punishment of offenders, the regent was often excessive, although he was by nature extremely humane for the age, and he was never wantonly cruel.

Towards the end of 1422 Jean, Bastard of Thian, was ordered to guard Paris, in the company of Guy Le Bautellier. They took up a position in St Germain-en-Laye, a town some twelve miles from the capital, even though such a site for defensive action was unusual in being so far removed from the city itself. A nearer locality, at which they established a military post, was in the major suburb of St Marcel, although even this area was practically a separate town, proud of its independence and already partly fortified.

Yet, in fact, Paris was more vulnerable to invasion by deception rather than to any direct assault.[7] The walls of Paris, south of the Seine, had been built by Philippe-Auguste in the twelfth and thirteenth centuries, and were some 30 feet high. The city's northern walls were erected in 1356 and were known as the walls of Charles V. They covered a much larger area, and were described as 'very high and strong, with great towers'. Beyond these walls were two moats, the inner one filled with water, the outer deep but dry. The greatest weakness was where the walls met the river, especially on the right bank. It was claimed in the very hot summer of 1422 that, were it not for a small ditch running from the walls to the river, one could walk into the city without getting one's feet wet, and some walls could be easily climbed in some places.

In the first three months of his rule the Duke of Bedford did wonders in replacing his dead brother. True, there was a swing in the military fortunes of the English, but this was entirely to be expected, and Bedford would shortly demonstrate his own abilities as the commander-in-chief. But since, in the eyes of his new 'subjects', he lacked the high position and enormous prestige of Henry V or the consummate martial reputation of his other dead brother, Thomas of Clarence, he had first to establish himself as the logical leader.

His main problem from the outset was that his English troops were spread out over an enormous area, and they were miserably lacking in numbers. Bedford had probably fewer than 15,000 men prepared for combat at any one time. Because of this general weakness, the regent saw clearly that his task could only be accomplished if the Burgundian alliance was kept up, and he did everything in his power to keep Duke Philippe in his camp. (His brother Henry, in his dying hours, had impressed this point upon him.)

Yet the Anglo–Burgundian connection had always been under strain, and Philippe the Good quickly revealed that he possessed much of his father's troublesome lack of loyalty. He had already shown by his irrational behaviour at the battle of Cosné that his conduct was not to be relied on. The town had been due to surrender and the day fixed for a battle, but the dauphin had again fought shy of matching up to his enemies and had retreated towards Bourges, leaving only a few patrols on the other side of the river to defend his flight. Yet with the town wide open to attack from the combined Anglo–Burgundian forces, and with the possibility of then pursuing the fleeing Armagnacs, Philippe had taken the extraordinary decision to fall back on Troyes, and to disband his army.

Clearly, his heart was not in the struggle, and it would require all Bedford's tact and patience to keep the Burgundians on his side. Fortunately, he was not lacking in experienced generals – chief among them being the Earls of Salisbury and Warwick – with Salisbury recognised as a leader of genius. Bedford's army, too, although lacking in numbers, had been built up by King Henry V on the strong foundation of discipline and religious fervour, with patriotism and religion being intertwined in the manner peculiar to the English. Indeed, it was the most disciplined army of any in Europe, and even the king's death had not impaired its morale.

8

But such military operations as took place were sporadic in nature. They consisted, for the most part, of sudden raids by one side or the other, followed by the sieges of castles, their capture and recapture. All Bedford could do, initially, was attempt to keep up the military situation as he found it before proceeding to further advances, all the time following his brother's strategies. For some months after the accession of Henry VI, the situation in France may be said to have been in stasis, with both sides being disinclined for movement. Even so, at the beginning of 1423 the prospects were not bright.

The Paris Mint struck a series of coinage in early November 1422, which departed in design from any used before. Up to this time the English had followed the Valois pattern in the coins they circulated in the territories they conquered, but the new issue was quite original in concept (even if it closely resembled the coins created to celebrate the union of Flanders and Burgundy in 1378). There were four new coins: silver *blancs* and *demi-blancs*, gold *salutes* and *angelots*. Common to all of them were the shields of the arms of England and France. But the traditional position of the Annunciation was reversed in the *salutes*, so that the Angel Gabriel, protected by the arms of England, appeared to be announcing the coming of a Saviour – who was, of course, the infant Henry VI. Much would be made of Henry's birth, so close to the Nativity.

On 12 December, shortly after the acceptance of young Henry's claim to the French throne, a local election was held in the capital, which was generally considered to have been held under political pressure, although there is no proof of this.

It was by now the custom to appoint the town provost and his aldermen at the 'Pillared House' in the Place de Grève (the forerunner of the present day Hôtel de Ville). Only the bourgeoisie, however small their influence might be, could elect the officials, and they were sent for in stages to attend. The Place de Grève (the 'Strand') was an open space by the river, sloping gently down to the Seine, from where boats were loaded.

The appointments were traditionally made by 'acclamation', but in 1422 three of the aldermen were elected by a secret ballot in the house of the chancellor, Jean de Clerk, disregarding the age-old practice. And although there was an appointment four days later of a fourth councillor, Jean de la Poterne, at the Pillared House, by the nomination of former officers, this process was also considered to be highly irregular. There was no evidence to suggest that any of these appointees were in any way tied to the English cause, and thereby forced upon the municipality, but the elected men *were* extremely pro-Burgundian. (Jean de Belloy's father had been executed in 1416 for plotting against the Armagnacs, and he himself was in the service of John the Fearless from 1413 to 1418. Jean de la Poterne was from a well-established family of goldsmiths, and his brother was a royal secretary.) Nor was the man in control of the proceedings ever shown to be an active supporter of the Lancastrian regime, despite the fact that three of the men were elected under his roof.

The true motive for these 'private' elections, it would seem, was not so much to impose unwelcome civil servants upon the public, but to avoid a major gathering of the citizens in the Place de Grève. This busy square was the centre of Parisian life, where most official festivities, the annual St John's bonfire, and the more spectacular executions took place.[8] As such, it was a notorious 'flash-point' for insurrection, and as the elections were held at a particularly sensitive time, when the dual monarchy was only a few weeks old, it was regarded as a doubly dangerous area for such a public manifestation. After the riots of 1418, all popular assemblies had been banned, this measure being aimed in particular at the 'people of small estate', but any large gathering of the principal inhabitants would have been regarded with alarm by the new authorities.[9]

NOTES

1 *Cambridge Economic History.*
2 Bourgeois de Paris.
3 The Parisian ambassadors to Henry V at Gisors had extracted a promise from him that he would uphold the rights and privileges of the city. Rymer, *Feodora.*
4 The official view of young Henry's right to the crown of France was expressed in a poem of 1423, written at Bedford's command, and which accompanied a pictorial family tree, showing Henry's descent in the 8th degree from King (St) Louis IX (1214–70) through both parents. On the paternal side he was a direct descendant of King Philippe IV (1268–1314), and on his mother's side he was descended from a nephew of the same king. In this pedigree, his uncle – the so-called dauphin – was shown to have no right to the throne, and other members of St Louis' family with a claim on the throne were similarly ignored. The poem and the picture were hung together in a prominent place in Notre Dame Cathedral. Rowe, *The Grand Conseil.*
5 Chastellain, *Oeuvres.*
6 He was provost until 1436.
7 de Metz, *Description de Paris.*
8 The midsummer bonfire was an important festival, and important people often lit the fire with great ceremony.
9 Even the simplest and most innocuous meeting was subject to such scrutiny. For example, the election of new church wardens at St Merri required the presence of a sergeant from the Châtelet. *Archives Nationales.*

CHAPTER II
1423: The Transfer of Power

On 5 January, the eve of Epiphany 1423, the Duke of Burgundy arrived in Paris, bringing with him many soldiers who did a great deal of casual harm to the villages around the capital, with much vindictive plundering. It was said that they left nothing portable behind them, except the goods that were too heavy to carry. To make matters worse, Armagnac bandits were operating on the south side of Paris, beyond the Porte St Jacques, St Germain and Bordelles, as far south as Orléans. They did 'as much harm as ever the tyrant Saracens did'.

The Duke of Burgundy did little that was good for the citizens during his stay in Paris, a city 'that loved him well', and which had suffered so much in his father's cause.[1] Philippe maintained contact with certain people in Paris, and he almost certainly nurtured his own spies there, but he always tried to distance himself from the capital as much as he could, reluctant to become too closely associated with the Lancastrian cause. His failure to ever act directly in the Parisian interest, though, was not because the duke bore them any ill will, but simply because he was a 'dilatory, negligent man'. It was said that he 'took three years to do what could have been done in three months'. He was also said to lead a 'damnable life', being ruled entirely by stupid and arrogant young knights with whom he surrounded himself. 'None of them cared for anything but having their own way.'

It was about the time of Philippe's arrival that the Provost of Merchants, Le Verrat, was dismissed by the Duke of Bedford, to be replaced by de Champluisant, the former Bailiff of Vermandois. This had considerable impact upon the running of the city, since de Champluisant was known to be a creature of the English, whereas Le Verrat had been a more independent overseer, and consequently more to the liking of the citizens, who always wanted a greater degree of self-determination. For Paris was unusual among the chief cities of northern Europe in that it had never acquired an independent executive of its own, and it had never had a charter of customs and privilege. The power of the crown seems to have stifled other growth, and this power was personified in the dignity of the provost marshal, who was the head of the 'city police', and sometimes of the local militia.

The Provost Marshal of Paris was not to be confused with the Provost of Merchants (or 'town provost') who, along with four aldermen, constituted the municipality of Paris insofar as it had one. The aldermen, or *échevins*, were also called 'jurors of merchandise' or 'jurors to the fraternity of merchants'. Elected for a period of two years, they managed the commercial life of the city from the town hall, which adjoined the bustling Place de Grève. This square was one of the two major trading areas of the capital, the other being the Porte de l'École-St-Germain, both situated by the two main bridges of Paris. The first was at the Pont au Change, and the second at the Pont aux Marchands.

The office of Provost of Merchants had originated as the head of the Watermen's Corporation. The tradesmen he represented had originally been 'river merchants' who had formed a rudimentary sort of union, to protect their own trading on the Seine and, as far as possible, to discourage that of every other town along the river. They had been given the right to confiscate the goods of traders who infringed their rules, and they and the crown shared the proceeds from these seizures. Over the decades, with the aid of Italian bankers, the provost and his 'corporation' had helped to develop the luxury industries for which Paris was to become famed throughout Europe, and it was from this corporation that such local government as Paris enjoyed had grown, but only in order to deal with the rules of trading and to settle the disputes of the business classes.

The municipal authorities had so far never achieved real political power, as had their equivalents in London, for example. Indeed, the disturbances in the minority of Charles VI, and the uprising of 1380, had resulted in the municipality being abolished and the city coming under the direct administration of the King's Provost Marshal. After the Duke of Orléans was killed in 1407, the Parisians had taken advantage of the confusion that ensued to have their negligible rights restored, and these were returned to them in January 1412. But the butcher's faction, led by Simon Caboche, a flayer at the slaughterhouse, then dominated the city for the Burgundians, and Caboche had installed a reign of terror that lasted from April to July 1413. Supported by the moderate bourgeoisie, the Armagnacs had later regained control of the city; but they, too, had alienated the population, who happily welcomed the Burgundians back in 1418.

Having learned their lesson, then, the corporation generally left national politics well alone, and Le Verrat may have been dismissed for making the mistake of trying to interfere too strongly in matters the authorities felt were not the concern of civilians. Under the new provost, the corporation concentrated purely on commerce and finance, where their influence was considerable, since their jurisdiction included the assessment and collection of local taxes, and all matters of trade – weights, measures, the sale of wine and firewood, and the control of prices and quality. They were also responsible for the upkeep of roads, bridges, hospitals without a religious foundation, and river matters such as wrecks.

They were not entirely without power though, for they had certain rights of arrest and their own sergeants to carry them out, though they sometimes used the royal officers for that purpose. The arrested were tried by the corporation's own judicial process, for it had its own court of law, and from which appeal lay to the Provost Marshal of Paris, and from him to the *parlement*. But the importance of the municipal establishment waned when royal power increased, and this power, as represented by the new English authorities, would be very strong under the Duke of Bedford, although he allowed the Parisians a level of autonomy in most matters.

With the death of the two kings, the Paris municipality established limited links with their compeers in England. The corporation took the step of writing a formal letter to their counterparts on the Corporation of the City of London, in which they stated that the Parisians were ready to show their allegiance to King Henry VI. Expressing their own belief in the dual monarchy, and of the benefits that could be derived from Anglo–French rule, they asked the Lord Mayor of London and his councillors to maintain their efforts for the recovery of the whole of France, adding incongruously that they in turn would grant similar aid to the Londoners if the positions should ever be reversed!

At about the same time that the municipality was making contact with their equals in London, the authorities of the university tried to initiate a relationship at a higher level, with no less a figure than Duke Humphrey of Gloucester, the king's Protector, a man of the highest culture.[2] Gloucester, a patron of the arts and letters, and a man of the greatest 'affability', took up their offer willingly, and French envoys were soon invited to England. They stayed in the residence of the Bishop of Bath from 21 January to 9 March.

It is doubtful that the average Parisian either had much interest, or took much part, in these representations, and encouragement largely came from the royal council, who had an obvious interest in the general questions of strategy that were raised by both these delegations. At the beginning of the dual monarchy, it is safe to assume that the role of the average Parisian was at best described as 'passively antagonistic'. It is certainly true that if the citizens did originally encourage the sending of representatives to England, they soon abandoned this policy. It was left solely to the royal council to maintain contact with England, or more specifically London. Similarly, there was no sign that the authorities in England wished to interfere in the administration of France, and particularly in that of Paris. Even the sending of an Englishman to serve on the royal council in Paris was a rare event. Separate masters ruled each country, despite being joined together in the name of the infant king.

*

13

By a bold stroke Meulan had been surprised and taken by the enemy, and the regent ordered a siege to be laid to it in January 1423. The ever-victorious Earl of Salisbury was sent to retake it.[3]

More seriously, and damagingly, Sir John de la Pole carried out a raid into Anjou, up to the gates of Angers, with a small force of about 1,600 men. But a superior French battalion, led by the Sire Aumale, cut in behind him, waylaying him near Laval on his homeward journey; the English force was cut up and its commander deservedly made prisoner. (He had been instructed to take a force to reduce the formidable fortress of Mont St Michel, orders he had inexplicably disregarded.)

Up to this point, Bedford had been pursuing a largely defensive policy for which he was forced to ask for 50,000 pounds *tours* from the Norman estates at Vernon (as well as for the clerical tenth) to be used for paying the army engaged in counteracting aggression against Norman frontiers. Now, in February 1423, he was drawing upon the French receipts to pay the force besieging Meulan, and another battle had been fixed for 24 February, which the English were anxious to fight. For a Scottish contingent was to take part in this, led by the Earl of Buchan, who had been made Constable of France after the defeat of the English at Baugé, and Bedford's men were keen to avenge the death of so many of their best soldiers.[4]

Bedford also attempted to tax the French clergy, always a popular move among the less devout, but a source of great contention among the pious; though whatever their religious persuasion, all Frenchmen were allied in their horror of taxes. But in late February, when every Parisian was asked to take a personal oath to be loyal to the regent, excess taxation seemed a small matter, for the imposition of the oath was a radical move that aroused strong protest. Burgesses and peasants alike were asked to 'obey him in all things and in all places' and were pledged to do all they could to harass Charles, who 'called himself the King of France'. The requirement provoked a broad range of reactions, with some being glad to do this, but as many being reluctant, and these pledged themselves with great ill will. Among them, indeed, were those who saw Bedford and his associates, and not the hapless dauphin, as their chief enemy.

Many, of course, like the 'Bourgeois of Paris' realised that it was in their best interests to ally themselves with the English, and some Parisians grudgingly agreed that they were quickly proving to be the most even-handed of their occupiers. The Bourgeois came to the conclusion that if you were to be captured and ransomed, it was better to be taken by the English than by anyone else. Yet he still saw them as a mean and warlike people, doing little for the general good of Paris, and spending their money grudgingly, whether publicly or privately. They had also, of course, 'highly uncivilised notions about catering'.

Some Parisians made their objections felt to the regent's demand for a sacred oath by expressing their defiance in singular ways. Clément de

Fauquembergue, the registrar of the *parlement*, although having taken the oath, pointedly omitted the name of the monarch and the regnal year at the head of his annual records. He normally also included a phrase adapted from the Book of Ecclesiastes: 'he that diggeth a pit shall fall into it' and 'whoso breaketh an hedge, a serpent shall bite him'. This rebuke implying that it was through their own fault that the French now had foreign rulers.

French forbearance of the English presence in Paris, of course, was in some ways always conditional upon the occupiers upholding standards of behaviour, at both a high and a low level. But there were inevitable lapses, and the soldiery at times behaved with the arrogance of conquerors rather than the comradeship of allies. Many officers insolently disregarded the rights of even the most highly placed French citizens, but the common soldiers often treated them with equal disdain. There were a number of belligerent incidents, and many of them were senseless.

Once, for example, a group of soldiers – after being given a free crossing by a friendly ferryman – then threw one of the barrels he was transporting into the Seine, 'out of devilment'. On another occasion a group of soldiers forcibly confiscated wood from some river traders and sold it on at their own price. In 1421 the English garrison at Monteran had stolen a boat and then brazenly hired it out to merchants at a lower price, an offence for which they had signally gone unpunished by their superior officers.

However, the Parisians could call on the law – in the shape of sergeants from the Châtelet – to their aid in matters of extremely abusive behaviour, or in simple cases of shoplifting. The provost marshal's sergeants were always ready to become involved on their behalf, although they usually stressed that they were acting in the name of the English king rather than that of the municipal corporation when dealing with recalcitrant soldiers. But neither did the royal council particularly favour the English military against French civilians in the type of offences for which pardons were granted.

Yet soldiers were always difficult criminals to apprehend, by virtue of the fact that the men were as often as not simply passing through the city and were often gone before their crimes could be registered, let alone before they could be arrested. Even during civil litigation, the accused Englishman was liable to disappear to the battlefield for weeks at a time, and afterwards, knowing what awaited them in Paris, some simply headed for the Channel ports, and home.

Parisians, then as now, were a contentious people, and disputes with the English soldiery were common throughout the early 1420s. Many of these clashes were largely born out of misunderstandings, and were for the most part simply a matter of language, since the average English soldier spoke no French, nor felt that he had any need to (beyond his immediate need for food, drink and sexual gratification). Equally, there is no evidence that the average Parisian made any great effort to learn English throughout this period. The inhabitants of both countries already held the other's language in contempt.

The ordinary law-abiding English soldier undoubtedly found his truest social level with the same kind of decent citizens that he had left at home, if he was so inclined, and there are some cases recorded where such men were made welcome in French families. But most soldiers were happy just to have casual relationships with the whores who were always ready to accommodate them. It is likely, though, that these soldiers more readily understood the argot of the Parisians in a way that was denied their 'betters'. For just as the cockneys of London had begun to create their own language in order to avoid being understood by the rest of the population, especially the law, the Parisian underworld had also created their own *jobelin* or jargon. The average English 'goddam'[5] very possibly understood this language better than he understood the French of the non-criminal classes.

By this time, too, the enlisted man's superiors were almost as helpless as he was linguistically, for in the past few decades French had become a dead language to them, taught in the same way that Latin and Greek were taught, as the language of the scholarly. Yet until a few decades earlier the English aristocracy had spoken French more readily than they had used their own language, although it was not a version easily understood by the sophisticated, since the French spoken by the English had remained static, whereas in France the vernacular was constantly evolving. The divide had been growing for more than a hundred years, long before Edward III had laid claim to his French mother's right to the throne of the Valois, the genesis of the wars that had culminated in the English possession of Paris. French instruction books had been known in England from the end of the thirteenth century, and by the time of the occupation the most elementary grammars were needed for high- and low-born alike.

Even those English in Paris who could take pride in their command of French had also to grapple with the highly stylised usage of the capital, whose inhabitants, as ever, took pride in being extremely fashionable. Their up-to-the-minute idiom was as incomprehensible to their new masters as it would have been to any Frenchman from the provinces (who, perhaps, more readily understood the French of the invaders). In the first decade of the fifteenth century, John Barton, who had studied at the University of Paris, and who dearly loved the city, composed a little book, *Donait François*, in which he gave a concise introduction to the Parisian speech that was known in England as *'doulce France'*. But since few common soldiers could read – and many of their commanders were as unlettered – it meant nothing to them, and they and the Parisians continued to struggle to understand each other verbally, which on occasion led to outbreaks of incomprehensible violence.

Yet even though the people of Paris had difficulty in coming to terms with the cruder class of the occupying force, they recognised that the English aristocracy was a different breed of oppressor to their home-grown autocrats, and they were infinitely preferable to the hated Armagnacs. But on a more deeply patriotic level, which had less to do with flag-waving than with a religious impulse, there was still the question of fealty towards the old royal house, the Capetian line, as represented by the dauphin. The detested Armagnacs were still the strongest of the French factions who had rallied to his side.

If the northern part of the kingdom of France was divided by differing loyalties throughout its length and breadth, this situation was intensified among the inhabitants of the capital. The divisions were not only between the municipal districts but also within them, and there was now a multiplicity of such flashpoints, as in 1380 Charles V had extended the area of Paris by building a new city wall. This had brought the number of districts to sixteen, with the creation of eight new quarters on the Right Bank: St Anthoine, St Gervais, St Avoyé, St Martin, St Denis, Les Halles, St Eustache and St Honoré, all of them filled with a diversity of people.

Religion partly helped to define the 'Armagnac' and 'Burgundian' sections in these new sectors, but they were further divided when various parties within them went on to establish political confraternities as an expression of their factionalism. The Blancs-Manteaux district, for example, was at the heart of the Armagnac refuge in the centre of the Grève area, while the principal church in Les Halles, St Eustache, was a spiritual stronghold for the Burgundians, and this pattern was repeated throughout the quarters. But the most important faction of all was the *Grand Confrérie* of Notre Dame (the religious voice of the Parisian elite), although it attempted to avoid committing itself to any one faction in the political divisions while retaining its theological supremacy. Even so, the Grand Brotherhood was biased enough politically to welcome Anne of Burgundy into its numbers, and her brother the duke was held in high regard by them. In these conditions of appalling patriotic confusion, the citizens still loyal to the exiled French royal family could do 'nothing but endure', although there were sporadic if somewhat muted, protests.

During the week before the English were to meet the Armagnacs on the appointed day to do battle, 24 February 1423, there were constant arrests of Parisians suspected of belonging to the Armagnac party. These arrests were carried out both day and night, though largely in the early hours of the morning, and those arrested were routinely imprisoned. Processions, both in support of the English action and in protest against it, were made for four days running during this week of general chaos. 'No one in Paris did any work of any kind on these days.'[6]

Fortunately, the siege of Meulan was short-lived, for the town surrendered on 1 March; and then the severest frost that anyone could remember arrived ten days after its fall. It froze so hard that even vinegar solidified, and icicles hung from the cellar roofs. This bitter weather lasted for seventeen days, and it also snowed heavily. The cold was so intense that few people worked. Instead, they played games to keep warm – among them an early form of football, hockey and fives.

Meulan's fall was followed by the surrender of Marcoussis, Montlhéry, and other places, and the English also enjoyed military successes to the north-east of Paris, where the forces of Jacques d'Harcourt, the bane of the Burgundians, were challenged and roundly defeated by the Earl of Warwick. D'Harcourt, the Sire de Tancarville, had defected to the side of the dauphin after serving with the Anglo–Burgundians. He was a bold and enterprising soldier, who had quickly overrun the valley of the lower Somme, severing communications between the English and their allies in Flanders. But now Noyelles, on the estuary of the Somme, was retaken, and the town of Le Crotoy was vigorously besieged. With its fall, the harrying and plundering of Picardy was brought to an end, to the great relief of the populace.

A further tax was levied in two parts in 1423. It took the form of a loan to be collected from those with the money to pay at once, which was collected between 15 March and 4 July, and this was followed by a straightforward tax of almost 10,000 *francs*. The loan was to allow military operations to be undertaken swiftly, and it was supposed to have been collected by August at the latest, but in fact was not secured until April 1424, by which time many of the lenders had still not been repaid. The taxes raised early in the period were for specific purposes, although most related to the ongoing business of war in some way.

Yet by the summer of 1423 the regent found that the expenses of these operations far exceeded his resources. By June 1423, he could not pay his troops engaged in the defence of Normandy, 'For there is nothing to give them, because the funds intended for the soldiers have been spent on the siege of Crotoy, which still drags on . . .'[7]

Bedford therefore had to convene the estates once more at Vernon, and try again to persuade them to vote another 60,000 pounds *tours*, in order to pay for the army defending Normandy and operating southwards from there. This sum, though, did not prove sufficient, and for a third time the Norman estates were summoned, on this occasion at Caen. They assented to the government's request for a grant of 200,000 pounds *tours*, for the recovery of certain places and for the suppression of brigandage, which was almost the worst danger the Normans had to face. Although the border viscounties could produce no adequate funding, the collections made elsewhere were pretty successful, but the money collected was only sufficient to finance the war for about nine more months.

Meanwhile, the regent made strenuous efforts to secure the goodwill of the Duke of Burgundy, since English power in the important buffer provinces of Champagne, Artois and Picardy rested on keeping the Burgundian alliance active. A pact with Brittany was also highly desirable, as in partnership with the Burgundians and the Bretons, the English would be the masters of the whole north-west coast of France.

These three alliances almost depended upon each other, because the brother of Duke Jean V of Brittany, Arthur de Richemont, was about to marry Philippe of Burgundy's sister, the Duchess of Guienne, which might have united the two duchies against England. This was a very strong possibility since Philippe was once again wavering in his allegiance, this time because of his displeasure over the actions of Bedford's younger brother, Humphrey, Duke of Gloucester, the King's Protector. Duke Humphrey was then in rivalry with Philippe over the rights to his new wife's lands, which Philippe considered to be in his protection.

This had come about because in the autumn of 1422 Humphrey had married the Countess Jacqueline of Hainault and Holland, who had divorced Philippe's cousin, the boorish Duke of Brabant. As her marriage had been annulled by Benedict XIII, a schismatic pope, it was consequently considered by some – notably Philippe of Burgundy – to be invalid. Fleeing her ex-husband, she had afterwards taken refuge in England, where she had fallen in love with the attractive and hugely eligible Duke of Gloucester.[8]

Although her divorce had been obtained with some difficulty, and even at the time of her second marriage, was still regarded by many as being dubious, Humphrey considered that his union gave him a right to Jacqueline's inheritance. Or failing that, as her husband, he should fight for his wife's just rights. Philippe, however, had counted upon making the government of Hainault and Holland his own (in his cousin's name), for the security of Philippe's empire in the Low Countries depended upon advantageous marriages, such as that arranged between Jacqueline and the Duke of Brabant. Duke Humphrey crossed the Channel in defence of his wife's heritage.

Because of this quarrel, the regent had been forced to work harder than ever on the diplomatic front and, in order to prevent Burgundy's complete estrangement from the proposed alliance, Bedford had suggested that he himself marry Philippe's sister Anne, a girl of 18. By doing so, he managed to suggest that, in the matter of apportioning Jacqueline's legacy, he would be in his future in-law's camp rather than that of his younger brother. Philippe agreed to this engagement, perceiving perhaps that a marital alliance was a stronger bond than a political one. In December 1422 it was agreed that Anne's dowry should be 150,000 gold crowns, and if Philippe died without a male heir she would succeed to the county of Artois. If Philippe was blessed with a successor, she would receive a further 100,000 gold crowns.

Bedford then arranged a meeting with the Dukes of Brittany and

Burgundy at Amiens in April 1423 to finalise these arrangements and, in order to overcome Duke Jean's reluctance to attend, he paid all the expenses of Brittany's entourage, amounting to six thousand pounds. Then, having successfully brought both the resentful Philippe and the hesitant Jean V to the negotiating table, the three dukes signed a triple alliance on 17 April 1423. With this treaty, the regent proved himself to be the equal if not the better of his brother Henry, as the tripartite contract was distinctly in favour of England, for in it all three dukes mutually agreed to work together to terminate the wars in France, in other words to defeat the best efforts of the still uncrowned 'Charles VII'. (The fact that the Duke of Brittany had contracted a similar alliance with the dauphin only a year before at Sable somewhat lessened the importance of the Amiens treaty, and perhaps both Brittany *and* Burgundy were acting insincerely when they put their names to the document.)

On 9 May 1423 the regent married Philippe's fifth and favourite sister Anne, with great magnificence at Troyes, while Arthur of Brittany (who fought in the English ranks) married Philippe's eldest sister. Neither of the sisters was a beauty, and Anne was considered very plain. (As she rode through the streets of Paris with her mother and sisters, somebody shouted that they were 'as ugly as screech owls'.) All the Duke of Burgundy's sisters possessed heavy Flemish features, with fair hair and washed out blue eyes, though Anne was proud of her long, delicate hands. She made up for her lack of looks, however, by being animated and high-spirited, and was considered 'livelier than all the ladies of her day'.[9]

The Duke Philippe delighted in pageantry, and he was determined that his favourite sister should be married with every circumstance of pomp and ceremony. The Bedford retinue was also imposing, as befitted his status, and the regent's behaviour after his marriage was kingly. On the way back to Paris, in a repetition of his brother Henry's military-style honeymoon, Bedford took Pont-sur-Seine by assault and captured it. The garrison had only recently fallen into dauphinist hands, and its entire complement of troops was put to the sword. Bedford followed this up by clearing up other rebellious townships along the way.[10]

At Paris, the married couple resided at the palace of the Tournelles, which had been repaired for the reception of the regent's new duchess, and which the duke was intent upon redesigning as a luxurious home from the time of his marriage. He had employed an army of workmen, whom he paid well, and this added to his popularity with the Parisians. The couple preferred the Tournelles palace, as that of St Pol was gloomy, the rooms panelled in dark oak and with low massive ceilings, while the walls were hung with age-darkened and threadbare tapestries.

But it was generally understood that Bedford had declined to take over the Hôtel St Pol because he did not wish to disturb his nephew the king's French grandmother, the dowager queen, who lived 'shut up all the time there, where her husband had passed from this world'. For some years Queen Isabeau, who was now very elderly, had been freakishly fat and a prey to gout, and after 1415 she had been confined in a chair to which wheels had been ingeniously attached.

The queen, who was otherwise mentally sound, was known to suffer from a number of abnormal fears, thunder and lightning among them, but above all a fear of open spaces, which led to her being virtually incarcerated in her own palace in her old age. The citizens of Paris found her behaviour very strange. It was one thing, it was thought, for her to remain quietly at home, as a widow should; but as the only truly royal representative of the French line still resident in the city she was expected to play her part in various ceremonies. (The Duke of Bedford, although the son of a monarch, was never seen by the Parisians as being truly regal, almost certainly because he was English, and his father had been a usurper.) But Isabeau had been their queen for decades and she had always insisted – to the point of almost bankrupting the state – on living in the style befitting her image of royalty. Yet, now, the old woman never stirred beyond her door, and she lived unseen in her grandson's capital as 'though she were a foreigner'.[11]

However, it was no hardship for the duke to live in the alternative palace that had been granted to him, for most people accepted that there was little difference between them in terms of grandeur. Both were a collection of modern buildings, with galleries forming cloisters around gardens, and with a succession of courtyards planted with vines, cherry and pear trees. King Charles VI had installed aviaries, a menagerie and an aquarium at St Pol, but Bedford embellished the Tournelles equally. The important fact was that both palaces were safe, built within the protective wall created by King Philippe Auguste on the drained wetland of the Marais, and both were within striking distance of the great fortress of the Bastille, the last resort of any ruler faced with insurrection.

Of the valuable book collection built up by Charles VI, some 853 volumes were still in the Louvre a few months after his death, and they had been valued at 2,323 pounds *tours*. In accordance with normal royal practice, the late king's possessions had been valued with a view to sale. The regent felt it incumbent upon himself to buy a portion of the library, which he did for the sum of 2,000 pounds *tours*. Later, when King Charles' executors were unable to pay for the monuments to the late king and his widow, it was rumoured that the regent had bought other books from the collection in order to help defray the cost. And although the books were now officially his, the duke allowed them to remain at the Louvre. For while he was Regent of France, and felt secure in this position, Bedford was content to leave the books *in situ*, and he even retained the late king's librarian, Garnier de Saint-Yon, as his librarian.[12]

The rich collection of tapestries that Charles VI had acquired over the decades was treated in much the same way. Of 325 items in the inventory of 1422, roughly half were purchased by the regent and his wife, with the rest being bought by members of his household or by loyal supporters of the Anglo–Burgundian regime. As the sole representative of his nephew, the 'true King of France', Bedford clearly felt that he had the right to dispose of the French royal possessions as he thought fit, even if this meant selling them to his friends at greatly reduced prices. But it was hardly good policy from the point of view of winning the support of those Parisians who were not given the same opportunity.

The Bourgeois of Paris complained in his journal that the regent 'always enriches his country at the expense of the French', and while this was true to some extent, the Duke of Bedford was no more acquisitive than his predecessors had been. The journal-keeper claimed that even the beautiful gold cup of the King of France, made for Charles V, had been taken to England by Bedford (although it was more likely that the duke had acquired the cup as part of some ransom payment).

The regent's men were said to have plundered the churches at times, and Parisians certainly believed that the English were responsible for the disappearance of a much-prized relic from the Church of the Innocents at Les Halles. (It was undoubtedly stolen at this period, but whether by an Englishman, a Burgundian, or even a Frenchman, was never proved.) However, whatever their capacities for larceny on a grand scale, some of the English were also capable of generous gestures towards the citizens. In his will, the Earl of Salisbury left an annual endowment to the hospital of the Hôtel Dieu, and although the regent's acquisitions were strongly resented, his expenditure on local artists and on architecture was princely, and his charitable donations to the poor were unstinting.

But although the regent was generous in bestowing property that had once belonged to the enemy to his favoured friends, only one great house was given to an Englishman in the early years – the Hôtel des Preaux in the rue des Barres, which was granted to Richard Wydeville, Bedford's chamberlain. The regent was always more open handed with the foreigners who favoured the English cause, particularly the Burgundians, as it was his policy at that time to build up support among them.

At first, the Duke of Bedford's military operations consisted mainly of lightning raids and 'castle fighting', that is sieges. The English were largely successful in these raids, but there were significant defeats, most notably the raid by John de la Pole into Anjou, which was crushed by superior forces. The siege of Mont St Michel was also a humiliating failure, and one that would have far-reaching effects within the next five years.[13]

While the regent remained in Paris, his forces took d'Orsay, after a stiff defence of six weeks. The soldiers of the garrison were sent into Paris bareheaded, and were imprisoned in the Petit Châtelet, the grim fortress that straddled the rue St Jacques and commanded one of the bridges over the Seine. (This gloomy place served both as prison and courtroom for those who waited for judgement, and it was also the official residence of the provost marshal.) The entire garrison of d'Orsay – like that of Pont-sur-Seine – had been condemned to death, and awaited summary execution. But the regent's young wife interceded for them, and – as had happened when Bedford's great-grandmother pleaded with her husband Edward III at the siege of Calais to spare the burghers of that city – the duke now gave the garrison their liberty without conditions. The duchess would prove to have a gift for ingratiating herself with Bedford's 'subjects', and this act of compassion was the first in a series of shrewd public moves on her part.

For a time, Bedford did not risk any major movement, although he used his best soldier, the Earl of Salisbury, to clear Champagne by first besieging Montaiguillon, some fifty miles south-east of Paris. (The main aim was always to protect Paris, at whatever distance.) The besieged town offered considerable resistance, and it was here that Salisbury heard that the dauphin had formed a new army at Bourges, with a substantial Scots contingent under Sir John Stewart of Darnley, who was put in command of the whole force. (This was one of the first examples of the cooperation between the Scots and the French in their mutual collaboration against English control of their mutual territories.)

Stewart's main aim was to remove Burgundy from the triple alliance, and so he concentrated upon attacking his regions to keep him occupied. By capturing one of their main strongholds, Cravant, as a first step, he hoped to re-establish contact with the dauphinist forces in Picardy and Champagne, while at the same time relieving the pressure on Montaiguillon. This move was at once countered by the Earl of Salisbury, who had received a new English contingent into his regiments, led by the Earl Marshal and Lord Willoughby. With the aid of a contingent sent by the dowager Duchess of Burgundy, the two corps made their rendezvous at Auxerre, and on 29 July 1423 they were joined by the English troops. Together they marched upon Cravant, nine miles to the north-west, made contact with the Burgundian leaders from within the town and decided to form a single army.

Their arrival came not a day too soon, for the Cravant garrison was so short of food they were reduced to eating their own horses, stray cats, mice and even sparrows. The captains of the garrison, thrilled that the English had also come to their rescue, came out of the town on their approach and escorted them with some ceremony into the cathedral city. Although the English and the Burgundians had been allies for four years now, no pitched battle had yet taken place where both were present, and so relations between the two parties were extremely cordial. Moreover, the two armies of the Burgundians, the besieged and the relievers, were happy to place themselves under the orders of the great Earl of Salisbury. The earl, it was said, was touched with the military good fortune of his late master, Henry V.

On 30 July the united force took the offensive against the dauphinist army in the valley of the Yonne. The size of the English army is given as 4,000, while about the Burgundian army there is no information, but since it was collected hastily it is likely to have been neither large nor of great quality. Nothing is known of the size of the Franco–Scottish army, although – to judge by the number of its casualties – it must have out-numbered the Anglo–Burgundians by at least three to two.

The Earl of Salisbury's army was now ranged on the western bank of the river and the other side was lined with the French in considerable numbers. The English, who composed the major portion of the army, were placed in the front ranks, with Lord Willoughby having command of the right and Salisbury the left, and reconnaissance showing that they were also in a commanding position about a mile and a half north of the town. So Salisbury decided to outflank the French, and he marched his troops round to the south-west where a bridge gave access to Cravant. The French, detecting this, moved from their high position down to the vicinity of the bridge.

To get at the enemy, the English had to cross the river, with their archers providing a covering fire for them as they did so. The earl himself, with a sudden shout of 'St George! Banner advance!' dashed into the water, closely followed by his bodyguard. Waurin says that the men crossed 'each as best they could', with the water sometimes reaching the knees of some and with others the waist, and the English men-at-arms forced to strip off a great part of their armour to avoid sinking further.[14] When they managed to reach the far bank, the Burgundians were encouraged to follow them into the water, where a bitter fight ensued in the narrow strip of ground between the river and the town.

Willoughby, meanwhile, attacked the bridge over the Yonne. This was held by a Scottish contingent that resisted valiantly, and the contest was fierce, with the many skeletons later dredged from under the bridge being a testimony to their valour.

After tremendous hand-to-hand fighting, the French gave way. But in moving to the security of the south, they were attacked in the rear by the garrison of Cravant who, although the men were weak with hunger, was nonetheless able to stagger out and to inflict some damage. To reach safety the dauphinist army had to pass between the garrison at their rear and the English now lining the east bank of the Yonne, and very few escaped. The French lost between two and three thousand troops, the Scots perhaps a thousand men. As a fighting force the dauphinists were almost wiped out temporarily, and many prisoners were taken, among them two commanders of the army, the Constable of Scotland and the Count of Entadour. Darnley lost an eye.

The battle of Cravant was a clear, crisp affair, and it bore the distinct stamp of the great soldier, Thomas Montagu, Earl of Salisbury. To cross the river (a shallow one, but with deep pockets) in the face of the enemy was a dangerous operation, but the earl saw from the beginning that it would have been more dangerous still to have tried to dislodge them from the high ground. In a bold move, Salisbury clearly counted on help from the defenders of Cravant, and in this his faith was justified.

With the dauphinist forces scattered like sheep, a contingent was sent in pursuit of them, while the remainder of the allies entered the gates of Cravant to receive a tumultuous welcome. Two days later the two armies took leave of each other at the city gates and marched their separate ways: the Burgundians to Dijon and the English army back to the siege of Montaiguillon. The dauphin's army had almost ceased to exist, and it had been a complete Anglo–Burgundian triumph, the dauphinist offensive for the year 1423 broken beyond repair. When news of the victory reached Paris, the overjoyed citizens lit bonfires in the streets.

The results of the battle went even further than this, as Bedford intensified the policy of close cooperation with the Burgundians. Salisbury, with Burgundian aid, continued with the clearing and subjugation of strongholds to the east of Paris. But the time was soon approaching when the regent could feel surer of undertaking offensive, rather than largely defensive operations, beginning with the conquest of Maine and Anjou.

There were, however, other problems to be dealt with within the capital itself, which although they outwardly bore on the military situation were actually more subversive, for they were concerned with a small group of civilians acting as spies and messengers for the dauphin's party.

Contact between the two rival parts of France had been heavily regulated from November 1420, but it was still possible to evade the restrictions if one knew how to, or if one knew the right people, or if one persisted. (In November 1420, for example, the canons of Notre Dame had sought permission to send messengers into the 'other obedience' (the kingdom of Bourges), to summon absent colleagues to the election of the Bishop of Paris. The royal provost had ruled that it was not in his power to grant the request. Chancery had given the same opinion, and it was only after they had received letters of approval in the name of King Henry VI that the men were allowed to leave. Others would pursue these same channels, with varying degrees of success.)

Except with the special permission of the Parisian authorities, any communication with the 'enemy France' was not allowed, and the provost marshal had done what he could to stamp out all secret correspondence in the short time of his command. But in 1423 it was discovered that

Michelette d'Auxerre, the widow of an Armagnac sympathiser, Giot de Bossu, had received and concealed a messenger from the enemy at her house in Paris, and she had been subsequently sighted delivering seditious letters.[15]

She had, apparently, been involved in this conspiratorial work for some time without being discovered, and she was certainly very active. Two years before, for example, when one of the dauphin's spies was captured by the garrison at Chevreuse, fifteen miles south-west of Paris, she had put up forty out of the hundred *francs* demanded for his ransom, to prevent him being brought to Paris for questioning, an interrogation that might have had disastrous results not only for those who had sent him, but also those who received him.

It is likely that Michelette was the daughter of a leading Armagnac, Guillaume d'Auxerre, who had been executed by the Burgundians in 1418, and whose widow was still living in Bourges. If this was so, Michelette had both cause to hate the regime that had killed her father and the opportunity, through her mother, to remain in touch with people in the other 'obedience'. Surprisingly, though, after being found guilty of sedition, she was then treated with unaccustomed leniency by the authorities for, on appeal, her sentence of standing in the pillory, banishment and the confiscation of her property, was commuted to a period of house arrest.

She was however, as would increasingly be shown, only one of many, drawn from all walks of life, though the largest number of these messengers, who negotiated the hazards of encountering not only the Anglo–Burgundian sentinels but also marauding soldiers and bandits, were priests, usually either monks or friars. Their clerical garb usually acted for them as a protection, almost a form of safe-conduct, for they were known to be great travellers on holy business, and more often than not they could plead that they were either on some form of pilgrimage or on a mission of spiritual mercy.[16]

Any contact between the citizens of Paris and the kingdom of Bourges was treated by the authorities as a crime, a situation that was tightened up by the English. But it was not always the case that only politics was involved, for quite often the messages that were carried between Bourges and the capital were simply concerned with whatever family business the exiles in Bourges still kept up in their home city. Most of the Parisian families who had followed the dauphin into banishment were people of property, whether patricians or of the merchant class; fleeing almost without exception from the possibility of Burgundian brutality rather than from fear of the English. But those who had left with the Armagnacs hoped soon to return, and it was therefore important to try to safeguard their property for such time as they could reclaim it. Many people did cross from one part of France to the other, sometimes to secure an inheritance on the death of a relative, but more often because they simply wished to return to their families.

Those of the dauphin's adherents who had not left the city largely survived by avoiding any confrontation with 'the enemy'. The most eminent of these to pull through the Burgundian occupation was Robert Louvel, the town clerk who, even though one of his assistants was suspected of being 'Armingeois', himself appears to have escaped any censure for many years. (Until, that is, his involvement with Michelette d'Auxerre's secret communications network became known.) When Louvel finally fled to Bourges, to escape retribution, the post of town clerk was given to a reliable Burgundian.[17]

Up to this time there had been no invariable system of military command, and no clear succession of the 'Captains of Paris', although from July 1420 two English dukes – Clarence and Exeter – had shared this office with Jean de la Baume-Montrével. But the regent saw that it was a mistake to give such a sensitive position as the captaincy to an Englishman during this transitional period. He instinctively felt that the Parisians were not to be subjugated by displays of force, as had happened in the two previous regimes, but needed instead a leader with whom they could work in partnership. The pugnacious Clarence and his men had done the city very little good, and the equally combative Exeter had also been notably unsuccessful.

Bedford had the much respected Burgundian, Jean de Courcelles, as his lieutenant, and he made him Captain of Paris in 1424 (although Courcelles was by this time, in any case, using the title on his own initiative). But the new captain appears not to have been all that effective, despite the trust that Bedford had in him, and it was at this time that the provost marshal began to assert his position in the running of the capital's military system. Little was heard of the Captains of Paris after 1424.

The main English presence would always remain at the Bastille, which was in their hands by September 1420; its garrison composed of men from the retinues of Walter Hungerford, John Robesart and Richard Wydeville. On 24 January 1421 its captaincy would be entrusted to Sir John Fastolf, and his successor was another knight, Sir Roger Fiennes, followed by John Midelstret in September 1423. Midelstret was a competent man, and he remained in charge of the Bastille until October 1428, when Ralph Butler succeeded him. In times of crisis the English did provide a greater show of strength than in normal times, and the sight of scores of English soldiers mustering in the squares would always remind Parisians of where their loyalties lay.

(Amazingly, the normal English garrison seems to have consisted of no more than a hundred soldiers in periods of relative calm; though this slim force would, on occasion, be expanded by the armed retainers of visiting nobles, who would bring with them as many as 300 men. But it was always the regent's policy to keep the various garrisons small, and not only because of the cost. Excessive numbers of idle soldiers, often spoiling for a fight, would only add to his problems.)

But military displays aside, the regent was keen to show that both he and his council were fundamentally only a part of the Parisian system, which in the end proved a bad decision, since diversity and confusion were often the most striking characteristics of the city's administration. For example, seventeen religious bodies alone had the privilege of 'high justice', claiming jurisdiction over all civil causes, and many criminal matters were still in their power.

At the beginning of the dual monarchy, the Paris council of Henry VI, wishing to make a clean start, made vigorous efforts to clear out the corrupt practices that had troubled the establishment for decades. Among the many misdeeds they uncovered was the mysterious dispersal of the French royal jewels, which had begun to disappear both before and after the entry of the Burgundians. In particular, they tried to trace the jewels that were missing from the crown of Charles VI, and one trail led to a Lucca-born merchant, Michel Totti, who was temporarily imprisoned in May, although the English seem to have acted too quickly in his case. The arbitrary manner of his arrest was denounced by his advocate who claimed that it was not carried out in due form, even going so far as to accuse the council of racial discrimination. (Totti was possible Jewish, which at that time would have predictably made him open to suspicion, Jews being generally distrusted.) The inquiries did not lead to the recovery of the missing jewels.

In August 1423 the Dukes of Brittany and Burgundy visited the regent at Paris, and Bedford tried to settle Philippe's claims arising from his marriage to his late wife Michelle, an elder daughter of Charles VI.[18] As a result, the regent placed Peronne, Roye and Montdidier in the duke's hands, which pleased Philippe, but he was unable to satisfy him regarding his brother Gloucester's marriage. Duke Humphrey was determined to recover his wife's inheritance, and all agreed that there was something to be said for his contention that Jacqueline's marriage to John of Brabant, Philippe's cousin, had not only been illegal but was very probably unconsummated, and therefore invalid anyway.

As always, the people of Paris welcomed the Burgundians warmly and, as ever, Philippe did little to earn that affection. Only in the months following the Treaty of Troyes had the duke formed a constructive relationship with the citizens of Paris. He had entered into the siege of Melun with vigour, and brought numerous weapons to the capital for its defence. Afterwards, he kept in close touch with his principal officers in Paris, but only in his own interests. Whenever in need of reinforcements, he had sent urgent letters to Paris, and the citizens had always responded to his appeals by raising a troop of militiamen. The Burgundians, however unworthy, would always be preferable to the Armagnacs, who were then as near to Paris as the countryside beyond the Porte St Jacques, St Germain and Bordelles, 'doing more hurt to honest citizens than ever the tyrant Saracens did'. (To the Bourgeois of Paris, the Armagnacs would always be unfavourably compared to the much-feared Saracens!)

To the continual bafflement of the English, the Parisians continued to prefer the Burgundians to them, despite the fact that there was now more order in the city than there had ever been before. In his government of Paris the regent had shown himself comparatively just and humane, and anxious to remove abuses; he had largely checked bribery, and had forbidden many of the cruel practices to which prisoners were subjected. His regency was vastly superior to the rule of the dauphin, with his corrupt officials, or even that of John the Fearless. Yet the well disciplined English troops were still not welcome on the streets of Paris, and the citizens' resentment was shown in a hundred ways.

Throughout 1423 the two successive Bishops of Paris had been confronted with the case of Jean le Ferre, a monk of Ste Geneviève and the *curé* of St Étienne-du-Mont, a dependent parish church next to the abbey. An Armagnac sympathiser, he had once been captured by them and imprisoned for two years, during which time he had most probably been recruited to the dauphin's service. For upon his release, he had returned to Paris to preach a campaign on his behalf, which was denounced officially as being 'zealously dogmatic, and abominable in several ways' apart from being 'seditious, perilous and criminal'.

In response to this highly political ministry, the Bishop of Paris, Jean de la Rochetaillée, took action against le Ferre. But because the offender was a monk of Ste Geneviève, the accused was given over to the abbot for the appropriate steps to be taken there, but the monks were disinclined to punish one of their brethren. As the monks took no action in the matter, the case was revived by Rochetaillée's successor, Jean du Nant, who became the Bishop of Paris in September 1423, and it was recorded because of a dispute about jurisdiction. The brethren were clearly un-enthusiastic about the Anglo–Burgundian cause, but whether they actively supported le Ferre's militant brand of politics is not known; they may simply have wished to protect a fellow monk. But what is evident from the account of this case is that, from the beginning of the Bedford regency, there were men who were sent from enemy territory to preach in favour of the 'uncrowned king'.[19]

These dissident preachers were comparative rarities, but they were important for two reasons; firstly because they had easy access to a multitude, and also because any political message delivered by a holy man would be clothed in religious authority.

The balancing of the books for 1423/24 would show that an Anglo–Burgundian regime based on Paris, and ruling slightly less than half of France, could be a viable economic proposition, as was exemplified by the influx of traders from the towns of northern France, who were once more allowed to occupy the market stalls at Les Halles, after years of fearing to make the journey through hostile territory. A proclamation to this effect was issued in June 1423.

Politically, this alliance would also prove to be to the liking of a considerable number of the occupied French. As for the Parisians, they could expect to maintain their independence of the French 'pretender'; and, where possible, do likewise with their English rulers.

NOTES

1   Bourgeois de Paris.
2   Youngest son of Henry IV, he had been wounded at Agincourt. Monstrelet records the embassy to him.
3   Bourgeois de Paris.
4   Afterwards, Buchan quarrelled with the Armagnac leadership for failing to show him proper support in battle. Partly to keep the peace between them, the dauphin sent him back to Scotland to collect reinforcements. Stevenson, *Letters and Papers.*
5   'Goddam' was a French epithet for English soldiers, because of their frequent use of this, their favourite oath.
6   Bourgeois de Paris.
7   Williams, *My Lord of Bedford.*
8   She married Gloucester in late 1422.
9   Bourgeois de Paris.
10   Newhall, *The English Conquest of Normandy.*
11   Quicherat, *Chronique.*
12   Saint-Yon was more politically important than his office of librarian suggests. He remained, throughout the dual monarchy, a loyal servant of the English regime. *Archives Nationales.*
13   'A glance at the strength of that fortress will explain why they failed to breach it.' Burne, *The Agincourt War.*
14   According to Burne. Jean de Waurin, who was an eye-witness, does not mention it in his account. Waurin was the bastard son of the Seigneur du Forestal, one of Burgundy's councillors. He lived until about 1471.
15   *Criminal Cases in the Parlement of Paris.*
16   Longnon, *Documents parisiens.*
17   Ibid.
18   Philippe was married three times. Michelle had died in 1422.
19   Bourgeois de Paris.

CHAPTER III

1424: A Second Agincourt

On 22 February 1424 the English Council in London drafted a message to all the important people in Paris. In a *pro forma* letter the king, then two years old, assured his loyal subjects of his health, and thanked them for keeping the city in peace under his lordship since the death of his *'grandpère de France'*. It was explained that he could not yet come in person, but he promised military aid so that his subjects could live in peace and security.

Such a formal letter, in fact, stressed the remoteness of the English government from the needs of the Parisians, although this was actually to the benefit of the citizens. As a result of the English reluctance to interfere in the way they were governed, they succeeded in maintaining their independence for a number of years to come, in a way that was never possible under the two previous regimes. The Paris council remained in contact with their colleagues in London, and each drew upon the expertise of the other, but without the Parisians calling for the practical assistance of their English equals.[1]

On the Sunday before Easter, the Bishop of Paris went in procession with the canons of Notre Dame to the abbey of Ste Geneviève. As he approached the building, three monks rushed out from it to confront him. Seizing the cross that was borne at the head of the column, they broke it into pieces, to the horror of both the bystanders and the people taking part in the religious ceremony. An act of such desecration had not been performed in public within living memory, and for such a sacrilege to be carried out by members of a religious community was beyond all understanding.

But the monk's astonishing act of violation had little to do with religious belief in itself. It was done because a processional cross was seen by them not only as a symbol of the bishop's spiritual authority but also of his temporal powers, and these monks were not prepared to tolerate such a claim when he moved into their own terrain. Their community had been seriously provoked by the bishop undertaking the trial of one of their number, and they were outraged when he had gone to the extreme of imprisoning their abbot and their almoner in his displeasure at their

31

shielding the culprit. The three monks had interpreted the bishop's purely devotional excursion – to worship at the site of the second most important saint in Paris – as just one more example of diocesan despotism, and had found this new assault on their religious privileges too much to bear.[2]

The Anglo–Burgundian allies had enjoyed a good year in 1423, but that of 1424 was to bring even more amazing successes, despite the fact that they would not only have to contend with the forces of the dauphin but also those of his Scots supporters. Scottish troops had been landing in France in a steady stream for some years and, in April 1424, a complete army of 6,500 men, under the 'war-battered' Earl of Douglas, had joined up with the forces of the dauphin in the south. By doing so, Douglas betrayed his promise to King Henry V, for he had agreed to remain neutral if his king, James I, still a prisoner of the English, was restored to Scotland. Yet within a month of King James being returned to his capital, Douglas had landed in France to give his support to the dauphin, who had created him Duke of Touraine. 'To the alarm of the people of Tours.'[3]

But throughout 1424 the English successes continued unabated, largely under the leadership of the inexhaustible and unbeatable Salisbury who, with Burgundian aid, subdued all the towns and castles that still held out to the east of Paris, while, in the north, Le Crotoy fell to the English in March.

Up to this time, the regent had confined himself to the instructions bequeathed to him by King Henry V, and had carried them out to the letter, and with considerable success. Not only had he established a sound and settled government in Paris, he had safeguarded the English conquests in Normandy, and had 'regularised' the whole of the region of northern France. Above all, he had managed to maintain both a friendly relationship and a mutually satisfactory cooperation – through his young, spirited and highly intelligent wife – with her brother Burgundy. But he now felt that the moment had come to strike out on his own, following policies of a more ambitious nature than those outlined by his late brother.

Bedford's main policy was to carry the war into the enemy's country, initially by invading and then conquering Anjou and Maine. He was perhaps inspired to this aim by the arrival of numerous detachments of Englishmen, voluntary and professional, but equally impatient to fight, who had crossed the Channel to join up with his resident forces. However, as most of these soldiers were immediately swallowed up in the ever increasing number of garrisons the English were forced to maintain, or were absorbed into the units laying siege to towns and castles, or even repelling local raids, Bedford's first imperative was to collect a field army together.

To do this, he drew upon the full strength of the new arrivals from England, half the number of the men then manning the garrisons, and eventually the mobile military trains that were acting independently of his other forces (including that of the Earl of Salisbury, now operating so far to the south that even a town such as Lyons, up to now safe from the threat of assault, began to fear for its immunity).

By mid-July the regent had managed to assemble an army at least 10,000 strong. They gathered at Rouen, where he himself travelled on the 20th of the month, for he had determined to lead the army himself, so important did he consider this enterprise to be. (His decision may have been affected by the news that reached him at Rouen that the Armagnacs were also gathering a huge army together, the dauphin apparently having decided upon one final and decisive confrontation. It was very strongly rumoured that the French command was at long last ready to face up to the English, throwing off the cravenness that had immobilised them since their failure at Agincourt, nine years before. It was also rumoured that this army would be the largest ever assembled against the invading English.)[4]

A levy had been declared throughout southern France to meet the cost of this new confrontation, and this imposition was not resented when it became known that a new influx of Scottish fighting men had rallied to the dauphin's cause. (Their enthusiasm was fuelled equally by a need of a currency stronger than their own, and the long-enduring hatred of their English oppressors at home.) The Armagnacs, meanwhile, fighting largely for financial gain – both for the fortune to be paid to them by the dauphin's financiers and for the treasure to be stolen from the people they were being paid to protect – had also raised a mercenary force in Lombardy and elsewhere. And once again the French forces outnumbered those of the English, for altogether the dauphin's army mustered over 15,000. It assembled along the lower Loire, with the advanced headquarters being settled on Le Mans, some forty miles north of the river.

While making preparations for action, Bedford did not neglect Paris, although the city could always be said to have been a town at war during this turbulent period, which had long predated the English occupation and which would also outlast it. Even when the battles were far away, danger could still be near at hand. War, more peculiarly civil than state, was an inescapable fact of life for the citizens. Farmers, driving cattle to the butchers of Les Halles, had done so under armed guard for decades.

But despite his martial deliberations, the regent still managed to concern himself with the civilian side of life, particularly with regard to justice. The new ordinances for the administration of the Châtelet prison were first drafted around this time, decrees that were perhaps to be the best legacy of the English domination of Paris, for such matters were overdue for reform, the practices at the prison being highly disorganised and often openly corrupt.

The regent had long planned to regularise the situation at the Châtelet, most notably to rid the institution of the judicial pretensions of the provost of merchants and his untrained aldermen. The municipal court had been founded to deal with matters arising out of trade disputes, but over the years it had taken to judging graver types of case. Now, all that was to change. On 1 April 1424 the Châtelet's claim to hold a 'grant to hear causes' was summarily rejected, and an attempt was made to limit its competence to the most minor disputes among the river merchants, all of which took the entire summer to complete. On 5 August Bedford and his council commissioned *parlement* to draw up new regulations.

The regent then returned to the business of prosecuting the war against the dauphin.

By a coincidence both the English and French armies were fully assembled at the same time and, by an even stranger coincidence, their commanders had settled upon the same objective, directing their main forces to the same town, Ivry, thirty miles west of Paris.

Both the town and its garrison had been captured from the English by the French in a sudden raid, but the town had been retaken by the Earl of Suffolk in June, although the French garrison had retreated to the castle, shutting themselves up within its keep. Frustrated, the English resorted to a mining operation, inserting explosives into the castle walls, the intention being to blow them up. As a result of this unprecedented move, and realising the hopelessness of their situation, the besieged garrison agreed to surrender to the English on 14 August, the eve of the Feast of the Assumption,[5] unless, that is, they were first relieved by their French compatriots. Because of this decision both armies set out in the same direction, with the French determined to release their compatriots and the English to take on both relievers and defenders. An all-out battle at last seemed imminent.

The Duke of Bedford's army arrived at Evreux, twenty miles north-west of Ivry, on 11 August. He was joined there by a contingent of Burgundians, under L'Isle Adam and, at the last moment by the Earl of Salisbury. His opponents, approaching Ivry from the south-west, had reached Noancourt, fifteen miles short of the town. On the 13th Bedford moved his army south to join forces with the Earl of Suffolk before the castle of Ivry.

Both armies were now within a day's march of each other, and the English expected to do battle on the following day, the day fixed for the surrender of the castle. The regent drew up his army, ready for attack, but to the astonishment of Bedford and his commanders, the French garrison marched out and surrendered to him without a fight. This was entirely due to a marvellous misunderstanding on the part of the advanced scouts of the French army, who had come into contact with their English counterparts and been informed that Anglo–Burgundian forces were now in control of the castle. The main French army, advised by their scouts of this, then decided to hold off, and when news of their resolution reached the beleaguered garrison, and it became clear they would not be relieved by the date agreed, they surrendered as previously arranged.

The French then held a council of war with their Scottish allies, which proved to be a turbulent meeting, with the Scots eager to forge ahead and challenge their opponents, while the French, anxious to avoid an outright battle, had decided to fall back from their present position. The Scots had been kept waiting at Tours for four months, and they were spoiling for a fight with their ancient foes, but older counsel prevailed. (The French aristocrats had not forgotten the humiliation of their defeat at Agincourt, even if they had never entirely learned from it.)

A compromise was eventually reached, which partially satisfied the honour of both the seasoned French leaders and the more impetuous Scots. It was decided that an outright battle with the English was to be avoided, but the dauphin's army was to try to capture as many towns on the Normandy border as could be done without provoking a direct confrontation. A start was to be made with the walled town of Verneuil, which the French had passed on their way to Ivry.

The French forces about-turned and marched directly to this small town, and on the next day took possession by simply announcing to the townspeople that the English army had been defeated at Ivry, and was in full retreat. (To make their story more plausible, they paraded some half-naked Scottish soldiers in sight of the town walls of Verneuil, tied to their horses' tails, giving out that the Scots were captured English troops. Since the Scots dialect was as unintelligible to the inhabitants as English speech, the townsfolk fell for this ploy.)

The Duke of Bedford had, meanwhile, received the keys of the abandoned Ivry castle, but had decided upon an astonishing step. Leaving a substantial garrison behind him at Ivry, and after sending the Earl of Suffolk's company to 'shadow' the French army, he also about-faced and returned with his main army to Evreux, a move that has baffled almost every military historian since. Having regained Evreux without a fight, he spent the next day, the Feast of the Assumption, at prayer in the cathedral. As pious as his late brother, King Henry V, little came between the duke and his devotions. But it could also be that the regent, having taken the measure of the French military, had decided that there was no immediate danger of attack; although his decision was not, in the opinion of most military historians, the mark of an outstanding commander.

It was not the first time that Bedford had contravened the elementary principles of strategy, and neither would it be the last, and he was capable of some astonishingly arrogant blunders. For example, in the course of the summer of 1424, he had received a visit from the Duke of Burgundy and Arthur de Richemont. (The meeting held at Amiens in the previous

January had produced no positive result.) At this reunion, to Bedford's consternation, the elderly Richemont had demanded the command of an army, and the regent, in a rare slip of diplomacy, had deeply offended him by refusing his request. Bedford very possibly doubted the Breton's good faith, although he gave as the reason for his refusal the somewhat insulting suggestion that the old soldier had not fought in the field since Agincourt nine years before, and he must by now have forgotten the arts of war! Any attempt to appease the insulted Richemont failed, and he retired to the seclusion of his brother's domain, where he brooded upon the slight with inevitable consequences for the English presence in France. Within a year he would change sides for the last time, and he would later accept the office of Constable of France from the gratified dauphin.

It was an astonishing blunder for so prudent a leader to make, as the English needed the support of all their allies, and the quarrel still simmering between the Duke of Burgundy and Bedford's brother Gloucester was becoming dangerous. (In order to secure Philippe's continued partnership the regent had made over to him the counties of Mâcon and Auxerre.) Within weeks, too, the English would be faced with a new threat, and a danger that promised to overwhelm them when, by an amazing act of recuperation, the ineffectual dauphin somehow managed to assemble an imposing army of some fifteen thousand strong. That it was composed largely of Scots and Italian mercenaries only added to the fears of the Parisians, for the Scots were thought to be barbarians, and the Lombards were well known to be devoid of scruple, at least in financial matters. To be faced with a Scot–Lombard–Armagnac occupation was the stuff of nightmares.

But the regent felt strong enough for a delay. Indeed, he was so confident of beating the Franco–Scottish army, that he further depleted his own force by sending L'Isle Adam with his Burgundian detachment, as many as 3,000 men, to continue their operations in the north of the country. By showing such contempt for the enemy he was, perhaps, remembering his brother's famous rallying cry on the eve of Agincourt, when the English had been similarly faced with overwhelming numbers, and with which King Henry had stimulated the pride and confidence of his troops. Bedford's gesture in sending so many fighting men away was as magnificent – if more foolhardy – than that of Henry, and when some Norman contingents afterwards deserted his side, abandoning the battle, the regent undoubtedly regretted his decision to part with the Burgundians. Among the deserters was the 'Lord of Torcy', whom Monstrelet lists among the knights who, 'on the very day of battle', broke their oath to the regent and deserted him.

It was 16 August before this methodical leader brought his troops along the road leading from Danville to Verneuil, where they halted for the night, surprising many, as his men had marched for only twelve miles that day and were sufficiently rested. But Bedford may have been in possession of information that forced his hand, as it would seem that, once again, the French were undecided as to what to do next. Controversy raged within their ranks, and the question was whether to fight or not to fight.

The regent must have felt supremely sure of his position, for he arrogantly sent a mocking message to the Earl of Douglas, the leader of the Scots contingent, referring to his ignominious retreat from the battle of Roxburgh in 1417. Though the news must have reached him that the Scots were emphatically for facing up to their traditional enemy, and even as he mocked them, the regent must have been aware that his army was opposed by a military force far superior to his own, at least numerically. Yet he still gave battle.

The Scots prevailed over their hesitant allies, and on the next morning, 17 August, their combined armies were deployed for battle on the open plain one mile to the north of the walls of Verneuil. Spectators were to have an excellent view of the battle from the town's ramparts. Both sides fought mainly on foot, save that two thousand French and Italian men-at-arms were sent to attack the regent's army on the rear.

The regent's troops faced an army drawn up into two divisions, with the baggage trains well back, in front of the forest area through which the road ran. The French occupied the left and their Scottish allies were on the right of the position, and each division was nominally in three lines, but the three soon became submerged into one. On the two flanks were posted small bodies of mounted men – the French cavalry having learned nothing from being routed at Agincourt due to their adopting the same pattern – with the remainder of the army being dismounted. Crossbowmen were interspersed among the men-at-arms. The length of each division was about 500 metres, with the Danville road dividing the two divisions.

It was a conventional battle plan, on the accepted chivalric pattern – now beginning to be outdated – and the regent decided to follow the military formation that his brother had deployed so brilliantly at Agincourt. A glance at the way the enemy had drawn up their units was sufficient to show Bedford that their flanks were still unco-ordinated, and even disorderly, but that they were supported by mounted troops. He therefore determined to dismount his men, with a front in two divisions (of which he himself commanded the right and his most trusted lieutenant Salisbury the left). The men-at-arms occupied the centre of each division, the archers were placed at both flanks, and the rank and file consisted of a single line at the front. Outside missile range, Bedford halted his troops and deployed them, drawing them up parallel to and along the same lines as his opponents, although cavalry were on the French wings, and archers on the English.

But, remembering the type of raids that had taken place at the battle of

Agincourt, the regent took the precaution of having a mobile reserve of two thousand archers stationed to the west of the road, to safeguard his baggage train. In fact, far in advance of his time, he took novel steps to defend it by drawing up the vehicles in close order along the perimeter, while the horses, tethered head to tail in pairs, were placed immediately outside the baggage carts. This left the pages and varlets, having no horses to hold, free to use their weapons in active defence.

Nonetheless the Lombard horsemen, assisted by the French cavaliers, succeeded in pillaging the baggage enclosure, but they were met and put to flight by the English reserve. Otherwise, the battle that took place was an ordered affair on the part of the main armies of England and France, the only irregularity being that the French were not led by their head of state, the 22-year-old dauphin. However, in a sense, it was also a battle between three nations, for the Scots were fighting as much in their own cause as in that of France. They had, after all, their humiliation at Cravant to avenge. When Bedford sent a herald to the Earl of Douglas, to ask what rules he proposed to observe in the coming fight, he received the grim reply that the Scots would neither give nor receive any quarter.

At about four o'clock, according to Bedford's own account, the two main armies advanced against each other simultaneously, as they had done at Agincourt, a battle that must have been at the forefront of every soldier's mind. The regent gave his men the traditional signal, 'Avaunt, banners!' and the troops, after kneeling down and reverently kissing the ground, responded with 'St George! Bedford!' The French countered with 'St Denis, Monjoie!' The English lines then stepped forward, slowly and deliberately uttering 'a mighty cry'. The French, by contrast, advanced rashly and erratically, for which they afterwards blamed the untrained Scottish troops.

Each English archer carried a double-pointed stake, and when they were within range of the French missiles, they halted, to plant the stakes in front of their most advanced military units. This procedure had been carried out at Agincourt, but because this battle took place in high summer, time was required to hammer the stakes into the hard ground. The French mounted forces, again as at Agincourt, were under orders to open the battle with an attack on the flanks or the rear of the archers, and they took advantage of the difficulties faced by the English, to charge before the hedge of stakes was fully erected. The western body of the French cavalry took the archers at a disadvantage and broke through their ranks. The English instinctively herded into closer formations, and the French horsemen surged around and past them, pushing on against the reserve.

Because many of the archers were swept aside, the right flank of Bedford's division was left exposed, an anxious moment for the regent in this, his first important battle. But his men-at-arms immediately came to his rescue. Disregarding the peril on their right, they strode straight into the ranks of their foes and laid into their French counterparts who were stationed in their immediate front.

The struggle proved to be much more strenuous than that at Agincourt. But after forty-five minutes the superior prowess of the English, though fighting against odds of over two to one (the French army consisting mainly of men-at-arms), gradually forced their way forward. The regent is said to have led his men, wielding a two-handed axe after the manner of King Harold at Hastings. He had dismounted from the bay charger that had carried him into battle. 'The regent was there that day as a lion,' John Hardynge declared.[6]

After three hours of indecisive fighting, but by a sheer display of toughness against greater odds, the English routed the Duke of Aumale's forces. Gradually crumbling under the pressure, they finally broke, and a complete formation turned and fled from the field together. Their men-at-arms also scattered and made for the sheltering walls of Verneuil. But the pursuit was so close, and so hotly carried out, that many of the French could not reach the gates in time, but plunged into the town ditch, where large numbers of them were drowned. The disgusted inhabitants were reported to have closed the gates in the faces of their fleeing warriors. The Duke of Aumale was killed, and the regent called off the pursuit, collected his dispersed troops and returned to the battlefield, where fighting continued.

At the Duke of Bedford's left side, the Earl of Salisbury engaged the Scots who were putting up a stiffer resistance than the French, seemingly undismayed by the sight of their allies quitting the battlefield. Largely young and untried, the Scots proved to be heroic fighters, but the defeat at Cravant was not to be avenged. The English archers, freed from attending to a mounted attack by the Lombards, went on to launch a firestorm of arrows over the French cavalry, with the result that the French finally gave way. Bedford's forces returned from pursuing the opponents who had fled beyond Verneuil, and the return of the regent's troops decided the final action, for the Earl of Salisbury's soldiers were still being hard pressed by the Scots. Relieved of fighting the French, Bedford turned his attention to aiding his second-in-command. The Scottish soldiers now found themselves hard pressed from two sides at once.

The summer day was dying, but the heat could still be felt on hot metal, and all the combatants were parched. Yet Bedford's weary troops plodded back into the fight, charging into the exposed right flank of the Scottish division, uttering a diabolical cry. Now completely surrounded, the northerners sold their lives dearly as they went down before this new assault. Escape was impossible, and surrender unthinkable, for had their leader not declared there would be no quarter on either side? The Scots were slaughtered where they stood, hacked down by the exultant English, with triumphant cries of 'For Clarence! Clarence!' – taking a final revenge for the debacle of Baugé.

The outcome of the battle was disastrous for the Scottish contingent, which was nearly destroyed. They lost the Earl of Douglas, with his son and his son-in-law, the Earl of Buchan, along with some fifty Scottish gentlemen of rank. A great part of the French soldiery had escaped, but their leaders had stayed to fight on, and so the battle was also calamitous for the French nobility, being almost as disastrous to them as Poitiers or Agincourt. Aumale and three great lords were killed, while the Duke of Alençon and Marshal Lafayette were taken prisoner.

Two days later Bedford, in a letter to Sir Thomas Rempston at Guise, stated that – by a count of the heralds – no fewer than 7,262 of the enemy had been killed, which seems an accurate assessment. The French losses were round about 1,500 killed, and of the 6,000 Scots, it was said that only a handful survived. The battle was the regent's greatest triumph in the field, to be compared with that of his brother and described by some French writers as 'un autre Azincourt'.

Bedford's combined forces have been estimated at ten thousand troops, but some had been sent away. His losses were set at about a thousand men, a noteworthy figure, but to the commander well worth the sacrifice. The French army would remain leaderless, dispirited and largely dispersed for some years to come, while Scottish reinforcements, a force that had regenerated confidence in the French position, had virtually ceased to exist.

When, that evening, the English troops entered Verneuil, the triumph was complete. On the following day a solemn service of thanksgiving was held in the great church, and the regent must have given thanks indeed for a 'second Agincourt'. He had much to thank God for.

The total English force at Verneuil was between eight and nine thousand, facing somewhere between fifteen and seventeen thousand opponents. Among the prisoners taken by the victorious army were a number of French and Normans, who had deserted from the English ranks on the eve of the battle. They were beheaded by Bedford's order, his wife not being present to plead for them.

After the battle of Verneuil, the English cause had never looked brighter. A French field army no longer existed, and the dauphin had not the financial resources to raise a new one, for he had spent all his available money on equipping the army the regent had just crushed. (At this, one of the lowest points in the dauphin's fortunes, he reacted by allowing himself to be seduced into 'feasts, dances and pleasure', seeking to 'wish away' the calamity that had overtaken him.)[7]

In August of 1424 Arnoulet Ram, who had favourably bid for the management of the Paris mint a year before, had by this time discovered that it was impossible to obtain the silver that was necessary to sustain the true value of the coinage. And this was chiefly because the only silver he could draw upon came from the mints of the Duke of Burgundy, whose weaker coinage was then circulating in France, with the permission of the regent.

Ram complained that 200,000 marks had been taken out of the kingdom, and that at the Geneva fair Lancastrian coins, worth two *deniers*, were being bought in bulk – at three times the rate of the equivalent Flemish rate. (Flemish merchants had, in fact, taken six packhorse loads of coins and silver back to Flanders, the purpose being to melt down the coins and then reissue a larger number of coinage with a lower silver content.)

Now, with Burgundian coins circulating freely in Paris, forgeries appeared within months of the issue of Anglo–French coinage, and with the running of the mint being always a hazardous investment in times of instability, profits to the English crown (and Ram) were minimal. Forgeries had been circulating as early as March 1423, and a year later an English soldier was found in possession of forged coins received from a Paris merchant, a crime for which he was hanged.

Taxation was then created to fill the gap in the royal finances that was left by the reform of the coinage. Indirect taxes were spread broadly, and they were bitterly resented. The *quatrième*, a tax of 25% on all wine retailed in Paris, was the most obviously unpopular, because the commissioners also insisted upon investigating stocks in private houses. Cattle, fish, firewood and exports of luxury goods also suffered from impositions that many saw as hitting traders and trade.

But it was the added cost of imported necessities (largely from England) that was the greatest burden for most Parisians. Even the Duke of Brittany's New Year's Day presents were not immune from confiscation when the export tax was not paid. (The regent considered this case personally, doubtless because he did not wish to alienate an already uncertain ally, but nonetheless rigidly allowing the impost to be exacted.)

Militarily speaking, an advance on the enemy stronghold of Bourges by the English army at this juncture might have given the best hope of putting an end to the war. For even the most fervent dauphinists, seeing the utter impotence of the armies they had raised for their leader by excessive taxation had now lost heart and given up the apparently unequal contest. Clearly, God was on the side of the infant Henry VI rather than that of his uncle, Charles VII. (It did occur to some of his advisers that the dauphin should fall further back from his temporary capital of Bourges. If he could set himself up in a southern city such as Toulouse, this would give him more time to build up a greater army to face those who wished to rob him of his birthright.)

But Bedford himself played into the dauphin's hands in this. An advance upon Bourges would have been decisive, in that its capture would have brought an end to all hostilities. 'Charles VII' might have become a prisoner of war, with no possibility of the enormous ransom the English would have demanded from his 'subjects' ever being raised. Yet inexplicably for one so politically astute, the regent missed this opportunity to anglicise France at one blow in the name of his nephew. Instead, he stubbornly clung to his original plan to conquer the counties of Maine and Anjou, to reduce the territories north of the Loire, and to capture the almost impregnable fortress of Mont St Michel.

To these ends he divided up his army among its commanders, entrusting the campaign in Maine to Sir John Fastolf and Lord Scales, the advance to the Loire to the Earls of Salisbury and Suffolk, and directing Sir Nicholas Burdet to mount a campaign against Mont St Michel. Bedford himself retreated to Rouen, ostensibly to punish the Norman deserters from Verneuil. The military situation remained favourable to the English, and would continue to improve over the next few months as the greater part of Anjou and Maine were overrun. Moreover, the campaign designed to topple the Loire strongholds was set in motion, and the fortresses still holding out in Picardy and Champagne surrendered.

Not that any of these future developments would have been evident to either the English or their French allies when the regent re-entered Paris on 8 September 1424 where, as the conqueror of Verneuil, he was received 'with great rejoicing'. By this stupendous victory, he had saved the capital from any further depredations by the Armagnacs for many months, if not years, to come. The city was decorated in every street that he was expected to ride along, and the pavements were especially cleaned. To express their joy in his triumph, the citizens went out to greet their deliverer, gaily dressed in red and yellow clothing.

The regent arrived about five in the afternoon, though the citizens' procession went as far into the country as the other side of La Chapelle and St Denis to welcome him. When they met up with him they loudly sang the Te Deum and praises to God, and so he came into Paris with an unaccustomed escort of citizens. It formed, in fact, a popular procession.

Wherever he passed by, the people shouted 'Noël', and the corporation had arranged for various diversions to amuse him. When the regent came to the corner of the rue Aux Lombards there was an acrobat, 'performing as cleverly as anyone had ever seen'. In front of the fortress of the Châtelet was a very fine mystery play of the Old and New Testaments, performed by the children of Paris. It was all done without speech, and often without movement, the children freezing into tableaux as though they were statues against the wall. The regent looked at their performance for a long time before going on to celebrate a special mass. He was 'received as if he had been God'.[8]

The processions that had not gone out to meet him in the countryside accompanied him to Notre Dame, and the canons welcomed him with singular honour, 'singing all the hymns of praises that they could'. He entered the cathedral to the sonorous rumble of the organ, the braying of trumpets, and the great bells pealing out. 'In short, more honour was never done at a Roman triumph than was done that day to him and his wife.'

It was beginning to be noted that his duchess accompanied him everywhere. The duke was clearly besotted with his clever and lively young wife, and she had begun to appreciate her extraordinary role as the wife of the virtual ruler of northern France, performing her duties with grace and charm. It is significant that, however reserved the Parisians would remain in their attitude to the regent, they spontaneously took his wife to their hearts.

Yet even though he was met with the most solemn of masses, and with a general rejoicing in his victory, another conspiracy in favour of Charles of Valois had been discovered in his absence, by those who wished to see the old line restored. However, it had been swiftly dealt with, and it was agreed by most that the victory at Verneuil had given English rule in France the greatest strength it had so far attained.

There was also much else to please the Parisians, as that year was the finest vintage within living memory. (The Romans had introduced wine growing to Paris, and the heights dominating the city were covered with vineyards. It was a very profitable business, even if the wine was generally mediocre.)

But that year so much wine was produced there was a shortage of casks and they became very dear. Three empty hogsheads went for the price of one full cask of wine, and to counter this a lot of citizens put their wine into vats, which they then had sunk into the ground. Wine was, in fact, so cheap, even before the harvest was over, that by the festival of St Rémi one could buy a quart for a penny.

A consequence of this was that men of all ranks – except for those in control – paid a very heavy levy on every hogshead of wine they harvested. All those who had wine in the Porte St Jacques and the Porte des Bordelles area paid 3sp 'good currency' on every large hogshead, and on puncheons, small casks and barrels at a matching rate. They also had the upkeep of an armed English picket to their cost, as small groups of Armagnac brigands still infested the district beyond the southern gates. On the near side of the bridge, purchasers had to pay only half a *thin*, as the 'false traitors' left that boundary alone and had no troops there.

In November the Lord of Toulougéon (Jean de la Trémoïlle) was married to Jacqueline d'Ambroise, one of Queen Isabeau's ladies-in-waiting, in the Duke of Burgundy's mansion. (Trémoïlle was grand master of the duke's household.) Jean was the younger brother of the man who would soon become the dauphin's favourite, his 'evil genius' according to many, Georges de la Trémoïlle, and this soon-to-be notorious brother, at that time no known threat to the English, was present under a safe-conduct.

Lord Scales was also married in that month. Present at that marriage were the Earl and Countess of Salisbury, and the Duke of Burgundy was said to have offended the earl by trying to make love to his countess. (Philippe, who would be married three times, had a notable eye for the ladies, but this insult to Salisbury's wife may well explain the support the earl later gave to Humphrey of Gloucester in his campaign against Burgundy in the Low Countries.) In celebration of the two marriages, jousts were held every day for six weeks, until the Duke of Burgundy went back to his own country.

After he had gone, the regent took over the palace of the Bourbons for his own use on 1 December. A very large feast was held there, at tremendous cost, which resulted in a heavy charge on the citizenry to pay for it. This feast took place two weeks before Christmas, and when it was ended all the great lords went away to Rouen, where Bedford also kept court.

To add to this burden of taxation 'for pleasure', there was another crisis with currency. Some coins that had been minted during the late Duke of Burgundy's command of the city were now devalued. These little coins had originally been valued at 12d, and that had been reduced to nine pence, but now, on 2 November 1425, it was proclaimed throughout the streets that they were only worth eight. This was much resented, but it was only the first devaluation. There were other coins called '*blancs*', worth about 8d. These *blancs* bore both the French and English arms, which seemed to guarantee their stability, and so many citizens felt that they had been twice swindled when it was suddenly announced on 9 December that these coins would only be worth 7d. 'So that all the people who had any lost one eighth of their wealth.'

The citizens blamed the English for this devaluation, but the currency in Paris (or indeed France) had long been subject to financial manipulation.[9] Money had, in fact, ceased to have any fixed value for over sixty years. The Treasury, which could draw on no established system of taxation, had only one way to ensure revenue: it increased the quantity of money in circulation by minting inferior alloys. Gold and silver coins had been debased sixty-four times under Philippe VI, one hundred and four times under Jean II, and forty-one times under the late king. His father, Charles V, had issued what amounted to a counterfeit coinage, because he had taken care to disguise its true value. The dauphin, it was said, had been more honest than most in that he had publicly pronounced in 1422 that his *florette*, which weighed 2.04 grammes, with a face value of twenty deniers, contained only ten milligrammes of silver. This was the lowest point reached by the process of monetary debasement, but for the Parisians at least it had one comfort. How could the dauphin hope to fund any sort of resistance if his finances were in such bad shape?

But this mad dance of money, and a shortage of goods, had meant a corresponding rise in the price of almost every commodity (except land, which nobody wanted to buy at this period). Since the Parisians already faced a 'city toll', an indirect tax that was collected on all articles of consumption that entered the capital, the prices of consumer goods were already raised substantially, without further impositions. By 1213 a long list already existed of the duties to be levied on all goods, and the list had grown appreciably over the years, while the Parisians thought up every possible trick to avoid these heavy tolls.

For many years thousands of refugees from the surrounding country-side had sought shelter within the walls of Paris, swelling the hard-pressed population; but now the population began to decrease, perhaps as a result of the devaluation of money, with many people deserting the city. As a consequence workmen were proving harder to find, and the wages to secure their vanishing services had risen correspondingly. The 'English' wars had ruined many of the great capitalists (except, of course, for those they had enriched) and they had also reduced the fortunes of the middle classes (except for those who had the enterprise to avail themselves of the new opportunities). But they had not much affected the purchasing power of the humbler citizen, for whom times would never much change, regardless of who was in power, since they would always be at the mercy of greater forces.

But additional miseries were in store for them.

The Burgundian and English marriages in Paris, mounted with such splendour in November, had both masked a deeper purpose. For the Duke of Bedford's brother, the Duke of Gloucester, had invaded Hainault in October 1424 with a contingent of English mercenaries, to claim the province for his wife, and Philippe of Burgundy was now decided to lead his forces into that country to defend his cousin's rights. The Duchess of Gloucester regained possession of her old domains very quickly, due to a brilliant campaign by her husband, and Duke Humphrey then sent a force into Brabant, which ravaged the country up to the gates of Brussels. At which outrage the Duke of Burgundy felt it incumbent upon him to threaten an outright war with England, in defence of what he saw as his cousin's (and his own) property.

Gloucester wrote to Philippe of Burgundy, informing him heatedly that it was his duty to espouse Jacqueline's cause rather than that of the Duke of Brabant, and most witnesses to the conflict agreed that there was much to be said for this view. But Gloucester also aroused Philippe's wrath by accusing him of making a statement that was 'contrary to the truth' in defence of his cousin's claim to the lands. Philippe saw this accusation as a reflection on his honour and challenged Duke Humphrey to a duel, with the Holy Roman Emperor to act as the arbitrator. This challenge was at once accepted, but as the emperor refused any role in the quarrel, it was decided that Bedford should act as judge. That this suggestion came from Philippe himself is a testimony to the regent's extraordinary impartiality.[10]

The conference between Bedford and Burgundy that lasted throughout November was designed to call off this disastrous confrontation, which would rob the regent of thousands of Burgundian troops, leaving the English forces, already undermanned, exposed to Armagnac incursions into their occupied territory, including the environs of Paris. Once it was known that the Burgundians had departed for the Low Countries, the French would obviously augment their divisions, and the English presence might not be strong enough to keep the enemy away from their prized possession, the capital.

So, although Duke Philippe continued to be unimpressed by any arguments that might dissuade him from his chosen course, the regent was constant in his endeavours to conciliate him, and it required all his tact, diplomacy and patience to soothe the feelings of the irate Burgundian. His efforts even extended to taking part himself in a joust, a passage at arms in which he was not skilled.

But once Gloucester's army arrived in Hainault, to try to get possession of his wife's lands, any further attempts at appeasement by the regent between his brother and the Duke of Burgundy were impossible. Then, on visiting Philippe at Hesdin, the regent was mortified to see the Burgundian lords sporting a badge that indicated their resolve to maintain the cause of John of Brabant against the Duke of Gloucester. Realising how strongly his allies felt about this matter, it was at this point that Bedford decided to hold a great council in Paris, under the guise of celebrating the two marriages. Here, he believed that his judgement would prevail; and he could proclaim that the challenge between his brother and his major ally should not be followed through, in the interests of keeping their mutual gains in France. Unfortunately, two weddings and six weeks of jousting could not break the impasse, and his judgement went for nothing. Gloucester's greed was greater than his patriotism.

The regent was tactful, conciliatory, resourceful, unselfish, both a skilful soldier and a capable administrator. His role as the leader in France was both arduous and frustrating, and although he laboured unceasingly to uphold his nephew's claim to the French throne, his efforts appeared to founder under this new threat to the English presence in France. He had the confidence of both men, but he was toiling in vain. For his grasping brother Gloucester could only see his own financial interests, and the Duke of Burgundy had no wish to admit an Englishman, even as the protector of his wife's property, into his dominions.[11]

Identifying with the Duke of Bedford's dilemma, the Parisians saw this war in a distant county, between their two protectors, as more a matter of pig-headedness rather than one of commonsense and, to them, the regent's brother was clearly in the wrong. His wife, after all, had been married in France to the brother of the Count of St Pol, and the first husband had clear rights to his wife's property. Nothing could be gained from such a conflict, and Paris would be at risk if English troops were to be taken away to fight in such a lost cause.

Besides which, always a consideration, a war between the regent's brother and the Duke of Burgundy would result in a heavy tax to be raised to assist the Duke of Burgundy, which could only further distress the poor, and serve nobody's purpose . . . at least in the capital. When this tax was duly levied, there was the inevitable outcry against it, but it proceeded as ordered, for the Parisians knew that such a tax was a necessary evil. Paris needed the English presence, the English needed the Burgundians, and so that presence had to be paid for, even if the price was often exorbitant.[12]

But, to the relief of all in northern France, the threatened breach between the two countries was healed in an unexpected way. The tide of war turned against the English in the Hainault cause, and Duke Humphrey went back to England without further attempting to prosecute his wife's cause. His reasons for returning without putting up a greater show have never been explained, but whatever persuaded him to abandon the fight was very strong, for he never returned to the continent. Gloucester, a 'high-metalled youth', would inevitably have taken his wronged wife's side in the matter, and his conduct was understandable and even in many ways laudable. But the consequences for the English were almost disastrous, as they would have ended in an open breach with Burgundy and the end of all English influence in France. Without Bedford's magnificent diplomacy the situation could not have been saved, and even though the quarrel was patched up it was to have unfortunate after-effects. It had slowed up the tempo of the war at a time when it was looking so promising. (The victory at Verneuil gave English rule the greatest strength it was to attain during their occupation of Paris.) But more fatally, it was the beginning of a rift between England and her closest ally.

NOTES

1   This was because the English wanted the French kingdom to pay for itself as far as possible. Messages from Paris to London, at any level, were mostly declarations of formalised loyalty to the young king. Otherwise, the dispatches were appeals for more troops to be sent to the front.
2   *Archives Nationales.*
3   Monstrelet, *Chronique.*
4   Newhall, *The English Conquest of Normandy.*

5 Date fixed by Martin Simpson in the *English Historical Review*, 1934.
6 Hardyng was also present at Agincourt, about which battle he wrote a rhymed chronicle.
7 Basin, *Histoire de Charles VII*.
8 Bourgeois de Paris.
9 Henry V tried to fuse together the various financial structures which at that time prevailed within the Paris region. He had also tried to modernise the antiquated methods used by the Treasury. This had been partially successful, but his attempts to establish a strong coinage had inevitably led to the re-introduction of unpopular taxation. Wyllie and Waugh, *The Reign of Henry V*.
10 Bourgeois de Paris.
11 Vaughan, *Philippe the Good*.
12 Bourgeois de Paris.
13 Williams, *My Lord of Bedford*.

CHAPTER IV

1425: Business as Usual

In the first week of January 1425 the labouring men of the surrounding countryside brought a petition to the great council of Paris. In it they protested against the distress and hardship caused by the actions of the many 'thieving brigands' who infested their land for some twenty leagues around the capital. These men had no allegiance to any of the three main war parties, their only interest was in immediate gain, and their marauding did great harm to the rural population. (These raiders were, in fact, a league of 'poor gentlemen' who had been impoverished by the wars, and who had turned 'robbers by day and night'.)[1]

The regent did not offer the services of his troops to round them up, but suggested that the Provost Marshal of Paris should himself raise a force to deal with this matter. The provost marshal did as he was ordered and summoned the forces of the city, along with sixty archers and crossbowmen, whom he then personally led to the robbers' reported base. In less than a week Morhier had captured over two hundred of the raiders, and had incarcerated them in various prisons in the nearest 'good' towns – that is to say those communities that were sympathetic to the English. On Wednesday 9 January 1425 he brought two wagonloads of the worst of them to Paris, and about twenty were executed.

During this time, the regent's brother had not completely abandoned his wife's cause, and the remnants of his troops were still making spasmodic war on the Duke of Burgundy. Accounts of the several skirmishes between Gloucester's private army and the Flemings were reported back to Paris, and the citizens knew that for as long as it continued they would have to pay for it, even though it was so remote from their concerns. Although it would all come to nothing, the people were still asked by the Duke of Burgundy to send men and money to his cause.

The burden was aggravation enough – although, as ever, the citizens grudgingly contributed – but more worryingly many Parisians saw this event as a bad portent for their own future, as it clearly exposed the breach between their two main supporters. If the English and the Burgundians were to fight among themselves, exhausting their inadequate forces in a conflict so far removed from Parisian concerns, who would protect them from their main enemy, the Armagnacs? It was well known that the dauphin, since his expulsion from Paris, had conceived an aversion to their city after being so violently rejected by the citizens. Who was to know what his actions would be, should he bring his army to reclaim the capital when it lay defenceless before him, while the English and Burgundian troops were at each other's throats in the Low Countries?

Yet, contradictorily, the military operations their protectors did actively pursue 'in the interests of Paris' were considered by the citizens to be almost as unimportant in the greater scheme of things during this period, the expenses for which could barely be justified in their view. Fortunately for their purses, the English advances in Maine and Beauce, in the land between Chartres and the Loire, came to a standstill, and were not resumed until the Earl of Salisbury returned in the summer with re-inforcements from England. (The earl paid frequent visits to England, not only to recruit new troops, but also to oversee their training before they were sent to the front.)

But although there was little military activity, there were other bad omens for the Parisians that year, even if it had begun well enough once the brigands were dealt with, and food could be brought in without harassment. Fresh herrings had been on sale until halfway through Lent. Peas, 'as good as they had ever been', were selling at three *blancs* or fourteen pence a bushel, and beans were selling for ten pence for a similar measure. It seemed that for the first time in many years, the citizens could look forward to full bellies during the summer months at least. Then a plague of caterpillars infested the plants after Easter. All the fruit was spoiled, and many vines. 1425 was not going to be a good vintage.

Yet there were some signs of improvement in the general life of the populace, which could only be attributed to the protection afforded by the English garrison, and the unaccustomed sense of security the Parisians now felt under their aegis. After Easter, before St John's Day, the people who lived in the rue Martin and the streets nearby were given permission to have the Porte St Martin opened at their own cost, in time for the great fair. The people of the quarter were pleased to undertake this major opera-tion, even though it would be very expensive, as it included repairing the drawbridge, the barriers and everything that was connected to the gate. For it had been much damaged over the years of the civil war, the arch of the bridge was broken, the walls were starting to crumble in places, the barriers were rotten, and even the locks had rusted.[2]

Elated by the fact that they were now safe enough to open an important gate, and equally inspired by their desire to keep the hated Armagnacs from their walls, the citizens spent money and labour so well that 'one could truly say their hearts were in their work'. Even priests and the clergy worked willingly alongside the citizens (a sight not often seen).[3] They did so much in fact, both personally and by paying for 'proxies' to do their share of the labour, that in seven weeks the builders were able to do more than people had ever thought possible. It was said that more people passed through the St Martin's gate on opening day than had passed through it for thirty years. The guardians of the quarter kept 'watch and ward' here, and the consecration of the gate was a cause of great celebration.

But soon after the gate was opened, the Parisians were faced with a new taxation. The Earl of Salisbury was back on the military front in the summer of 1425, when he pushed through more of his victorious campaigns, all of which had to be paid for, and to which the Parisians contributed more than most. Fortunately, the earl – as was his reputation – took little time in cutting through the enemy forces. After a final 'mopping up' operation in Champagne, he pushed westwards into Beauce, captured Etampes and Rambouillet, and drove forward into Maine. Le Mans, the capital of the Sarthe, fell to him on 10 August, and Mayenne capitulated soon after, by which surrender the English forces completed their conquest of the Maine area.

After this, hostilities flagged, and the people of Paris had a brief respite from the continual levies that had been forced upon them by the English prosecution of these battles, that is until a fresh quarrel broke out between the Duke of Burgundy and Duke Humphrey of Gloucestor, and the two men resumed *their* war. Philippe, as always, demanded a heavy charge to be once again imposed upon the Parisians, greatly to the distress of the poor, who could least afford such allegiance to him.

But life went on much as it had always done. Bedford, who had a policy of 'bread and circuses', ensured that the Parisians were provided with spectacular events, although the citizens could always devise their own more primitive amusements. On the last Sunday in August, an entertainment was given in the Hôtel d'Armagnac in the rue St Honoré, which was very much to their liking. Four blind men, each wearing armour, and each carrying a club, were put into an enclosure along with a strong pig, and this would be their prize should they manage to kill it. They fought a very odd battle, to the extended amusement of the crowd since, instead of hitting the pig they for the most part hit each other, giving themselves tremendous blows with their clubs. Only their imitation armour protected them from real injury. On the day before they had been led in a mock procession, with a man beating a drum.[4]

This contest proved immensely popular and on the day of St Giles and St Lupus, which was a Saturday that year, some members of the parish council suggested putting on another entertainment. This consisted of sticking a thirty-six-foot long pole into the ground, with a basket at its tip, in which were a fat goose and coins to the value of six *blancs*. Then the pole was greased, and it was announced that whoever could scramble up the

51

pole unassisted, to capture the goose and the money should have the prize. But nobody succeeded in climbing the treacherous pole, though a boy who had managed to climb higher than anybody else was given the goose as a reward, but the money was taken back by the council.[5]

On the following Wednesday, a knight was beheaded in public by order of the regent, which was also much appreciated by the crowd. This man, 'an evil brigand' called the Messire Etienne de Favrière was known to be a great thief, who had caused much misery to his victims, and the people were happy to see him parted from his head. As an extra precaution, the regent also hanged some of his disciples from the Paris gallows, and the crowds were as eager to see them dangle.

Death, in fact, was very much in the air that month. The gruesome mural of the 'Danse Macabre' was made at the church of the Innocents; begun about August, it would not be finished until the following Lent. People said that the word 'macabre' related to the Maccabees, who were associated with death because of the prayers for the dead, in their book in the Old Testament, but by chance it was also the name of the painter. It very quickly became accepted that to 'dance the dance', meant to have danced with the Dark Angel of Death. As a work of art it was satisfyingly horrifying, and it would prove to be very influential.[6]

In September the Armagnacs abandoned Rochefort, the dauphin's only important seaport, where 'our people' (a body that was largely made up of volunteers from Paris) were besieging them. The city could regard this triumph as their own particular achievement and, perhaps as a consequence, the authorities felt so confident of their safety they opened the Porte de Montmartre in that same month, although work on the drawbridge was not finished until a few weeks later, and even then it was lowered only in the daytime.

Not only common soldiers still had difficulty in making the French understand them, for much higher placed individuals still struggled with the language, for even when their French was good enough, their English accents were too broad for the Parisian ear. After the Treaty of Paris, the first president at the parliament had been forced to address the court in the name of some of the English members, since none could follow their manner of speaking. The dean of the regent's chapel, John Estcourt (himself of an old Norman family), was a highly placed member of the French royal council. In October 1425 he explained to the chapter of Notre Dame (presumably in Latin) that it was impossible for him to hear the annual confession of those chaplains who spoke only French because he had difficulty in following them. A French priest was appointed to fulfil this task.

Rouen, the second city of the Northern Kingdom, was ideally placed between Paris and the sea, and both cities were in a position to benefit from each other, yet there were conflicting interests, and continual friction between them. While the merchants of Rouen felt they were denied the same level of commercial success as their Parisian counterparts, their council controlled access to the sea, and both cities jealously guarded their individual privileges. At the same time, they each sought to encroach on the preserves of the other, with the result that conflict between them was inevitable.

Although occasionally hazardous, since boats and barges were often at the mercy of river pirates, the Seine was still the safest of the supply passages for the capital, and the Rouennais were only too keen to exploit this advantage. They had challenged the privileges of the merchants of Paris, as granted by the crown between 1315 and 1380, and they had repeatedly attempted to gain control over the trade of the Seine, navigable for sea-going vessels as far as their city. The Parisians could not accept this situation, so detrimental to their own commercial interests, and their objections were swelled by the councils of several Norman towns who also objected to the growing power of Rouen. But, partly because it was now the acknowledged capital of 'English' France, Rouen was never happy to accept the supremacy of Paris, and throughout the early years of English triumph the second city took on the aspect of the first.[7] *Parlement* was, naturally enough, always firmly in favour of the old capital against the upstart, but by 1425 the matter was still unsettled.[8] Both the city council and the University of Paris joined to argue the case in front of the Duke of Bedford, but again it was left unresolved.[9]

This problematical matter created great tensions throughout Lancastrian France, and the Parisian *chambre du roi* was forced into a secondary position. Bedford, always anxious to placate the Parisians, sought to rectify the situation. To diminish Rouen's dominance, patrols of the major roads that ran between the two cities were organised, in an effort to limit the problems of raids by brigands and enemy soldiers, and to leave the Parisians less dependent upon the river. This solution, of course, proved expensive, and was – as always – reflected in the cost of foodstuffs.

To the consternation of the Parisians, the regent was requested to return to England by a letter from the English council, dated 31 October 1425. At home, he was required to settle a quarrel between Henry Beaufort, the Bishop of Winchester, and the Earl of Gloucester, who had returned to England from Hainault. Gloucester had been named as the protector of his nephew Henry VI, but Beaufort – the richest man in England – was the practical head of government.[10] Born in 1374, he has been described as a 'rich, resplendent, domineering prelate, and one of the few men in England who could stand the financial risk of making loans to England, and who did well on it'. As grasping as Gloucester, but much more accomplished and sensible, the bishop would have been far too strong for the duke, had the charismatic Duke Humphrey not been personally popular with the mob, and third in line to the throne. The struggle for power between these two dominant men, both so close to the king, would last for almost twenty years, dating from this period.[11]

Real power in England, though, was more properly invested in an aristocratic council that controlled all official appointments and the royal prerogative. Inclusion in this council was highly lucrative, as the members were paid for attendance, but they were as often as not at loggerheads over the spoils of government. Both Beaufort and Gloucester had their adherents among this influential body, and when the council finally split into two camps, one was headed by Duke Humphrey, and the other by his uncle.

By 1425 Bedford's presence in England was very necessary, for the quarrels between the two men had become extremely violent, and there had been armed attacks upon Beaufort's life. (The bishop was a half-uncle to the royal family, a son of John of Gaunt, through a bastard line that had been legitimised, and which would eventually produce a pretender to the English throne in the person of Henry Tudor.)

The bishop used his enormous wealth largely for his own political ends, and his influence upon the English government was extensive, largely because it was almost permanently in debt to him. Therefore Bedford knew that because of Beaufort's vital importance to the royalist cause in France, he must conciliate him, even if it meant doing so at the expense of his brother. Parliament was growing increasingly reluctant to pour money into the bottomless pit of war, the financial deficit was becoming ruinous, and the English position in France depended upon Bedford's ability to placate the two warring men, and to squeeze more money out of both parliament and the bishop.

Committing the prosecution of the war, and the protection of Paris, to the Earls of Warwick, Salisbury and Suffolk, the regent left the capital on 1 December, in the company of his duchess and a small regiment of soldiers. Before quitting the city, he distributed a number of valuable gifts to highly regarded colleagues – among them the Royal Secretary and his own four trumpeters. Fine houses, confiscated from the Armagnacs, were given to the Earl of Warwick, Sir John Handford, and Sir Walter Hunger-ford. It was Lord Willoughby, though, who received the greatest prize – the enormous mansion of the Duke of Orléans, which straddled the old walls of Paris in the area of Les Halles.[12] Willoughby was the second major English landowner in the city, after the Duke of Bedford.

The regent's entourage then headed for Amiens and the coast, but an attempt was made to surprise and capture them on the way, by a local chieftain called Sauvage de Fremainville, who was at the head of a band of freebooters. A ransom for a man so vital to the Anglo–Burgundian cause would have been more than his dependents could ever raise, but Bedford cannily avoided the trap that was set for him, and he made his way safely to England. He landed at Sandwich on 20 December, entering London on 10 January 1426.

On All Hallows Eve 1425, in fear of his life, Beaufort had written to Bedford in France, imploring him to return to England, post haste, to prevent a pitched battle with the Duke of Gloucester. Meanwhile, he had taken refuge from the duke at the fortified priory at Merton, south of London. He and the regent would enter the capital together in early January 1426, escorted by the Lord Mayor and other dignitaries. The city was *en fête* to greet Bedford, but London was not considered a suitable venue for the act of reconciliation between the two men and, over the next few months, Duke Humphrey would resist any attempt to get them together. All this would keep Bedford away from his duties in France.

One of his last acts before leaving Paris had been to devalue the coins called 'blacks'. This devaluation, as we have seen, was much resented, and the regent left his nephew's capital an extremely unpopular man.

NOTES

1   *Archives Nationales.*
2   The Porte St Martin (like the Porte St Denis) is not to be confused with the gates now standing, which were erected in the 17th century, though based on similar structures dating from a much earlier period. By late medieval times, Paris had outgrown this inner wall (demolished in the 19th century to create the Grands Boulevards). By the early 15th century, another wall had been erected beyond this, a more truly defensive wall, as described by de Metz.
3   Bourgeois de Paris.
4   Ibid.
5   Ibid.
6   The word 'macabre' was associated with death before this date. To 'dance with death' is thought to suggest that someone has come close to dying.
7   Bedford eventually decided that at least one particular set of cases, those involving disputes over royal gifts of lands and benefices within the duchy of Normandy and the lands of the conquest, should be heard outside Paris. To deal with these actions, he created new committees, which heard them in the Council of Rouen. The *parlement* of Paris found this difficult to accept.
8   Burney, *English Rule in Normandy.*
9   Allmand, *Lancastrian Normandy.*
10 Williams, *My Lord of Bedford.*
11 Holmes, *Cardinal Beaufort.*
12 Fauquembergue, *Journal.*

CHAPTER V
1426: Interregnum

Bedford was away for over a year, and yet he had left matters so well organised that the governance of Paris was relatively little affected by his absence. That life in the capital continued as normally as it did in the circumstances is a tribute to the strength of the English presence, even though it had been greatly reduced, but it can also be charged to the ordinary Parisian's strong need for life to go on as usual.

But much as they wished for a peaceful routine, and for the fighting to be kept as far away from them as possible, the Parisians were always prepared to serve in the defence of their city, even when the action lay beyond the city walls. On 24 January, for example, Guillaume Jouan, a master of crossbowmen, mobilised nineteen other archers to serve under the Earl of Warwick in a campaign east of the capital, which was by no means unusual.[1] (It is not known how many Frenchmen actually served in the ranks of the Anglo–Burgundian armies, but there must have been hundreds of men who were as keen as Jouan to enjoy military service.)

In other years the pillaging that had taken place throughout the countryside had made it impossible for men to work their fields, and so little ploughing or sowing had been done anywhere. The people had complained to the great French lords, but they were only sneered and laughed at, and their troops had then behaved more criminally than before. As a result many of the labourers had stopped working in despair, and some had even abandoned their wives and children, forsaking their strips of land. 'Let it all go to the devil,' had been the general attitude. 'Just as well do the worst we can as the best.' Yet under the regent's protection this situation had been vastly alleviated, and life had returned to something of its old normality.

The citizens, always ready to take advantage of any opportunity offered to them by nature, particularly in times of hardship, often flouted the law in order to do so. On 14 January the authorities banned people from descending into the moats in search of fish for themselves and grass for their animals, although this decree was generally ignored. During the spring flooding of the Seine, particularly strong this year, when large numbers of small fish took shelter in the stiller waters of the moat, many enthusiastic anglers over-fished these waters, and a large number of arrests were made. The authorities believed that the fine nets used not only gave the fishermen an unfair advantage, but could lead to a depletion of the river's stocks.[2]

Although they would never warm to them, the majority of the Parisians at this time were beginning to see the English as their shield, a shield that had been temporarily withdrawn with the departure of Bedford for London, with a corresponding cutback in the number of the garrison. They marvelled that the dauphin still made no attempt to recapture the lands between his forces and the capital while the city appeared to be relatively defenceless, and they put this down to the fear in which the English were generally held, even when they were temporarily leaderless. (They were not to know that Charles's financial problems, from 1424 onwards, would preclude any further assault on the English possessions north of the Loire for some time to come. It was not simply a question of the superiority of English army tactics, the dauphin lacked the money to revitalise his army, virtually dismantled at the battle of Verneuil.)

In fact, while Bedford was in England, the only operations to need the attention of the resident English army were in Brittany, where the turncoat duke, Jean V, had now decided to share the fortunes or – at this stage, misfortunes – of the dauphin. As a result of the duke's defection, a small English force under the leadership of Sir Thomas Rempston invaded Brittany in January, to the stage of reaching the capital. Although Rempston, with no reinforcements to back up his action, soon retreated from this exposed position to establish his base at St James-de-Beuvron – at that time held by Suffolk – a little town on the border of Normandy, midway between Avranches and Fougères.

Arthur de Richemont then raised an army to assist his renegade brother, and in February he advanced to besiege the English-held St James. As ever, in these contests between the French and English armies, the English were outnumbered but not outclassed. In this encounter Richemont's forces were truly alarming, being about 16,000 strong, while Rempston could only muster a paltry six hundred men.

For a time it looked as though the English would suffer intolerable reverses. The newly created French constable had brought with him a powerful artillery force, and by using it he soon made two breaches in the walls of St James. He then made an outright assault on the town, as a result of which a long and very fierce struggle took place, which lasted until the evening. The hard-pressed English garrison, after holding a council of war, decided on a desperate expedient. Leaving a portion of his already defective force to hold the enemy in the breaches, Rempston took a small group of men through a sally port, and by doing so was able to attack the enemy in the rear with the cry of 'Salisbury! St George!'

The French, thinking themselves assailed on two sides, at once gave way, many of them being driven into a nearby lake, where some were drowned. The others fell back to their camp, after suffering heavy losses. However, that was not the end for them, for during the night a considerable number of their men panicked and deserted their comrades, after burning their tents. This set up a chain reaction, and group after group, the French army abandoned their artillery and stores, not stopping in their breakneck flight until they reached their original point of departure near Fougères. 'Thus fled his army,' de Beaucourt wrote of Richemont's defeat, 'routed by an enemy twenty times its inferior in numbers. Thus terminated in a most lamentable reverse an expedition in which he had placed all his hopes.'

The English were said to have captured fourteen 'great guns' and fourteen barrels of powder, along with three hundred pipes of wine, and hundreds of pipes and barrels of provisions. This extraordinary 'Rout of St James' was one of the most astonishing episodes in the English wars against France.

Not that this was apparent, even to the French chroniclers of the time, and for the inhabitants of Paris it was a great deal less remarkable, and the year proceeded much as other years had done. All the battles that were essentially fought for the preservation of their way of life were carried on far from their walls, and their defences were designed only to stand against siege and assault.[3]

Yet it needed only one man to obtain the key to a gate for disaster to strike, and so the keys were now closely guarded; there would be no repeat of 1418. There was also some concern to limit the number of entries into the city, although it was soon realised that the authorities could not contain or exclude isolated individuals. But when danger drew near, ingress and exits were reduced even further, to the point at times when only one gate in the north and one in the south were left open, and they were always heavily guarded.

There were two watches in Paris – the gentlemen of the *guet* ('look-out') *royale* and the citizens of the municipal *guet*.[4] The latter was divided into four categories, known as the *bourgeois*, the *métiers* (tradesmen), the *assis* (established) and the *dormants* (those who could only be called upon in an extreme emergency). The *Chevalier du guet* was in overall charge of the system, and his tasks were varied. For example, in 1426 he policed the great fair at St Denis, but in the following year he led an expedition to capture a notorious bandit. He was provided with a house at the centre of the busy Ste Opportune area, and his royal watch was composed of twenty mounted sergeants and sixty on foot. They patrolled the walls throughout the night, checking that those who were supposed to be on duty were present – and awake!

Yet it was surprisingly easy to obtain ammunition in Paris, and a dedicated and resourceful rebel could easily have armed a group for a coup against the government without much trouble, which makes it all the more extraordinary that so little was attempted in this line. There were some eighteen known arms dealers, five of whom had very substandard stocks of a variety of weapons, but many more suppliers worked secretly. Even some ordinary merchants included arms among their other goods. For example, Robin Clément, a moneychanger with connections to the Low Countries, offered saltpetre at twenty *ecus* per hundred pounds. Perhaps it was only the diligence of the secret police that checked such subversion.[5]

Both the regent and the municipality, of course, possessed stocks of arms, secreted around the city. Supplies were preserved for the use of the royal troops at the Louvre, and at other redoubts. The most important fortification was at the Bastille, the grim castle that guarded the eastern entrance to the capital, and a long-time symbol of royal strength.[6] Its military were capable of repelling attacks both from outside the city and from within. The bastion could be held even when the rest of Paris had fallen to the enemy, and it could also be used to wage war upon the citizens when they rebelled against the authorities. Not that it was ever required to do this in the early days of the English occupation.

The ordinary Parisian, like the corporation that represented him, was content to leave political and military matters well alone. Instead, he concentrated on commerce and finance. To his relief, although there were further reductions in the value of coinage during the regent's absence, taxes remained at the level that had been agreed upon before he left for England. In fact, during this interlude, Paris could be said to have ruled itself in a manner it had never known before. All matters of trade – weights, measures, the sale of wine and firewood, the control of prices and quality – were more in the hands of the corporation than had ever been the case when a king was established in his palace. Streets, bridges, hospitals, river matters and wrecks, were left to those best able to deal with them, and for a time all matters relating to ordinary life improved. As the royal power decreased with Bedford's absence, the municipality came briefly into its own.

Then nature struck. Unexpectedly, on the feast of St John the Baptist, in June 1426, an unseasonable volume of rain poured from the skies, the water level rose alarmingly all over northern France, and the land was broadly flooded. This continued throughout the whole month, with catastrophic consequences, some of which greatly disturbed the people. After the midsummer bonfire was lit in the Place de Grève, and even as the revellers were dancing around it, the Seine suddenly overflowed its banks, its waters extinguishing the festive fire. Surprisingly, since to many present this seemed an ill omen, the dancers unhurriedly gathered up what they could of the unburned wood and took it up the incline to the

Cross. This feast had proved more expensive than usual to prepare, and they were determined to enjoy the festival.[7]

More alarmingly, the entire area east of the Pillared House, the old marshlands – which was believed to have been fully drained over the previous three decades – filled up again with river water. Many great houses were flooded, including that of the absentee regent.

This flooding lasted from late June to 10 July, and all the crops from the low-lying lands were lost. The Parisians, overcome by this calamity, turned as always to God, making a holy procession on the Wednesday before St Peter's and St Paul's Day, which was very solemn and moving. An immense column of people passed over the bridge behind the Hôtel Dieu and along the first street beyond the Petit Châtelet, crossing the Pont Neuf and then the Grand Pont, and coming back again by the Pont Notre Dame. It seemed that half the population of Paris was present to implore divine aid, and certainly all the elders of the parishes went into the cathedral, strong-armed men carrying the shrine of the Blessed Virgin before them. There, the clergy celebrated a special mass, and a Franciscan monk, Brother Jacques de Touraine, preached a sermon that many considered to be deeply moving.

But even though the floods abated and the land dried out in time, the damage was done. Cherries alone were very plentiful in their season, but the markets were otherwise starved of produce.[8]

In September, by order of the English commander, the Porte St Martin was closed again, but it was not walled up. The gate remained shut from Holy Cross Day until 7 December. The guardians of the quarter had especially requested a re-opening of the gate, because its closure impeded the passage of goods on this important highway, which was true; but the English governors were still unwilling to leave the wall exposed to the casual marauding of the 'soldiers of fortune', men who were loyal neither to the French king nor the English, but who roamed the country, stealing, raping, torturing, killing and burning.

Notwithstanding, the will of the Parisians prevailed, and the provost and his aldermen attended the grand re-opening on 7 December, an occasion that was not popular with the English. Their garrison made its position clear. They told the citizens they were there to protect that if they wished for the gate to be left open it was up to them to guard it. '. . . At your risk be it defended.'[9]

Yet despite the calamities that seemed to overwhelm them in that desperately wet summer, the Parisians still clung to their normal pursuits, although they perhaps made more of those which appealed to their innate sense of religion, possibly seeing a divine hand at work in their tribulations. In the same month that the English closed the Porte St Martin, a general procession had been made to St Magloire, to protest against certain heretics who had 'erred against the faith'. It was announced that even the Holy

Father wished the University of Paris to do its duty in this matter, to which end his holiness had appointed four bishops to attend the colloquium that would try the apostates. The Bishops of Therouanne and Beauvais were among them, and they had the Chancellor of France to add his presence to the gravity of the proceedings, so seriously was this apostasy regarded by the Holy See. This sort of theological debate was entirely to the taste of the more discerning Parisian citizens, and so intent were they upon these doctrinal disputes they forgot, for the moment, the danger from their enemies, who could be presumed to be massing against them.

Finance, rather than any imminent onslaught, concerned them more. On 7 January 1426 the French *double* coin was said to be only worth one English penny each, while those bearing the arms of England were to remain unchanged at a higher rate. Gold crowns, current at twenty-three shillings, were reduced to eighteen. Small gold *moutons*, since they were French currency, were to be reduced from the exchange rate of fifteen English shillings to twelve. The day after this proclamation, neither bread nor wine was available to the ordinary citizen. Moneylenders would not give a proper rate for any coins, since they could not rely upon their face value being ultimately agreed upon. A good many people, it was said, threw their money in the Seine, their disgust against their rulers being so extreme.[10]

To the amusement of many, a comic relief among the daily miseries, the provost marshal, with the support of the lords of the *parlement*, decreed that no mounted serjeant, nor any tipstaff, could retain his office unless he was a *married* man. The present incumbents were given from All Saints Day (1 November) to Low Sunday (the first Sunday after Easter) 1427 in which to find a wife, or else they could not continue in their work after Ascension Day. (These officers had always to be laymen; such posts were denied to the clergy.)

As for the clergy, Nicolle Fraillon was made the Bishop of Paris on 28 December 1426, being received into Notre Dame on that day. But his rule did not last long, for he had been elected in opposition to the candidate of both the regent and the Duke of Burgundy, Jacques du Châtillier. Fraillon was a priest more to the liking of the citizens, but – as had happened in King Henry's time – Bedford and Burgundy quickly ensured that their choice replaced that of the Parisians. This was done in the face of fierce opposition from the chapter of Notre Dame and the electors of the university, who capitulated slowly. But what is most remarkable about their capitulation is that this change was made when neither of the dukes was in Paris during the selection process. Their disapproval, it would seem, was felt from hundreds of miles away.

What made this imposition more galling, in fact, was that the Regent of France was still in England, intent upon business that seemed to have nothing to do with the welfare, either spiritual or material, of ordinary Parisians. All in all it was a critical period for the English, since at this juncture, Bedford was seen as 'being no lord at all'.[11] Though much of the resentment against the absent duke arose from the fact that the Englishmen he had left in control had little of his aptitude for civil administration. 'Nothing was done by those he had left in charge to ease their situation,' the Bourgeois wrote. Had the regent still been in France, it was felt that matters would have been different, for he would have thus been aware of the general disaffection in Paris, and he would have acted accordingly.

Yet Bedford, throughout the time he spent in England, was still earnestly striving to keep the peace on which would depend the English presence in France. Only by acting as an arbiter between Beaufort and his brother could he hope to make a reconciliation take place, and only by effecting this reconciliation could he hope to keep Beaufort's supremely important financial commitment to the English forces in France. Without the bishop's appreciable aid, the English cause would have long foundered.

Despite his efforts to cultivate the bishop at the expense of Duke Humphrey, a bond of alliance seems to have been formed between the two brothers, and it was a bond in which Queen Katherine joined. For it was, after all, in her particular interest, as both the sister and mother of the two disputed Kings of France, that she should mediate in any English quarrel that could affect the possibility of her son being accepted as the rightful sovereign of the country of her birth. She, like Bedford, realised that her young son's tenure on the French throne very much depended upon them keeping the Burgundians on their side.

Mediation between the two royal brothers, though, was very protracted, and only a solemn command to attend the king at a parliament held at Leicester finally brought Duke Humphrey to the negotiating table on 12 March 1426. Conventional weapons were forbidden at this provincial assembly, and the delegates were reduced to carrying clubs for their own protection, and so the occasion became known as the 'Parliament of the Bats'.

Before reluctantly attending this session of parliament, the Duke of Gloucester made a wild attempt to have his uncle convicted of treasonable activities, a charge that was not acceptable to those present, and which was firmly rejected. Humphrey, claiming that he had been misled by 'malicious persons', was forced to retract his accusation.

Bedford and other lords then acted as arbitrators between Beaufort and Gloucester, and the two men made a show of being reconciled. To ease the situation further, the Council, headed by Bedford, granted Henry Beaufort formal leave to go on a long delayed pilgrimage on 14 May 1426, which – for the time being – gave the country some respite from the warring princes. Before the English parliament broke up on 1 June, Bedford knighted the young king, then aged 5.[12]

NOTES

1 *Archives Nationales.*
2 Glasson, *Châtelet: abuses of procedure.*
3 In 1417 the moat between the Porte St Jacques and the Seine had needed repairs. (The Canons of Notre Dame had given 100 francs towards the cost of the work.) But, on the left bank, the main problem was that a large section of the wall was beginning to crumble. General defences were overhauled by the municipality at the start of the Anglo–Burgundian regime, although from as early as January 1420 the city had received financial assistance towards the creation of a palisade and a bulwark to protect the approaches from the river. Allmand, *English Suits.*
4 Garsonnin, *Le Guet et les Compagnies.*
5 Chastellain, *Oeuvres.*
6 The armoury contained hand guns and cannons. The cannons that stood on the terraces could fire balls weighing from 5 to 20 pounds, with one device firing seven lead shots at a time. Bournon, *Bastille.*
7 Vidier, *Comptes.*
8 Bourgeois de Paris.
9 Ibid.
10 Ibid.
11 Ibid.
12 Gregory's *Chronicle.*

CHAPTER VI

1427: The Return of the Regent

At a council the Duke of Bedford held in London on 28 January 1427, an attempt was made to bind Gloucester to act constitutionally. The Lord Chancellor of England made a speech before the assembly, setting out their position with regard to the duties of the two protectors, Gloucester in England and Bedford in France. Bedford, who had no doubt planned the occasion, replied by promising to act in accordance with the will of the council. Political artifice apart, he was plainly moved when he opened a copy of the Gospels that was lying on a table in the 'starred' chamber and, placing his hand upon it, swore to abide by the decisions of the council. After this, Gloucester was asked for a like assurance.

Bedford was only too willing to abide by the ruling of the council, because two days previously it had been arranged that the expenses of his return to France should be paid out of the exchequer, 'because he was not in the King's pay'. On 25 February 1427 it was decided that he should return to France, 'inasmuch as the late King had desired that he should guard Normandy'. (It is significant that the council made no mention of the greater English title. Many highly placed men in London had begun to lose faith in the possibility of ever conquering the whole of France.)

Early in March, having raised a large body of troops and artillery, Bedford left England. Beaufort, who had largely funded this army, accompanied him, with an impressive retinue, across the Channel.[1]

In northern France it had been another very hard winter, and the Parisians had suffered more than the rest of the population, perhaps, for when foodstuffs became scarce the prices rose more steeply in the capital than elsewhere.

The ground had begun to freeze on the first day of January 1427, and it froze for thirty-six days without stopping. The meagre crop of vegetables that were grown locally, and upon which the citizens relied for sustenance in difficult seasons, perished in the ironbound earth. Not only such reliable produce as cabbages and beets were destroyed, but even many herbal plants died; no green stuff appeared above the soil until the end of March, the land being frozen throughout February. The ordinary citizen could buy nothing to sustain him for less than two pence, a sum beyond most people's pockets.[2]

The regent arrived back in Paris on Saturday 5 April, the eve of Passion Sunday. Most Parisians believed that his mission to England, after sixteen months, had been unsuccessful, for they understood that he had only been there in the hope of making peace between his brother Gloucester and the Duke of Burgundy, an undertaking in which he was thought to have failed. Very few Parisians had any knowledge of the tensions between these royal brothers in England, and even fewer realised that it was also important to appease Beaufort (who had now been made a cardinal), upon whose purse the safety of their city depended. To the Parisians nothing else mattered but that their English protectors should keep the Duke of Burgundy on their side in the battle against the Armagnacs. Yet there was little change in the relative position of the three parties in France.

Beaufort, the Cardinal of Winchester, arrived in Paris on the last day of April. To the astonishment of the Parisians, he had a greater retinue than the governor of France, and it struck them as the greatest ostentation. (On the other hand, as lovers of pomp and pageantry, they also highly approved of it.) They were not to know that, as the richest man in England, and one of the richest in Europe, it was largely the cardinal's money that had brought new English troops to guard their city. But they were deeply impressed by his flamboyance, and charmed by his efforts to amuse them. The regent was always willing to provide the Parisians with spectacular displays, but they had seen nothing to match the splendour of the cardinal's diversions.

The frost that had prevailed throughout April was present for most of May. It vanished only in the last four days of the month, and not a week had passed without an outbreak of this killing cold or heavy hailstorms. When the climate did finally thaw, it then rained without cease, in chilling downpours.

The regent, as a deeply devout man, had a particular appreciation of religious processions. On 7 May, when the arctic conditions had eased, he commanded the chapter of Notre Dame to hold a general procession for the deliverance of the town of Pontorson, where the long siege by the English was reaching a climax. The canons agreed, and a procession that managed to combine both piety and martial pomp was held the next day. This curious mixture of bellicosity and piety was greatly to the Parisian taste for paradox, and many thousands attended, despite the murky conditions in which the marchers walked.

Then, on the Monday before Ascension Day, more of the devout marched from Notre Dame to the shrine of St Denis at Montmartre, this time to give thanks to God for the return of spring, however illusory. (It was, indeed, somewhat warmer, but those who walked in the procession were soaked to the skin, for it did not stop raining from nine in the morning until three in the afternoon.) Yet, afterwards, to stress their piety, they walked on to St Lazare. It took over an hour to trudge through the muddy roads, with the rain pelting down harder than ever.

The regent and his wife, with a great company, happened to be riding out at the same time, passing through the Porte St Martin. At this point, they met the procession on its way back into Paris. Since the royal party was moving very fast, with the rain driving down, they splashed the procession 'of which they thought very little', before the people could escape them. Fortunately, nobody was injured in the headlong flight to escape injury by the horses' hooves, but the Bourgeois of Paris, who was present, thought very little of this display. 'Not one of the company had the manners to slow down a little, neither for the procession, nor for the shrine.'

The insult to the statue of the Virgin was, of course, beyond the comprehension of most of the followers who took part, but because of the pelting rain, Bedford's party was perhaps not aware of the religious nature of the occasion, and the regent would have felt deep concern for any affront to the sacred image. As it was, this meandering procession did not reach its final objective at St Merri until mid-afternoon, by which time all who took part were saturated.

The regent was quick to visit Duke Philippe at his city of Lille – which had been handed to the Burgundians by Charles V, and which had prospered under the old duke. Bedford went there on 26 May, deeply perturbed by the developments that were then taking place. Despite their agreement to act otherwise in England, he had learned that his brother Gloucester was again planning an armed expedition to the Low Countries on his wife's behalf and, although Bedford had written off to England to order him to abandon this ambition, the situation was still volatile.[3]

To aggravate matters further, the Duke of Brittany had followed his brother Richemont's example and again attached his cause to that of the dauphin's. Although upon finding that the Duke of Burgundy was still not prepared to desert the English alliance, despite the Duke of Gloucester's provocation, the Duke of Brittany quickly grew less devoted to the dauphin's enterprise. After Bedford again threatened his duchy, Duke Jean abandoned the dauphin anew and swore once more to abide by what had been agreed in the treaty of Amiens.

On 1 June the new Bishop of Paris celebrated his appointment in the cathedral with a solemn mass, after being confirmed in the post, and nothing more was heard of the election that had been made earlier. Fraillon was set aside and Châtillier installed, and after the obligatory objections, the majority of the people accepted the bishop who had been forced on them.[4] It was understood by the politically aware that the spiritual and administrative powers of a diocese were related to the civil aspects of government, and it was recognised that Châtillier was a more politically potent figure than the choice of the chapter. Châtillier was the Grand Treasurer at the cathedral of Rheims, and as such his position there was immensely important to an administration that was intent upon establishing the credentials of their claimant to the French throne. For since 496 AD, when Clovis I was crowned king of the Franks in an earlier cathedral, the coronation of every French king had taken place at Rheims. Bedford, intent always upon stressing his nephew's indisputable right to the French crown, knew that a coronation, to be fully sanctified, must be performed in this 'sacred' building. He had chosen Châtillier, with his strong affiliation to the 'coronation cathedral', to this end.

Apart from this, Bedford and his English council also wished to deprive the clergy in Paris of any real force, since it was recognised that many important clerics were still attached to the old ruling family. One way of withholding power from these hostile ecclesiastics, it was decided, would be to confiscate all the revenues granted to the Church by the city during the last forty years. (Why this particular period of time was decided upon has never been made clear. It could as easily have been for the past century, or even longer, although forty years had a satisfactorily biblical ring to it.)

This solution was inevitably deeply unpopular with pious citizens at all levels, and there was a strong movement against it. The governors of the University of Paris challenged the decision, and many of their students, who were directly sponsored by the Holy See, embroiled the English council in a series of conferences on the subject over a period of months, conferences so interminable and wearying that the regent finally admitted defeat and abandoned his plan.[5]

It was another summer to dishearten the most optimistic of the faithful. The Seine rose unseasonably high, and by Pentecost, on 8 June, its waters reached the cross in the Place de Grève, where they stayed until the end of the mid-summer festival. On the following Thursday, the waters rose again, about a foot and a half. In the next few days they covered the island of Notre Dame and almost all the ground 'where the elm trees grew', near St Paul's church on the north bank opposite the island.

To most Parisians, it seemed that it had never stopped raining from the middle of April until the Monday after Pentecost, and after that the weather had continued to be miserably cold. 'English weather,' cynics called it; brought to Paris by courtesy of the occupying forces.[6]

Again, this sign of divine reproach inspired some touching processions among the devout, both in Paris and in the outlying villages. These processions explain much about the formation of society at that time, for the clergy and the laity – however distinguished the latter – always walked separately. And even among the laity the men and women were segregated, with the women following the men.

The women and children, old and young, were also mostly barefoot.

They walked for miles in a slow-moving line, while singing hymns and raising their voices in praise to a God who seemed to have abandoned them. Women carried their personal sacred objects, while the sturdier men bore the heaviest relics; and the climax of the procession was always a sermon, filled with the strong imagery and high-flown rhetoric so cherished by the people.

Because of the cold weather and the floods, not a single vine had yet come into flower. The suppliants travelled incessantly from parish to parish, and yet their pleas were mocked; for the day of their lengthiest column, when thousands of citizens joined them, proved to be the hottest day of the year, and many of those who walked in the procession collapsed from heat exhaustion.

Yet within days the water had risen again, and the cathedral itself was under threat, as the flood covered most of the island of Notre Dame. Since most of the houses on the island had low-lying storerooms, even their ground floors were flooded, with, in some storerooms, the water 'deeper than the height of two men standing upon each other's shoulders'. In stables that were below street level, the confined horses were drowned before they could be released. Wine casks floated away and into the river, to be carried off to sea.

The water eventually reached the sixth step of the cross in the Place de Grève, and it actually threatened the Pillared House. The river level was almost two feet higher than the year before. Wherever it spread, it utterly spoiled everything. The corn and oats that were grown in the fields of the Marais area were beyond reviving, since the river had covered them for almost five weeks.

To make matters worse, a heavy tax had been decreed, which was 'mercilessly collected' during this time. For soon after his return to France, the regent had decided to resume operations against the Armagnacs, the arrival of fresh reinforcements from England putting fresh vigour into the campaign. He sent an army two thousand strong, under Warwick and Suffolk, into the eastern theatre of war. By 15 July this army had laid siege to the town of Montargis, sixty miles south-east of Paris and forty miles east of Orléans. Such an offensive had to be paid for, and the siege was to last for two months.[7]

This siege is of interest because it brought into prominence a man who would prove himself to be the first real challenger to English dominance in 'the dauphin's war'. This was a bastard son of the murdered Duke of Orléans (and therefore a possible half-brother of the dauphin), known as the Count of Dunois. Together with the adherents of the recently released La Hire, his soldiers fell upon a portion of the English besieging force, cut it into pieces, captured Suffolk's brother, and relieved Montargis. To the surprise of all, the hitherto invincible English troops retreated ignominiously, leaving most of their guns behind.

This unexpected success was the first 'ray of sunshine' (as de Beaucourt called it) that the French had enjoyed in five years of conflict. The dauphin himself described it as 'the start of our happiness'. (That is, as the beginning of his slow climb back to being regarded as the true claimant to the throne by a show of military prowess.) It was an undoubted setback for the English cause, although it may not have seemed so at the time. This victory certainly encouraged the dauphinists, and they received some further encouragement from their irresolute Breton 'allies' in the west, but the English – certainly at this point, when they seemed totally in command of the military situation – could not be discouraged from vigorously pursuing the war.[8]

Their trouble, as always, was a shortage of troops. (Since Agincourt the English had always fielded considerably fewer men than the forces that were lined up against them, sometimes by as much as two thirds.) But it should be noted that at the siege of Montargis, they were then working single-handed, a situation that had existed for almost two years. For the Duke of Burgundy, although he had not openly broken with his allies, had withdrawn his field troops into the Low Countries in his war against the Countess Jacqueline. The only Burgundian leader to keep faith with the English was John of Luxembourg, and he was operating out of the Argonne, in eastern France.

The Earl of Salisbury had been sent back to England to raise fresh troops, and he had spent the latter part of 1427 engaged in that duty. His task was not rendered any easier by the activities of Humphrey of Gloucester, who was once again trying to revive the cause of his wife in her homeland, for the troops that Gloucester recruited for this purpose consequently made large inroads upon the force that was intended for France. Eventually, the regent again managed to put a stop to Gloucester's project, and Salisbury was then able to build up a small army of some two and a half thousand men. He sailed with them from Sandwich on 19 July, and he landed at Calais five days later. From the port, he pushed on to Paris via Amiens.[9]

On 6 August it was decreed that only one-penny loaves should be baked, and the sale of these should be rationed, for the outcome of the rotten summer was beginning to show, and it was feared there would be a poor reaping. No loaf smaller than a two-penny one had been baked in the Parisian ovens for the last nine years and many Parisians resented this new constraint, with the inevitable result that the rich bought more loaves on the 'black' market, leaving less for the poor. To make matters worse, in that same week it was announced that gold crowns and gold *moutons* were to be current only at the value of their gold content. Money, like wheat, was getting scarce.

But there was plenty of excellent fruit. 'Good plums at a penny a hundred, and not one of them maggoty.' Almonds were so heavy on the trees they broke the branches. And after the worst summer, it was the finest autumn that anyone could remember, and to the astonishment of all, the ripened corn was plentiful and of the highest quality. '. . . God can work in a moment,' as the Bourgeois wrote.

The regent had left Paris on the first of the month. It was beginning to be said of him (and no longer only by the Bourgeois) that he always left the city in some way poorer, though he could not be blamed for the ravages of nature. Yet it was true that he always enriched his own country 'with something from this kingdom'.[10] It was also said that he never brought anything into France except for fresh taxes, and people were beginning to question these heavy – and excessive – financial demands. Murderers and thieves still infested the countryside around the capital, stealing and looting, 'and no one said Dimitte'. Why couldn't the English soldiery, sitting at their ease in their garrisons, protect the citizens better? That would be an achievement worth handing over one's hard-earned money for.

On Sunday, after the middle day of August 1427, twelve penitents – as they called themselves – arrived in Paris. Among them were a duke and a count, and ten other men of lesser degree, but all on horseback, their horses gorgeously caparisoned, and the riders clad in the richest and most elaborate clothing, with many strange ornaments.[11]

They said they were all good Christians, and that they came from Lower Egypt. They also openly admitted that their baptism had been forced upon them, as they had been compelled to become Christians or die. Their king and queen had only retained their sovereignty by accepting the word of Our Lord, and yet sometime after this compulsory baptism they had voluntarily adopted Christian beliefs and practices. Because of this the Saracens had then made war upon them and, being militarily weak, they had surrendered to the infidel and were forced to deny Christ. As a result of this apostasy, the Christian warriors in their country – on leave from fighting to reclaim the Holy Land – had also made war upon them. Defeated by the crusaders, a number of them – the present company included – had been sent to the Holy Father in Rome to seek his consent for them to hold land in their own country again.

The pope had imposed a formidable sentence upon them: that for seven years they should travel throughout the Christian world without ever sleeping in a bed or settling in one place for more than a few weeks. He had also ordered that, to provide some means for them, every bishop, and every abbot who bore a crosier, should pay them a single payment of ten pounds *tournois*. He had given them letters concerning this, addressed to the prelates of the church, and after his blessing they had departed from Rome to carry out his bidding. It was therefore the

71

religious duty of every great churchman and every devout Christian, they urged, to provide them with the means to live while they worked out their penance.

They had been travelling for five years before their arrival in Paris, and they arrived on the holy day of the beheading of St John the Baptist. Because they were regarded as being aliens, and yet because they were said to be under the protection of the Holy Father, they were not allowed to enter the city, but were lodged at La Chapelle and St Denis, by order of the authorities. Apart from their mounted leaders, there were not more than a hundred travellers altogether, for these were survivors, others had died on the way, including their king and queen. They continued with their penance, despite these tragedies, because they still hoped to return to their ancient kingdom. Or if they could not return to that much contested land, they still hoped for another country they could call their own, for the Holy Father had promised them a good and fertile land to live in once they had sincerely accomplished their mission.

Huge crowds went to view these strangers. The children in particular were a great source of pleasure; dark and vibrant, and astonishingly intelligent, they entranced the public with their ingenious tricks. Almost all of them, boys and girls, had their ears pierced, and they wore a silver ring in each ear; which was, they said, a mark of good birth in their country. Their fathers were very dark, with tight curly hair, and their mothers were considered to be extremely ugly, for a scarred face seemed to be their idea of beauty. They wore nothing that could be regarded as a gown, but only an old coarse blanket that was tied at the shoulder with a strap or piece of string, little more than a wretched shift or smock. Compared with their glitteringly dressed menfolk, the women were the poorest creatures that anyone had ever seen come into Paris, which even at that time was famous for its delight in dressmaking.

The crowds were thrilled to learn that the newcomers had sorcerers among them, particularly the women, who could look at a person's hand and tell their future from the lines that crisscrossed the palm. The outsiders, it was also quickly realised, were remarkably adept at making 'money flow out of people's purses into their own'. So skilled were they at fleecing the hordes that visited them, in fact, that within a short space of time they were seen as 'cunning people', who lived with the 'devil's help'.

It became a great scandal, to such an extent that the Bishop of Paris went to see them, along with a Minorite friar called the 'Little Jacobin'. At the bishop's express order, the Minorite excommunicated all the men and women who had been foolish enough to believe in the strangers' claims, and particularly those who had held out their hands to have their fortunes told, for such an act was in itself sinful. Having had his fill of these strange penitents, who seemed to have entranced the citizenry, the bishop banished the outlandish visitors on Lady Day, and in September they departed for Pontoise, presumably to tell the same exotic story. Paris had just encountered its first gypsies.[12]

It was as hot by the festival of St Rémi[13] as it had been at the feast day of St John, yet there had not been more than one month of real summer weather. The vines did badly, the most they produced was one cask per acre, some even less. All this had been due to the interminable winter. Almonds found on the trees after All Saints Day were as green and fit for peeling as they had been in mid-August. Yet they tasted good. As a result of this catastrophic yield, wine was very dear, and all exports were banned that year. Thin wine sold for 8d the quart, although the currency was very good.

A woman called Margot came from Hainault, where she had acquired great fame as a tennis player,[14] and at 28 years she was the most skilful player that anyone in Paris had ever seen. The best tennis in the city was played in the rue Grenier St Lazare and at the Petit Temple, the ancient game of real tennis, and Margot was the first player to use a racquet (which did not become popular until the end of the century).

Two weeks after St Rémi, a 'corrupt and evil air' descended upon the city in a sort of miasma, which caused a very unpleasant illness that people called the 'dando'. No one entirely escaped this unwholesome pollution while it lasted. The symptoms were very unclear: pain in the back and shoulders, and what seemed like the 'stone'. People had shivering attacks, and a violent trembling that shook their whole bodies. It was a week to ten days before people could eat or sleep, and all had fits of coughing which were so bad that those attending sermons could not hear what the preacher said for the almost continuous sound of coughing among the congregation. The illness lasted for two weeks until after All Saints Day. The Bourgeois said that there was hardly a person one saw whose mouth and nose was not swollen or scabbed with an abscess.

On 15 December Sauvage de Fremainville, who had been terrorising the area, was captured by force at the castle of L'Isle Adam, along with his two servants. (Colin Laignel, a sergeant was killed in this action. He left a widow, who later had great difficulty in claiming compensation.)[15] Fremainville was bound with rope and put on a horse, with his hands and feet tied, and taken to Bagnolet, where the regent was encamped. The duke ordered the man to be hanged immediately, even without hearing a defence, for Bedford was very afraid that the man would be rescued if there was any delay, since he came from a family of great lineage and had many powerful friends.

Fremainville was brought to the gallows, accompanied by the Provost Marshal of Paris and a man called Pierre Baille, said to be 'of low extraction and less valour', but who had flourished by his devotion to the English cause.[16] Pricking him with his sword, to encourage him, Baille forced the protesting Fremainville to climb the ladder to the hangman's noose, without the man being given leave to make a last confession. The hangman, who was as much intimidated by Baille as was the victim, in some way botched the matter, with the result that the rope broke and the condemned man fell, breaking his leg. Despite his evident agony, Baille compelled Fremainville to climb the ladder again, and a new rope being supplied, the man was hanged – or more properly strangled.

In Flanders, Sauvage de Fremainville was said to have killed a bishop with his bare hands, and most of his crimes were equally villainous, but many wondered why the Duke of Bedford had been so set on hanging a man without a trial or a shriving. The truth was that the regent had determined to be rid of him, for this was the same Sauvage de Fremainville who had earlier tried to ambush him on his way to England. (Waurin describes the trap that he had arranged for Bedford.)[17] So, even before the man's capture, the regent already had good reason to dislike him – he had 'felt great indignation' when he first heard about the attempt to entrap his party – and such an offence against a sovereign power in state could not go unpunished.

NOTES

1 Williams, *My Lord of Bedford*.
2 Bourgeois de Paris.
3 Without the regent's efforts, there would have been open breach with Burgundy, and the end of English rule outside Normandy. Burne, *The Agincourt War*.
4 Bourgeois de Paris.
5 Ibid.
6 Ibid.
7 Ibid.
8 Quicherat, *Chronique*.
9 Salisbury returned to England frequently to raise reinforcements. Burne, op. cit.
10 Bourgeois de Paris.
11 Ibid.
12 Ibid.
13 St Rémi (1 October).
14 'Tennis' is probably from the Anglo–French 'tenetz' ('hold'). It originates in the game of *la paume* (in which the ball was struck with the palm of the hand).
15 Monstrelet, *Chronique*.
16 Baille started out as a shoemaker's apprentice. He became a tipstaff, and then a public receiver. By the time of this episode, he was the Grand Treasurer in Maine. Tuetey (ed.), *Journal* of Bourgeois de Paris.
17 Ibid.

CHAPTER VII

1428: The Army of Invasion

There was a plague of caterpillars in April 1428. They ate the leaves of the vines, the almond and other fruit trees to such an extent that, two weeks before St John's Day, there was scarcely any foliage left on any of them. The walnut trees especially were laid bare by the powerful jaws of the larvae.[1]

The Duke of Burgundy arrived in Paris on 22 May, on the eve of Pentecost. He rode in on a small white horse, dressed like an archer. No one would have recognised him had the regent not been riding alongside him, with his wife behind.

The year was already being marked by several military successes. The Earl of Salisbury had taken Jargeau along with many towns on the right bank of the Loire. Charles of Valois had been reduced to the last extremity, and even his ally René of Anjou had been forced to enter into negotiations with the regent. The English and the Burgundians celebrated these victories over the Armagnacs, and the Parisians were happy to contribute to their celebrations. But the Duke of Burgundy stayed only until 2 June, leaving on the eve of the Holy Sacrament.

There had been more caterpillars that year than the old men could ever remember seeing, and the plague lasted until St John's Day, spoiling all the trees. They were present in their millions until St Peter's Day (29 June), even though the weather had proved very cold until St John's Tide, on the 24th. There was constant rain, thunder and both sheet and forked lightning; and on 3 June, during a heavy storm, lightning had struck the belfry of the Augustin's church, and blasted it on to the roof, which was of slate. The timbers cracked, and the damage was reckoned at ten thousand *francs*.[2]

Two isolated actions took place in Maine, both of which involved Lord Talbot,[3] who had come to France in the train of the Duke of Bedford upon his return from England in the spring of 1427. Talbot's first engagement had been the capture of Pontorson under the Earl of Warwick, and he had then taken part in the siege of Montargis. But in the spring of 1428 he collected a force at Alençon, in pursuit of some mysterious venture, and while employed in this, news came that the Armagnacs had taken back the city of Le Mans on 25 May, under the leadership of the vigorous and rampageous La Hire. (Baptised Etienne de Vignolles, his nickname of 'La Hire' ('the stamper') was probably acquired as the result of an accident in 1421 that left him lame and limping badly. The Bourgeois described him as 'the worst, most tyrannical and most pitiless of the Armagnac captains'. He was also one of their most successful.)

The retaking of Le Mans by the French was said to have been achieved almost entirely by treachery, with 'several of the townspeople being a party to it', and the English troops were now cooped up in the Richendale tower, where they were facing annihilation. Talbot's response was immediate, and typical of his chivalrous nature, for by marching overnight with only three hundred men, he arrived outside the walls of Le Mans between dawn and sunrise, at the most promising moment for attack. His men soon overcame the sleepy guards and stormed into the town with their spine-chilling cry of 'St George!' Taking the slumbering garrison by surprise, their success was complete. Then, aided by friendly citizens, La Hire's men were ejected from the town and the imprisoned English soldiers released.[4]

A second action involving Lord Talbot occurred shortly afterwards. In another swooping raid, using only a minimal number of troops, he captured the town of Laval – midway between Angers and Avranches. This was a particular triumph for the novice leader, since the town had up to that time always held out successfully against the English. Both these actions were to prove typical of Talbot's approach to military action, and his methods made a powerful impression on French martial opinion at that time, even though his English colleagues (including the Duke of Bedford) remained oddly unimpressed by them. However, they would soon come to appreciate Talbot's radical and remarkable talents, when English dominance would be challenged from a freakish and, to many, unnatural source.

The cold weather continued, so that there were no good cherries, hardly any fresh beans, and no corn. The blossoms had withered on the vine.[5]

Despite this, on St Leufredus's Day, 21 June, a most sumptuous feast was held at the palace. It was given to celebrate the receipt of four new doctors of canon law, two of whom were French, and two English. Everyone above a certain station was welcomed to eat there, each according to his rank. The regent, his wife, and the noblemen and knights were served in the palace, with food that was proper to their status. Prelates, abbots and priors were next to be served; doctors of all the sciences came afterwards; the *parlement*, then the provosts of Paris and the guardians of the Châtelet. The aldermen of the council and the merchants' guilds were all together, and even some commoners were served. At least eight thousand people sat down to this dinner throughout the course of the day, seven hundred dozen loaves were eaten and at least forty *muids* of wine were drunk, and there were 'eight hundred meat dishes, not including mutton and beef, which were past reckoning'.[6]

This huge feast was paid for out of a new charge raised by the regent; and for those who paid for the meal but did not get to partake of it, the event was a great affront. It seemed a senseless diversion at such a critical point in their lives. Were the English insensible to the fact that, in view of the abysmal weather, food was going to be scarce again this year?

Late in July the Earl of Salisbury entered Paris at the head of his army of 2,700 men, and the people 'groaned even louder' when it was learned that another heavy tax was to be levied to supply these troops with provisions. For how could this huge army be employed in their best interests, since the city was already better protected than at any time in its history? The problem was even further intensified when it became known that the English had been collecting contingents from all the provinces they occupied, and the numbers swelled to over five thousand.

To pay for this 'army of invasion' – whenever it was ready to set out from Paris – two hundred wagons had to be paid for, each drawn by four horses. Along with the foodstuff for the artillery, and the fodder for the horses, over two hundred hogsheads of wine were taken from Paris. And this at a time when even the poorest vintage was so expensive that very few householders drank wine.

(It was at this period, as a response to the price of wine, that many people began to brew beer; before All Saints Day came, at least thirty brewers were at work in the city. Ales were also brought in every day from St Denis and outlying places, and it was 'cried about the town like wine'. Paris beer sold at only two *doubles*, and the brew from St Denis at three. A *double* was then the equivalent of four English pennies.)

Prices, generally, rose alarmingly. Good peas and beans, when you could find them, were 10d a bushel. Eggs were 12d a 'quarter'. Grapes were still so unripe by Holy Cross Day in September that, according to the Bourgeois, 'no one could say ". . . Look, here's a bunch that's black all over".' The maturing had continued for too long and too late.[7]

In the previous August, an ordinance had been made about rents. Everyone who could afford it might pay by the English pound, equivalent to fifteen pounds *tournois*. This ruling only applied if the rents had been collected for a long time; and widows, minors and churches were exempt from payment. Several other ordinances were made about these rents, and they could be read at the Châtelet fortress. The main ordinance was published on the last day of July 1428, when Pierre Balley was Receiver of Paris.[8]

Long and careful councils were held in order to decide upon a plan to bring the war to a successful conclusion, but from the outset there was a divergence of opinion. One faction favoured the conquest of Anjou, which meant the seizure of Angers, its main city. The other group held out for the capture of Orléans. There was little doubt among this latter group, headed by the Earl of Salisbury, that the second scheme was a sounder strategy. For Orléans lay midway between Paris and the dauphin's 'capital' of Bourges, each city being about sixty miles from the other; whereas Angers was more than twice as far from the dauphin's 'realm'.

Those who wished to fall on Anjou did so from a patriotic attachment to the cause, as Anjou had been an old domain of the Plantagenet kings. The others argued, rightly, that its capture would serve no direct purpose, since such a triumph would have no real effect on the dauphin's movements, Angers was too far away from his main objective: the taking of his true capital, Paris. But to take Orléans would cut the dauphin's main artery, the Loire river, which had now become the northern boundary of his sphere of authority. The English had long desired to rupture this vital line, and there was another consideration, for – since it was the nearest point to Paris – an English army could be more easily supplied and re-inforced from there.

Bedford, however, favoured the plan to invade Anjou. It was a sur-prising decision for him to take, as his previous attempt to conquer the county, although it had made some progress, had not weakened the will of the dauphinists to fight on, and four years of intermittent warfare had not greatly altered the situation. It was precisely for this reason that the Earl of Salisbury now championed the direct approach, an attack on Orléans would hit the enemy where it most hurt.

Bedford recognised that Salisbury was easily the most experienced and successful general on the English side, and after some weeks of bitter wrangling, despite his continuing misgivings, he reluctantly consented to the second plan. (The regent was, perhaps, following the code of chivalry in his reluctance to besiege Orléans at such a time, for it was contrary to fifteenth-century military custom, as the Duke of Orléans, officially the city's protector, was at that time a prisoner in the Tower of London. Captured at Agincourt, he had since been unable to raise the huge ransom demanded for his release, and to attack his property when he himself was not there to defend it would have been a serious breach of chivalric etiquette.)

But Orléans it was to be, and in mid-August the English army set out, 'to drink in front of the town',[9] although Salisbury's army at first set off in the direction of Anjou, in a bid to deceive the enemy as to their actual objective.[10]

En route, Salisbury decided to make Chartres his first target. Retaking on his way four towns that had fallen back into the Armagnac camp, he entered the city in the latter half of August. He then turned sharply south-east towards Janville, some twenty-six miles away, capturing a number of small towns as he progressed. These put up the minimum of resistance, with the exception of Puiset, which had to be stormed. Janville would also be a different proposition, as it was a walled and moated town, which had a resolute garrison.

It was Salisbury's plan to reduce this garrison by siege, but his troops – angered by some action on the part of the French troops – went against this strategy within a few days of surrounding Janville. Assaulting the walls, they took the town by storm, 'after the most formidable assault that we have ever seen' as Salisbury himself wrote to the Lord Mayor of London. It was said that the garrison had already offered to surrender, but that Salisbury preferred to overrun it by a violent assault. But this was a highly unlikely manoeuvre, for no commander with Salisbury's experience would have endangered the lives of his men if he could secure his end without striking a blow.

Janville lay only fifteen miles north of Orléans, and Salisbury may have already decided to use it as a forward base or supply depot for his army, for he had the foresight to recognise that any siege of the great city would be long and arduous. The town of Janville was, indeed, well situated for his purpose, being on the direct road from Paris, and only a day's march to Orléans.

Their base once established, the next stage was to isolate Orléans by water. This could only be accomplished by capturing the towns defended by the Armagnacs who were immediately up and down river of the city, Jargeau, Meung and Beaugency being among the chief of them. Salisbury first turned his attention to the latter towns, twelve and twenty miles below Orléans, and both on the northern bank of the Loire, with Meung as his first objective, since it was necessary to use the road that ran from Janville to Meung for the passage of his artillery. On 8 September Salisbury posted a left-flank guard on the outskirts of the town to safeguard his guns, cannon and mortars, although in fact none of these weapons were brought into deployment, for the town surrendered without a fight, and the English swept on to the siege of Beaugency.

This proved to be more difficult, for the château and the abbey – now both heavily fortified – were just within range of a many-arched bridge. The French garrison confined their defence to the château and this bridge, but the English, having taken possession of the bridge at Meung, and thus being free to cross the river, were able to approach Beaugency from the southern bank. In this way they were able to surround its less protected walls, thus leaving the French guarding a largely redundant vantage ground.

The siege opened on 20 September, and on the 25th a simultaneous attack was made upon the château from the north and on the bridge from the south, after an artillery bombardment. There was a disorderly struggle on the bridge, which a small group of men-at-arms had decided to harry as a diversionary tactic while the bulk of the army made their attack on the northern wall, and this resulted in knights in armour being hurled over its parapet into the river. But the attack in general was successful and the beaten garrison surrendered within the next twenty-four hours; after which, the inhabitants were 'persuaded' to swear allegiance to their new king, the boy-king 'Henry II'.

The first stage in this great operation was thus successfully accomplished, and Salisbury had a justifiable pride in it, as he showed again in a letter to the Lord Mayor of London. He stated that forty towns, châteaux and churches had fallen into English hands, and this proved to be no empty claim. After this triumph, he immediately moved his troops to the eastern side of Orléans.

There were two more successful sieges. On 2 October Sir William de la Pole laid siege to Jargeau, twelve miles upstream and, even though formidable ramparts and a ditch defended the town, it only held out for three days. Châteauneuf, ten miles higher up stream than Jargeau, fell as quickly. The capture of these important riverside bases meant that the city of Orléans was now doubly blocked on each side and the English army could settle in for a long siege. Salisbury's audacious actions and the further successes of the English force seemed to proclaim the assurance of a complete triumph against 'the King of Bourges', for Orléans was the 'last rampart of his power'.

De la Pole advanced from Jargeau along the southern bank of the Loire, marching his men to the bridge that spanned the river into Orléans on 7 October. Five days later he was joined by the Earl of Salisbury at the head of the main army, which had marched from Meung. The two sides merged into one whole, and encamped in Olivet, the southern suburb of the city. Owing to the necessity of leaving detachments and garrisons on the escape route back to Paris, Salisbury's entire force did not exceed 3,500 men at this stage, plus some 900 pages.[11] This company was later joined by about 1,500 Burgundians, who had been allowed into the service – and above all, the pay – of England. The English artillery was fewer in numbers and less powerful than that of the garrison, but some of their guns could reach the centre of the city at a range of over one thousand yards.

But the citizens of Orléans were not unprepared for the arrival of the English. An attack had been feared for some years past, and as a result the city's defences had been greatly strengthened. For example, an earthwork had been thrown up on the southern bank, to serve as a walled outwork, creating an added protection. (A massive wall with towers and five strongly defended gates already surrounded the city, and bastions were placed to permit firing along the flanks of the wall.) Orléans was probably at this time the most impregnable town in the whole of the dauphin's area of influence.

It was also well provided with artillery and other ammunition, and it possessed at least one great catapult for hurling stones at an advancing enemy, while alongside this ancient weapon were modern cannon, some of surprising size. A number of their balls weighed as much as 192lb, and at least one of them engaged an English ferry at a range of 1,400 yards. In all, there were about seventy-one guns, many of them made of leather, mounted on the walls. The regular garrison was made up of about 1,500 men, although the civilian population provided another 3,000 for the *milice*, a natural form of Home Guard.[12]

The Loire river was in itself no great protection. Some 400 metres broad as it passed the city, although still navigable for a certain type of boat, it ran shallow and rapid, broken up by sandbanks and islands, and a bridge, some 350 metres long, joined the city to the southern bank. Built over thirty years from 1100, it consisted of nineteen arches, and on the southernmost of these, separated from the bank by a drawbridge, stood a fort with two towers, called Les Tourelles. These defences were the most formidable the English had faced since the siege of Rouen, and it was not surprising that the Duke of Bedford viewed Salisbury's attempt to take the city with mistrust, as he considered Salisbury's forces to be negligible in the circumstances.

The earl opened operations by directing a cannonade against the Tourelles and the city. After a few days he was convinced that his troops could now carry out an assault, and he launched an attack upon the outwork, but the resistance with which his men were met was so ferocious that Salisbury promptly changed his plans. He had brought with him a group of miners, and once having reduced the guns of the barbican to silence, he put these men to the task of digging out the foundations of the fort. After two days of this the French garrison abandoned the horn-work, and even more surprisingly the Tourelles, breaking down two arches of the bridge behind them as they retreated into the city, to hinder the Anglo–Burgundians.

Salisbury, encouraged by the success of his second attempt, then set about the third. He had his men hastily repair the Tourelles, on which he established an observation post, from where he could reconnoitre the area, and he would base his plan of attack upon these findings. His opportunity to do so came soon, when at a quiet moment during the dinner hour, after the French gunners had gone to their meal, leaving their cannon loaded and laid, the earl took a party of his chief officers and ascended to his observation post.

But it happened that a young boy, the son of a gunner perhaps, was at play among the French cannon; and either for a lark or because he had spotted the English officers looking out from the Tourelles, he touched off one of the cannons.

The result was devastating for the English, as they lost their finest soldier by it. Salisbury, hearing the shot coming towards him, ducked out of the way, but the cannonball hit the lintel of the window, dislodging an iron bar, and this struck the earl on the side of his face, removing half of it. He was at once transferred to Meung for medical treatment, but he died there, after eight days of agony, commanding his officers to persevere with the war until they had obtained complete victory.[13] There is little doubt that had Salisbury been spared he would have succeeded in taking the city, for the French garrison was by then completely demoralised.

The news of Salisbury's death was a 'very great blow to the English, especially to the Regent of France.' 'For he was resting comfortably, he and his wife, as she always went everywhere with him, and now, with Salisbury dead, it was up to him to carry on the war. He left Paris to go and do so on Wednesday, Martinmas Eve (10 November) 1428.'[14]

Who was to succeed the dead general, for who indeed could succeed him? Only the Earl of Suffolk was held in anything like the same admiration, and Suffolk was the Earl of Salisbury's opposite. Whereas the dead man was celebrated for the 'great doughtiness and manhood that was found in him, and in his governance at all times',[15] Suffolk was completely averse to any action of a hazardous nature.

This he proved now, since instead of carrying on with an operation that had begun to show signs of every success, he tamely withdrew the field army to winter quarters in the neighbouring towns. He left an isolated garrison under the captain, Sir William Glasdale, in the Tourelles, in a fortification they threw up around the church of the Augustins, to the south of the tower.

His decision largely baffled his officers and men, for the French troops who had been arriving in the vicinity for the past few days were now of an overwhelming strength, and they had been reinforced by the arrival of the Count of Dunois, the Bastard of Orléans. Dunois had already proved himself to be a formidable opponent, and the English expected him to take action against them at any hour. Yet to their continual astonishment the English who were left to defend their positions were saved only by the puzzling reluctance of the French newcomers to advance upon them, leaving Glasdale's men unmolested for three weeks.

Suffolk's action in withdrawing his men can be seen as a calculated risk, but the only rational explanation for his departure was a desire to preserve the health of his troops whilst billets were being constructed for them outside the walls. The citizens of Orléans had razed to the ground the suburbs outside the walls, including many small churches, in order that the besiegers could not find shelter against the coming winter. Perhaps, too, Suffolk concluded that an interval was needed for the heavy ordnance that would breach the city walls to be brought up.

Whatever the reasons for their withdrawal, the English began to return to the siege in December, although it was recognised that they had insufficient men to conduct a close operation. Lord Talbot arrived on 1 December, and he and Lord Scales were now associated in the chief command with the Earl of Suffolk, although there was no truth in the rumour that Talbot and Scales shared equal control with him. Either way, it was a strange and unsatisfactory arrangement and, clearly, the regent had little confidence in Suffolk as an independent commander. (Three years previously, the earl had been replaced while in command at Pontorson, the reason for which was never divulged.)

Talbot, by comparison, as we have already seen, was a truly remarkable figure. He had spent some thirty years under arms, and was at this time about 46. He would soon become known to the French as 'The English Achilles', and there is no doubt that his presence greatly revived the English soldiers and made the besieged more fearful. With the return of the English troops, a new plan of operation was worked out, for it was clear that any strategy to take the city by a *coup de main* would fail as it done before.

The tedious procedures of mining and bombardment would have to be adopted, although it was accepted that there would be abnormal difficulties in pursuing this course. The perimeter of Orléans was over two thousand metres, and to construct a besieging line some seven hundred metres beyond the walls would require almost four thousand metres of fortifications, which would exclude works on the south bank. These would require a long time to construct, and there would be insufficient troops to man them when they were finished. Yet the English still managed to elaborate a ring of fortresses, or *Bastilles*, around Orléans. Some of these, such as the Bastille of the Augustins, were constructed around partially demolished churches.

The aim in general was to prevent the arrival of large quantities of foodstuffs entering the city, for the great size of the population could be made to work against them as they began to starve. The besiegers had long accepted that they could not prevent isolated individuals from making their getaway, or even quite sizeable bands of men (there was a constant trickle of escapers throughout the English siege), but the main strategy was to prevent large numbers of people leaving. At this stage, certainly, the whole city could not be contained and there were many points of egress for those who were desperate to leave, even though most ordinary people seemed not inclined to do so. Commonsense suggested that the odd escapee should be ignored, but that any mass exodus should be firmly put down.

Work was first begun on the western side, the most vulnerable to attack from the dauphin's reinforcements, arriving from Chinon, his present headquarters. As the siege continued, the English army could be increased, and the line would then be drawn completely around the city, if it had not already surrendered before then. This, in fact, was the plan of action followed by the English high command. A great base camp was constructed around the church of St Laurent, which was on the north bank, and this was connected to the fort of the Tourelles by another fort on the Île de Charlemagne. A further line of forts, four in all, were constructed, all connected by trenches. These would take many months to build, and the besiegers, meanwhile, settled in for what remained of the winter.

NOTES

1 Bourgeois de Paris.
2 Ibid.
3 John Talbot (1388–1453). Created the First Earl of Shrewsbury, he became one of England's most famous medieval generals, extremely active in France and, at times, in Ireland. He was well thought of, even by his enemies, 'because he waged war honourably, and was a valiant man'. De Maupoint, *Journal*.
4 Cousinot, *Chronique de la Pucelle*.
5 Bourgeois de Paris.
6 Ibid.
7 Ibid.
8 Ibid.
9 Ibid.
10 It has been argued that Bedford was unaware of Salisbury's intention to assault Orléans, on the grounds that the earl set off in the direction of Anjou, and that the regent was known to be against the Orléans project, from first to last. In a letter to King Henry VI, at a later date, Bedford wrote: 'All things prospered for you until the time of the siege of Orléans, taken – God knows – by what advice.' In this letter, the regent obviously sought to distance himself from the disaster that followed, but he knew perfectly well that Salisbury's march towards Anjou was designed to confuse the enemy. Burne, *The Agincourt War*.
11 Molandon, *L'Armée Anglaise*.
12 Ferdinand Lot, *L'Art Militaire*.
13 Waurin, *Anchiennes Chroniques d'Angleterre*.
14 Bourgeois de Paris. Martinmas Eve is 10 November.
15 The *Brut*, possibly the only contemporary English account of the tragedy.

CHAPTER VIII

1429: The Siege of Orléans

On 16 January 1429 the canonical hours began to be said at St Jacques de la Boucherie as they were at Notre Dame, the first time that a minor church had been granted this honour. Some of the more pious Parisians regarded this act of religious parity as a regrettable 'English' tendency, for they considered anti-clericalism to be endemic in England, with established dogma having long been under attack there. Confession, the English held, was not necessary for salvation, and bread remained bread after its consecration. The English, too, wished to rid themselves of the priests, and especially the pope.[1]

Such a step did, in fact, seem to be in tune with the changes that were then being made in the English church, where, it was insinuated, papal authority could not prevail in the face of such a strong desire for reform. Devout Parisians saw the presence of the English in their city as an assault not so much upon their civil liberties, as upon their dearest religious beliefs (although, as it transpired, the decision to honour St Jacques in this way had had nothing to do with English influence).

But while the more conservative saw it as an attack on their religious practices, others found it liberating, since it also allowed the humbler worshipper to venerate God at the correct times. Indeed, they hoped that this new departure would spread to other churches in the city – or even throughout France. Many Parisians agreed with the English heterodoxy, in that they, too, felt the spirit of official Christianity was now too mechanically legalistic and authoritarian.

The new practice began on a Sunday, the Sunday letter being 'B', a Dominical letter that had to do with calculating the correct time to celebrate Easter.

At the beginning of February 1429 the dauphin at last stirred himself to assemble a relieving force, which was based on Blois, some forty miles downstream of Orléans. This sizeable army was put under the command of the Count of Clermont, Charles of Bourbon,[2] and this move would prove a major effort by the French to raise the siege of Orléans. Bedford's instantaneous answer was to assemble another army to deal with the new challenge, stripping his garrisons in Normandy and in other places to do so. Along with this new force, he sent a large convoy of victuals to feed the troops, escorted by Sir John Fastolf and the protection of about 1,500 men, most of them archers, but with a solid body of Parisian militia among them.

Some of this convoy had, in fact, been organised for some time past, since in the last two months of 1428 the citizens of Paris had been ordered by the authorities to provide flour for the troops besieging Orléans. They had got together more than three hundred carts full, all paid for by the people who lived in the open country around the capital, working the mills there. Such a sacrifice was held to be no more than their patriotic duty, and most people were happy to fulfil their obligations as, while the enemy was occupied with battling with the English for far-away Orléans, they would be free to farm their lands without the threat of harassment. On arrival at the collecting point in Paris, the millers were given sufficient expenses to cover a nine-day stay in the capital, but they were forbidden to stay for longer. If they did so, it would be at their own cost, 'to their great loss'.[3]

The provisions convoy was fully fitted out at Paris, and it was dispatched to Orléans early in February. But as Lent was approaching, when fish was the staple diet for both devout and impious alike, the victuals – apart from the great quantity of flour – consisted in large part of salted herrings and other 'Lenten stuff', which, even so, would have been enough to keep the troops active. They had survived on worse rations.

The food-convoy reached Etampes, some twenty miles south-west of Paris, without trouble, and from where it crossed the plain of La Beauce, again without challenge. On 11 February it had reached the village of Rouvray, five miles north of Janville, a safe haven, where it was decided the men should rest for the night.

But on setting out early the next morning, they almost immediately encountered a French mounted patrol, the vanguard of the dauphin's army. This patrol appeared on the skyline to the south-west, and it soon became clear that they were the advance guard of Clermont's relieving force. News of an English convoy rumbling its way towards Orléans had reached Blois, and the count had instantly made the decision to march north-east in an attempt to cut it off and so prevent the besieging English force from receiving provisions.

But Fastolf was a general of long experience and a commander of great ingenuity. Alerted to the danger, he took the unusual step – unprecedent-ed at that time – of halting his entire convoy and its escort in an open space on the road to Janville, one mile south of Rouvray. For he had instantly understood that his slow-moving company had little chance of reaching whatever protection Janville might provide. He had also realised that the line of wagons, some three miles long, could not be adequately protected by his small force against a mounted adversary whilst on the march. (The enemy numbers were, as ever, three times greater than the English escort.) Having halted the convoy, he then constructed a 'leaguer' around it for its protection. The leaguer had two openings, and these he defended with archers, while the remainder of his troops took cover inside. When the French came up to them, they found in their path a defence as 'compact as a hedgehog's bristles'.[4]

This entire military procedure was something new in the warfare of that time, but the Count of Clermont was also no stranger to tactical fighting, and he quickly adapted his own stratagem to this novel situation. Being provided with a large number of small-calibre cannons, he ordered an artillery bombardment, seeing that the English could not return in kind as they had no weapons of that sort. Fastolf's men therefore had to sit out this assault while their casualties mounted steadily, with many of their wagons being holed by the enemy cannonballs, resulting in a loss of many herrings, which spilled to the ground.

If Clermont had persisted with this bombardment there is no doubt that there could have been only one outcome, the utter rout of the English detachment (which would have marked the first total victory by gunfire in the history of warfare). But chance then came to the aid of the English in the form of Sir John Stewart of Darnley, the Constable of the Scots in France, an undisciplined man and an impetuous fighter. Disregarding the Count of Clermont's order that the whole army, apart from gunners and crossbowmen, should remain mounted, Stewart took his men into an attack, without waiting for the artillery bombardment to take effect. As a result his company encountered the deadly fire of the English archers, as effective here as at Agincourt, and they suffered a bloody repulse.

The French men-at-arms, unthinkingly following Stewart's precipitate lead, attempted a mounted attack, spurring on their horses, and this was equally disastrous. Their steeds were impaled on the stakes the English archers had stuck into the ground before them, and the riders were pitched forwards over their horses' ears. Seeing that the moment had come for a counter-attack, Fastolf now ordered his men-at-arms to mount. When the archers made way for them, two separate bands of cavalry surged out of the leaguer to meet the enemy, as a result of which the Franco–Scottish army was roundly defeated. Against the odds once more, what came to be mockingly called the 'Battle of the Herrings' was won by the English, and Sir John Fastolf delivered his precious supplies to the army surrounding Orléans, and then immediately returned to Paris for more provisions.

The carters, who had been pressed into service, and the Paris militia, who had volunteered for 'glory', returned with Fastolf, and it was found that only four Frenchmen among their number had been killed (along with a number of waggoners, who were there purely for payment, and who had understandably tried to run away from the engagement). There were, however, many wounded. 'How dreadful it is,' the Bourgeois wrote piously, 'on both sides, that many Christian men must kill each other like this without knowing why! One man might be one hundred leagues away from the other, and here they come together to kill each other, and all to win a little money – or the gallows for their bodies, or hell for their poor souls.' He seems, at that point, to have conveniently forgotten that the English who had died in the battle had done so in order that the Parisians might remain in control of their independence from their supreme enemies.

Unsurprisingly, this victory, the 'Battle of the Herrings', had a lowering effect on the morale of those besieged in Orléans. The spirits of the English force were raised, but the expectations of the French reached their lowest point. The dauphin's relieving army had once again been unaccountably trounced, and all hope of breaking the siege of Orléans must now be abandoned. Negotiations for surrender to the English were put in hand, and during the second half of February an embassy led by the dauphin's most famous captain, Poton de Xantrailles,[5] was sent to the Duke of Burgundy to ask him to mediate between the two opposing camps.

Philippe was pleased to receive the embassy, and on 4 April, when he went to Paris to meet the regent, he took some of the delegates with him, arriving in the capital with a splendid company of knights and squires. The settlement he proposed was that the siege should be lifted, and that he himself, in the name of the Duke of Orléans, his cousin, who was then imprisoned in England, should put governors into the city. Half their yearly revenues should go to King Henry and the other half to the captive duke for his maintenance. In addition to this, the English should be allowed free access to Orléans, and the community should contribute 10,000 *écus* a year to the English war chest.

About a week after Philippe's arrival, a Grey Friar called Brother Richard also entered the capital. He was said to be a man 'of great judgement, wise in prayer, a sower of sound doctrine'. He certainly worked tremendously hard at preaching, since he did so every single day, beginning at 5am and continuing until ten or eleven at night. Some five or six thousand people came to hear him, and he spoke from a high platform, with his back to the charnel houses opposite the Charronerie, near to the newly finished Danse Macabre, in which people capered to their graves. He had, perhaps, chosen this site very carefully, for while he preached eloquently against the temptations of this world, he spoke as vividly of eternal fire in the next, and of the torments of hell.

The regent, normally imperturbable, was extremely angered by what he thought of as Duke Philippe's 'meddling' in the problem of the siege of Orléans, for Bedford saw it as a matter for the English authorities alone.

Appearing to ignore the fact that the duke had been asked to negotiate terms, Bedford probably saw it as an attempt by Burgundy to profit from an enterprise that had not only been expensive for the English to mount but which had already cost them dear. The regent bluntly told the duke that 'he in no wise intended that lands which belonged to the crown of France should fall into other hands than those of the [English] king'. Adding that he would be 'very angry to have beat the bushes that others might take the birds'.[6]

It was not a good move on Bedford's part, for the Duke of Burgundy's reaction to this impolitic refusal was not only to precipitately return 'to his own kind' in Flanders, but also to withdraw all his forces from the siege of Orléans, which was a loss the English could not easily sustain.[7]

A result of this misunderstanding was to make food even dearer in Paris, for the Burgundian withdrawal also meant that the trade routes to the north were no longer so well guarded. To make matters worse, the citizens were now called upon to send larger quantities of their rations of flour, meat, vegetables and other victuals to sustain the troops engaged in the siege. Indeed, so much foodstuff was sent to Orléans that from one Saturday to the next, corn rose from 20 s.p to 40 s.p, 'and everything else that can keep a man alive increased similarly'.[8] Because of this, the Parisians blamed the Duke of Burgundy for leaving their city without having done anything towards protecting the peace, or – failing that – for protecting the poorer people. It was alleged that he had abandoned them to fight the Liégeois, when in fact he had simply quarrelled with the regent.

Throughout this controversy, the Grey Friar was still fervently preaching against covetousness, and something approaching a religious conversion occurred in Paris. Indeed, he moved the citizens to such an extent they built huge bonfires upon which to burn the 'visible tokens of their sinful fall'. Chess and backgammon boards, along with dice, cards, balls and sticks, and every other kind of gambling game was flung into the fire. Fine headgear of both sexes was confined to the flames, for the brother also preached ardently against vanity. Rolls, stuffing and whalebone, anything used to stiffen a headdress, was thrown into the fire, for this was 'an abomination', particularly the horned headdresses that noblewomen wore, a clear sign of the devil's influence. The length of their trains was simply an indication of their vanity, but their head-coverings were a sign of pure evil. In the ten sermons that the friar preached in Paris it was said that he had done more to turn the people towards piety than all the preachers who had appeared in the capital for a hundred years.[9]

Brother Richard said that he had recently returned from Syria, but he had also been in the holy city of Jerusalem. There, he had encountered many Jews – for not all the Jews had been expelled by the Romans at the fall of Jerusalem – and he had talked with them. The Jews, he said, insisted that *their* Messiah, the truly awaited 'King of the Jews', had now been born, and he was pledged to give them back their inheritance, that is the Promised Land. Even now, the Jews remaining in the Holy Land were flocking towards Babylon, where he had made his appearance. This, the Grey Friar asserted, was clear evidence that the End of Time was now approaching. For according to Holy Scripture, was it not written that the Anti-Christ was to be born in the ancient city of Babylon, to be reared in Bethesda, and to spend his youth in Chorazin – cities of which Christ had said '*Vhe, Vhe, tibi Bethsaida! Vhe, vhe, Chorazin!*'

Brother Richard preached his last sermon in Paris on the day after St Mark's Day, 26 April 1429. His last pronouncement was that the coming year, the year '30, would see the greatest wonder that had ever happened in the world after the birth of Our Lord. To back his claim, he swore that his master, Brother Vincent, would bear witness to this out of the Book of the Apocalypse and from the writings of St Paul himself. (Brother Vincent Ferrier, born in Valencia around 1350, was a Dominican who had preached amongst both Jews and Moslems throughout Europe and the Middle East.) Richard declared that Brother Bernard of Siena (1380–1440), an observant Franciscan, who was known as 'the people's teacher', had also affirmed his claim.

The Grey Friar only ceased to preach in Paris because he was denied permission to continue. But because there was such an outbreak of public grief at his going, he was allowed to stay on. Because he had so vehemently admonished those who came to hear him on the evils of property, many of his followers had a number of mandrakes burned as a symbol of their renunciation of worldly matters. For popular superstition held that if you kept a mandrake root wrapped up in fine linen or silk, it would bring untold riches.

Brother Richard left Paris on a Sunday, but before he went, it was reported that he would make one final appearance at the hill village of Montmartre. Six thousand people went to hear him, most of them leaving Paris in great crowds on the Saturday night, so as to have better places in the morning. They slept in the open country, wherever they could find a place to rest. But to their great anger, the sermon was cancelled and Brother Richard was peremptorily escorted from the area. His sermons were not to the taste of the authorities, for this was not the time to preach along the lines of a new Crusade.

The danger to the Parisians was, in fact, much closer to them, for those Armagnacs not engaged with the siege of Orléans had bypassed the English army, and now held much of the open country to the south of Paris, where they were, as always, rapidly devastating the land. (To the Bourgeois of Paris, the Armagnacs would always be more terrifying than the Saracens.) Some eight thousand English troops were sent to meet them, yet mysteriously, they only numbered some six thousand by the time they found the Armagnacs, who were said to be ten thousand strong.

The Armagnacs charged the English troops fiercely almost on sight, and they were given a 'warm welcome'. Both sides suffered heavy losses in the early stages of the fighting, but the English soon realised they could not hold out, for the Armagnacs were as many again in number. They hemmed the English in from all sides, making it impossible for them to adapt their usual tactics, or to retreat from the unequal battle. As a result the English were heavily defeated, and four thousand of their corpses were found on the battlefield. The casualties of the other side were not known in Paris, but the news of the English defeat reverberated around the city.

Xantrailles had returned to Orléans on 2 April, to report on Burgundy's terms. Now, he was followed back by those of his colleagues who had accompanied Philippe the Good to Paris, and who had witnessed his quarrel with the regent. They arrived on the 17th, accompanied by a trumpeter of the Burgundian army. His mission was to command his fellow troops to leave the area, on the instructions of their master the duke. This, the Burgundians did 'in great haste', to the consternation of their allies.[10]

By this time all sides were becoming weary of the siege, and it was costing the English regime sums that it could not afford, some 40,000 *livres tournois* a month. In the first week of March, the regent had ordered all his officials, of whatever rank, to make a forced loan of a quarter of a year's salary, their contributions to be used for the operations at Orléans. Those who refused were made to forfeit six months' pay. The regent naturally also gave up some part of his own emoluments, but as a result of this imposed obligation there were an increasing number of desertions from the besieging forces.[11]

A ring of forts had been constructed around the walls of Orléans, and these were by now almost complete, being ten in all. The main English camp was just south of one of them, La Croix Boissée, the last fort on the western side of the north bank, the camp being raised around the church of Saint-Laurent. But, even so, there was a considerable gap in the north-east, and the besieged had more or less free use of the 'Burgundy' Gate, and of the road leading to Gien. It was said that the English, thanks to the long duration of the siege, had settled down too comfortably within the elaborate structures they had erected, and the citizens of Orléans had, therefore, a greater freedom than they should have been allowed.

Yet the situation was still to the advantage of the besiegers, and what aided them most effectively was the continual expectation among the dauphin's followers that the city would fall, sooner than later. Even the dauphin himself, it was rumoured, seemed possessed of an almost superstitious belief that he would lose his most valuable city, although he made great efforts to pay his troops and kept in constant communication with his captains.[12] He also scoured his 'realm' for artillery experts to send to the aid of the besieged. Within a few months he would raise above ten thousand men, while the besieging force, after the defection of the Burgundians, would amount to no more than seven thousand. The garrison had fallen off from an initial figure of about two and a half, perhaps because the Count of Clermont had smuggled out those of his troops who were sick or were simply unable to face any further hardship.

But the wonder that Brother Richard had spoken of came much earlier than he had prophesied, within three days of his last fiery sermon in fact. On 29 April a relieving force of some ten to twelve thousand men entered Orléans by an apparent intervention of God. Incredible though it sounded to the conventionally faithful, and more specifically to the hardheaded English commanders, it was led by a peasant girl, although one masquerading as a soldier: a certain Jeanne d'Arc, who called herself the 'Maid'.

About 17 years of age,[13] she had been convinced from puberty, by what she called her 'voices', that it was the will of Heaven the English army should be thrown out of France, and that *she* had been chosen to bring about this military marvel. That she had somehow persuaded the highly intelligent and deeply sceptical dauphin of her divine mission was thought astonishing enough, and was regarded as something of a joke by courtiers and military commanders alike. But when her arrival at Orléans coincided with a comet in the sky, this unmistakable portent could only add credence to her assertion that she had been sent by God to defeat the English. Her main aim was to have her 'lord the dauphin' anointed with holy oil at Rheims, after which rite the English could no longer claim that Charles was not the King of France in the sight of God. For enthronement at Rheims was the ultimate sanction.

The Parisians first heard of Jeanne when she was in the Loire valley. From the outset most people thought her a sorceress, and even those who would later marvel at her victories firmly believed she had brought them about by witchcraft. It was said that she could foretell the future, and she had a strange power over natural creatures. Like St Francis she could call them to her, and wild birds would fly into her lap to eat bread from her fingers as though they were tame, although she bore no other resemblance to that gentle saint.[14] That her banner bore the one word 'Jesus' was thought to be a great sacrilege by the devout, and the Parisians would quickly come to regard her successful taking of Orléans as a supernatural act.

But on 27 April 1429 Jeanne d'Arc, resplendent in a gleaming suit of armour and riding with her own specially designed banner, arrived on the south bank of the river with soldiers freshly fitted out for the relief of Orléans. The Duke of Alençon was nominally in charge of the army, but it was said that the troops had been spiritually transformed, and that this had been the work of 'the Maid'. Whether they saw her as a living saint or simply as a mascot, she had put fresh heart into them, and to the astonishment of all, her most exacting orders were carried out without protest, even to the instructions that dealt with the men's general behaviour. Swearing was abolished, prostitutes were banned from the camps, every soldier attended Mass, and each made his confession.

To the further confusion of the English, a large body of priests marched at the head of this extraordinary army, chanting psalms. It was said that the French soldiers were elated by the presence of this mere girl, and she had convinced them that Heaven was at last smiling upon the dauphin's cause. No army had been so spiritually charged since that of Henry V's before Agincourt, and to the regent and his advisers it must have seemed that the French had found in this outlandish figure a leader as charismatic as their late king.

Before setting out for Orléans, the uneducated girl had dictated an astonishing letter to the English 'usurpers'. 'Jhesus Maria. King of England, and you, Duke of Bedford, who call yourself Regent of the kingdom of France ... You ... who call yourselves lieutenants of the said Duke of Bedford, acknowledge the summons of the King of Heaven, and render up to the Maid, who is here sent by God, the King of Heaven, the keys of all the good towns you have here taken and violated in France.'

She declared that she had been sent by God's will to reclaim the 'blood royal' and that she was 'very ready' to make peace, if they would acknowledge her cause to be right, by leaving France 'and paying for what you have held'. She was, she said, sent by God to drive them, 'body for body, out of the whole of France. And if they do obey, I will be merciful to them ...'

There was much else in this vein, including a threat to enter Paris 'with a goodly company'. But her main warning was that the King of Heaven had given her men a greater strength than could ever be commanded by those of the invaders. She begged Bedford not to let his men and himself be destroyed by these forces of Heaven. But if he did not agree to her terms, he would be 'reminded of it by your very great injuries'.[15]

This letter was dated Tuesday of Holy Week, 22 March 1429.

Bedford and his council were naturally dismissive of this aggressive, and highly illiterate, communication, as were most of his troops camped before the besieged city. It was said later that terror had been struck into the breasts of the besieging army on hearing of the Maid's approach. But the truth is that when she first appeared outside the city, most of the troops in the English camp, with the exception of their captains, were unaware of the existence of this phenomenon and would have seemed little better than a joke.

Later, when an English commander who had abused her verbally was drowned before the slaughter, it was rumoured that he had died due to the curse she had laid upon him. He was afterwards 'fished up', cut in quarters, boiled and embalmed, and taken to Paris, to the parish of St Merri. He remained there for a over a week, in a chapel in front of the crypt. Four torches burned before his body, as the Parisians came in huge numbers to pray for his soul, and then he was taken to England. This man could be said to have been the Maid's first casualty, which is perhaps why he was treated so royally in death.

A convoy of supplies for the city came with this new army, but there were only two ways of getting them into Orléans without having to risk a battle, which the French wished to avoid at this stage, the Maid not having yet proved her extraordinary claims. The first course of action for the relieving army was to make a wide circuit to the north by way of the forest, where they could approach through the gap between the forts of Paris and St Loup. The other was to approach Orléans by barge from Chézy, five miles upstream. This would land them at the Porte de Bourgoyne on the eastern face of the city, an approach made possible only by the neglect of the Earl of Suffolk to stretch a chain across the river, a barricade that would have caught any boat trying to break through the defence. This was the sort of carelessness that would have been unknown in the time of Henry V, and is perhaps symptomatic of the easing of military standards. The so-called Count of Dunois, in command of Orléans and undoubtedly in touch with Alençon, must have reported the absence of a river barrier and suggested this approach as being the best for the convoy.

Thus it was that Alençon led his army by the south bank of the Loire, which was contrary to the demands of the Maid that they should follow the northern bank. Since she was generally ignorant of the region, it was never clear why she wished to impose her view upon the recognised commander (except at the behest of her voices). As it was, the Duke of Alençon, for his own reasons, kept his plans secret from her.

It was decided by the French that, when the wind changed, a number of empty barges should be taken from beneath the walls of Orléans, to be sailed upstream to Chézy and at the same time a convoy would march on that place. There, the supplies for the city would be transferred to the boats, which could then slip back downstream. The French had meanwhile drawn up the relieving army in formation opposite the city, and in order to distract attention during the return journey of the barges, Dunois then arranged a demonstration against the Fort St Loup. Since this fort possessed few cannons, the project was successful, particularly when the wind changed in the favour of the French. All went according to plan and Joan crossed the river at Chézy with a small escort. She entered Orléans on the morning of 30 April, to be met with great rejoicing from the populace. It was already apparent that something without equal was taking place among the previously demoralised French forces.

Her escorting army, though, had not entered Orléans by the unguarded Porte de Bourgoyne, as the English might have expected, but had set off for Blois, to return a few days later with further supplies. This army entered Orléans on the morning of 3 May. Up to that date the English seemed hardly aware of the presence of the Maid, but they were to realise their mistake on the same day that her army entered the city. For a few hours afterwards another attack was made on St Loup, in which Joan, galloping out of town, joined with the attackers and inspired them with such military zeal that they captured and then burnt the fort. Both sides were equally surprised at this unusual victory, although the fact that the English had left the fort so dangerously isolated was a measure of the contempt the besiegers felt for their enemies. When Lord Talbot, moving from his headquarters in Fort St Laurent with the intention of going to St Loup's relief, saw the smoke rising from the devastated stronghold he knew that he was too late, and had no other recourse but to fall back within his own lines.

The destruction of St Loup was the turning point of the siege, although neither the English nor the French may have recognised it at that time, for the fort was little more than a church which had been put into a state of defence. The next day was the Feast of the Ascension, and some chroniclers asserted that the Maid refused to fight on such a holy day, while others said that she wished to attack but was held back by wiser counsel. So the attack took place on 6 May, soundly directed by the Count of Dunois against the English-occupied Tourelles. The striking force for this task crossed the river by boat and kept the garrison engaged, while a short bridge of two boats was constructed from the Isle of St Aignan to the south bank.

The fight for the Augustins' fort was a heroic affair, and, although the English were hopelessly outnumbered, it was an all-day struggle. But after several repulses, the fort was at last captured, a victory that was largely due to the stimulating presence of the Maid. The next morning the attack was resumed, this time against the barbican. The efforts of the previous day were intensified, with guns, scaling ladders and mines being brought up. A fire ship was rigged out and floated beneath the draw-bridge, which caught alight. Any retreat by the garrison was thus threatened, and as they fell back into the Tourelles across the drawbridge it collapsed, with the death of the gallant Glasdale who was cast into the river and drowned.[16] To worsen matters, the powder for the cannons failed, and the balls simply dropped from the muzzles to fall impotently into the water.

At the same time, the garrison – roused to action by the example of newcomers – rapidly assembled a temporary structure, with which they spanned the broken arches of the old bridge. Over it, they simultaneously attacked from the north bank as their compatriots struck from the south.

This was the last setback for the English defenders. Having fought an engagement as gallant as any in their history, they were forced to surrender. Three hours later, the siege was raised, and the triumphant Maid of Orléans proudly rode her charger across the bridge into a transformed city, where she was everywhere acclaimed.

The English were now forced to make an onerous decision, for the superiority of their position had vanished overnight, with the advantage straightaway passing to the other side. They could only abandon what was now seen as an impossible enterprise. Yet there was still one action open to them, one last proud gesture. On the morning that the Maid's army took formal possession of Orléans, the entire English forces were ordered into battle array and commanded to stand before the ramparts of the city, in an unoccupied zone. There, it stood silently waiting, challenging the French to emerge from the walls and engage it in open battle. After a wait of some time, with the French showing no desire to satisfy them, the English army quietly filed away to the north 'in good order', as even the French chroniclers were forced to admit.

NOTES

1   Bourgeois de Paris.
2   His father, the Duke of Bourbon, had been a prisoner of the English since the Battle of Agincourt.
3   Bourgeois de Paris.
4   Quicherat, *Journal du siège*.
5   Jean, Lord of Xantrailles, who would become the Marshal of France in 1454.
6   Lucie-Smith, *Joan of Arc* (quoting Antonio Morosini).
7   Quicherat, op. cit.
8   Bourgeois de Paris.
9   Ibid.
10   Quicherat, op. cit.
11   Williams, *My Lord of Bedford*.
12   Lucie-Smith, op. cit. (quoting Beaucourt).
13   There is doubt about her actual age, but 4 January 1412 is believed to be her date of birth. Burne, *The Agincourt War* (quoting Deprez).
14   This, like the myth that she was a child shepherdess, probably owes its origin to Perceval de Boulainvilliers, and was later repeated by Quicherat.
15   Lucie-Smith, op. cit.
16   Sir William Glasdale had also earlier insulted the Maid, who had prophesied that he would die in a state of sin. Quicherat, op. cit.

CHAPTER IX
1429: The Battle of Patay

A poem that was soon to do the rounds in Paris was given the title 'The Mystery of Orléans', for the raising of the siege seemed to the superstitious to have something of a divine mystery about it. To the more logical among the citizens, and to those who clung to their English protectors, it seemed to be a mystery of a different order. For how could it be that, at a time when English military supremacy was at its height, their commanders had erred in such a glaring manner, and then compounded that error by behaving so negligently afterwards? Many were willing to blame the Earl of Suffolk for his general incompetence, or else to blame Lord Talbot for his singular failure in not reinforcing the garrison in the Tourelles. A few were even prepared to blame the Duke of Bedford, who seemed to have distanced himself entirely from the conduct of the siege.[1]

After fourteen years of almost continuous victory, the English had the military ascendancy, but had now let it slip from their grasp. Only four days before the attack upon St Loup, a French attack upon Fort Paris had been frustrated simply by a general fear of the English.[2] Dunois himself would later testify that two hundred Englishmen would put a thousand Frenchmen to flight, prior to the coming of this 'Maid'. But with her appearance it seemed that French morale had soared, to match that of the English troops, while the confidence of the latter had dipped in consequence.

The news of the relief of Orléans came as a great shock to the English authorities in Paris, and the regent immediately set about gathering a new army, seeing that a defensive force must now be mustered between the two great cities. It was agreed that this line of defence must be far enough away from the capital to keep it untouched by the expected conflict, and yet near enough for the citizens to provide the defending army with provisions. The Earl of Suffolk had stupidly dispersed the besieging army before it could be recalled to duty, taking about seven hundred men to Jargeau, while Talbot had taken the rest of the men to Meung and Beaugency. The Count of Dunois pursued Suffolk to Jargeau, but was repulsed and forced to fall back on Orléans. The Maid rode off to Tours, to announce the glorious news to her king.

97

The dauphin held a war council to debate the next move, and Jeanne was all for raising another army to capture those towns along the Loire that were still in English hands. But Charles and his main adviser, the dominating Georges de la Trémoïlle, were still hesitant. News had reached them that Sir John Fastolf was even then approaching them with a new army, and despite the courage raised by the Maid's promised success, Fastolf's was still a name to inspire fear. Yet in the end the Maid prevailed, and she and the Duke of Alençon were dispatched with an army to Orléans, where Dunois' garrison was added to it. The whole then marched along the south bank of the river towards Jargeau. This was a well-equipped army, fully prepared for a siege, and said to be almost eight thousand in number.

Because the Maid's voice (and, through it, her 'voices') was heard for the first time at a war council, and because she was in favour of the capture of Jargeau, the French proceeded along the lines that she then laid down. Their army marched up to the town walls and, after a skirmish in which Jeanne distinguished herself, they drove an English sortie back into the town. In the evening the English defenders were faced with an unforget-table challenge by the Maid: 'Surrender the town to the King of Heaven, and to King Charles, or it will be the worse for you.'

The Earl of Suffolk took no notice of the ravings of 'the witch', but he did enter into negotiations with Dunois, which came to nothing. On the next day, Sunday 12 June, the French artillery was placed in position and a bombardment commenced. With only three shots one of the chief towers was demolished and the English position was greatly endangered. When, after some hours of bombardment, the French were still deliberating as to whether they should assault the town without delay or wait for further developments, the Maid insisted upon an outright attack and her view again prevailed. Scaling ladders were brought forward, with Jeanne herself mounting one of them. The French surged forward and the town was entered.[3] Once captured, the escape of the English over the bridge was blocked, and both the Earl of Suffolk and his brother John were seized. Suffolk seemed more distressed by the lowly station of his captor than by the disgrace of his capture. When the Frenchman admitted that he was only a squire, and therefore unworthy of securing such a high-ranking prisoner, Suffolk immediately knighted him, and then – honour being satisfied – formally surrendered.[4] Afterwards, the whole English garrison, except for the nobles who were held for ransom, was put to the sword.

Other disasters for the English followed, all within a week. Both Meung and Beaugency remained to be captured before the reluctant dauphin could be conducted safely to his coronation in the sacred cathedral at Rheims. For a change – largely under the inspiration of the Maid – the French generals acted decisively. Jargeau fell on the Sunday and, on the Monday, the army immediately returned to Orléans, where – on the

Wednesday – it marched along the south bank to Meung and Beaugency, and the bridge at Meung was reached at nightfall. Although this was defended by the English on its southern end, where they had established a position, the French won the bridge and left a small guard to defend it. (No attempt was made to take the town, for it was separated from the bridge by a meadow.)

Instead, the French continued along the south bank to Beaugency where it was found that the English were again holding the bridge. The siege artillery that had been so effective against Jargeau was soon brought into action, with some of the guns – in order to shorten their range – being floated upon barges. The cannonballs had not much effect on the grim keep of the château, but the bombardment was kept up all the next day, a Friday. That night the English defenders, feeling themselves hopelessly overpowered and despairing of relief, made an arrangement with Alençon, whereby they could quit the town the next morning, taking their arms and belongings with them. Had they known that Fastolf's relieving army had been halted only two miles from them on the previous day, and was even now preparing to come to their aid, they might have held out.[5]

Although the quality of this army of Fastolf's was unmistakably substandard and might have proved useless, for the best and most active English soldiers to be drawn from the northern garrisons had already been taken up by other forces. Fastolf's troops were liberally composed of *milice*, or 'faux Français', who had decided to fight under the Anglo–Burgundian banners, and their commander was under no illusions about the poor calibre of his men. Even when Lord John Talbot came to join him, bringing with him a tiny force of forty lances and two hundred archers, the relief army was hardly strengthened.

Besides which, both commanders were hopelessly in disagreement over the tactics that should be taken. Talbot, a man of ardent fighting spirit, argued in favour of an immediate advance to relieve the threatened towns of the Loire. But the more cagey Fastolf proposed that they should fall back to maintain a defensive posture, for he had learned that the regent was planning to send reinforcements to the area, with fresh troops from England. A more experienced general than Talbot, he was also aware that the loyalty of the French contingent was now in question. Since the triumph of 'the unnatural witch', Fastolf had seen how affected the spirit of their French volunteers had been. The English would always see Jeanne d'Arc as a creature of the devil, but even the French who were most opposed to the dauphin's cause were beginning to see that she was an amazing phenomenon, and had the authority of the church behind her. Fastolf began to believe from this time on that their trustworthiness could no longer be relied upon.

Talbot insisted that the English should go to the relief of their compatriots, stating recklessly that he would go off with his own troops should no one else follow. Fastolf, his hand forced, consented to march the next day. But even then he attempted to avert what he believed would be a disastrous operation by holding a last minute war council, at which he again cautioned delay. When the troops finally moved off, their leaders were still in dispute about the best way to proceed.[6]

The march, however, was carried out speedily, with Meung being their first objective. Because the bridge at Meung was still held by the French, the English troops advanced along the northern bank of the river. But outriders reported that, two miles short of Beaugency, a French army was being drawn into battle order, with the evident intention of giving fight. Fastolf immediately took measures to counter this action, halting his men and deploying them in the usual English battle formation with the archers planting their pointed stakes in what by now was a traditional way, to await the oncoming French.

To no effect, for the French, after having completed their arrangements for battle then sat firmly where they were arrayed. Seeking to stir them into action, Fastolf sent off heralds to propose that three knights from each army should fight out the issue on the ground between them, although the usual challenge was for single combat between the two leaders.[7] In any case, his proposal was disregarded, and they did not stir from their places, waiting for the English to come to them. Because Fastolf very sensibly had no intention of taking the offensive, seeing that the French position was too strong for his weak forces, he took the same course as the Earl of Salisbury on the eve of the battle of Cravant. He at once fell back to Meung, intending to cross the river there, and approach Beaugency from the south side, where the bridge was still in English hands. His army withdrew that evening and made preparations to capture the bridge. Cannons were put into position, and during the night they bombarded the defenders on the bridge.[8] This was one of the first instances of 'night firing' by artillery.

But as Saturday dawned, the bridge at Meung was still in French hands. At about eight o'clock the English assault party was ready to attack – using doors and shutters as improvised shields – when a horseman arrived with the disturbing news that Beaugency was now completely in the hands of the French, and that they were even then advancing towards Meung. In the face of this, both English leaders agreed that their puny army would be no match for the superior forces arrayed against them, and they would in fact be caught between two cross fires, north and south of the river. Retreat was the only course, and so they set out on the return march to Janville.[9] This was the first step, had they but known it, in a retreat that was to lead to the eventual expulsion of the English from France. Not that the English command in Paris could ever have imagined that two such minor 'victories' would be the forerunner of so many disasters for them.

*

100

Others might have foretold this impending reversal, for strange phenomena had been reported in Paris, all of which the superstitious took to be sinister omens for the safety of the city. On 6 June, at Aubervilliers, two children had been born with two heads, four arms, two necks, four legs, four feet, but only one belly and navel. They were christened, and kept alive for three days so that the Parisians could see this remarkable marvel. More than ten thousand people went from the city to observe them. In the same week, on the next Sunday, a calf was born in the Chanvrérie, behind the church of St Jean, and this animal had two heads, eight legs and two tails. The week after that a piglet was born near St Eustache, with two heads but with only the usual four legs.[10]

Perhaps as a result of these monstrosities, on the Tuesday before the Feast of St John the Baptist (24 June), there was a considerable disturbance in the city. A rumour was spread that the Armagnacs were going to enter Paris that night, with the result that a strict watch was enforced, and the walls were patrolled without pause for some hours. The defences were also strengthened, with a number of cannons and other artillery being mounted on the walls. No attack took place, of course, although compulsory sentry duty increased over the next few days.

Before the festival of St John, a new Provost of the Merchants, Guillaume Sanguin, was appointed, along with additional aldermen.[11] The provost was a moneychanger who had been the Master of the Household to the Duke of Burgundy, and had been ennobled in 1400. Tremendously rich, Sanguin had lent freely to both the regent and the Duke of Burgundy, and he had been the Parisian ambassador to England from 1423. (Fervently pro-Burgundian, he had early conspired against the Armagnacs, and he had been banished from Paris for two years in 1416 for his temerity.) Among his council he included men who had been equally loyal to the Burgundians and the English, who had also been banished by the Armagnacs. All of them were now rewarded for their allegiance to the Anglo–Burgundian cause, with Raymond Marc, a draper, later being put in charge of the artillery. But not all of them were worthy of their position, for despite their constancy, some of these men were outright rogues. The mercer Jean de Dampierre, for example, had been accused of selling defective gold belts in 1427, although he blamed this on the goldsmiths who made them. All of these men took office in the first week of July.[12]

There is some discrepancy in dates here. Papers in the *Archives Nationales* claim that the election was held on 12 July, 'under special circumstances', in a show of strength for the Duke of Burgundy, who had arrived two days before, 'to discuss the Lancastrian reverses'. Philippe had, indeed, arrived in Paris on the 10th and, in the face of the approach of the dauphin's inspired new legions, public demonstrations against Charles were to be encouraged, especially when the presence of so many pro-Burgundians rendered a large assembly of voters relatively harmless to the authorities. In creating an illusion of unity in a time of great crisis, a mass election was invaluable. And, by selecting Sanguin, the Parisians also showed that they would follow the Duke of Burgundy in any political direction he cared to take.

Having partially succeeded in making up his quarrel with Duke Philippe, the regent had written, begging him to come at once to the capital, and the duke made a surprise appearance in the city, arriving in the evening. He stayed for five days, during which time he had several consultations with the royal council where, to the relief of the English, he renewed his alliance with them. (It was said almost solely through the influence of his favourite sister.) A general procession was made in his honour, and a fine sermon was preached at Notre Dame.

At this time, when the allegiance of the average Parisian might be thought to be wavering, both the regent and the duke worked on the passions of the general populace by making the details of the assassination of John the Fearless public for the first time. A charter was published at the Royal Palace, and this showed how, in the time of the late duke, the Armagnacs had carried on a peace negotiation with the Burgundians, presided over by the papal legate. It also showed that both parties had forgiven the other for their mutual transgressions, and had sworn a sacred oath – the dauphin, that is, and the former Duke of Burgundy. To solemnise it, they had received the sacrament together. A number of distinguished knights from both sides had also sworn this oath, and all had put seals or signets to this charter, or letter. It revealed how the late Duke of Burgundy, longing for his kingdom's pacification, and being anxious to keep the promise he had made, had humbled himself to the point of agreeing to go wherever the dauphin and his advisers might require. So when the dauphin (or his accomplices) had named a place, the Duke of Burgundy had gone there with some of his most trusted knights, only to be treacherously murdered, while 'on his knees' before the dauphin.

When this letter was read out in public, there was a 'great uproar', and 'some [of the citizens] who were still closely allied with the Armagnacs' began to regret their loyalty to the dauphin.[13] 'They began instead to hate and detest them.' After the charter was read out, the regent called for silence, and Duke Philippe then spoke, mourning the breaking of the peace and his father's death. After this, a show of hands was called for, from all men who would be true to the regent or to the Duke of Burgundy. The Anglo–Burgundian lords then promised on their faith to 'defend the good town of Paris' and the principal burghers renewed their oaths to the Treaty of Troyes.

Philippe left on the next Saturday for his base in Flanders, taking his much-loved sister with him, but leaving a number of his men behind, promising the regent to send him further reinforcements. The regent and his forces went away to Pontoise, and later to Rouen, to meet additional troops from England, to gather together a local army, and to keep the Normans steadfast. The Lord de L'Isle Adam was made Captain of Paris.[14] He would prove to be the only man to make any individual mark in this command, and he would vigorously lead the citizens in the coming assault upon the city. Taking the post very seriously, he managed to streamline tasks that were normally delegated. In particular, he diligently guarded the gates, ensuring that no goods of potential use to the enemy were taken out of the capital.

After the loss of Jargeau (and the capture of the Earl of Suffolk), the regent had gone about raising troops with all speed, very quickly raising a large body of men, which he sent from Paris under the command of Sir John Fastolf to reinforce those of Lord John Talbot.

Now, with the attack on the bridge of Meung suspended, the English could only retreat to Patay, some eighteen miles north. Once again the French leaders exhibited their usual indecision, and it was only at the insistent urging of the Maid that Alençon ordered a vigorous pursuit. 'You have spurs, use them!' she cried passionately, and for once the French command took action, selecting the best-mounted men for the vanguard of the chase.[15]

This crack unit soon gained on the English, whose progress was adjusted to that of their baggage-train. By the time they had reached Patay, the French vanguard was at St Sigismund, four miles to the south. (Characteristically, they halted for their mid-day meal, resuming their pursuit some two hours later.) Before this time the French detachment had made no contact with the English army, but patrols were now sent out in all directions, and the English were then sighted to the south of Patay (perhaps also characteristically because the English had startled a stag from its grazing, and when it galloped into view had set up a cry of 'Halloo').[16]

Hearing from his own patrols that the French advance guard was close on their heels, Fastolf held a hasty council. But again both English commanders differed in their opinion as to the best way to confront this new challenge. Fastolf reluctantly agreed to stand his ground, while Talbot reinforced his small force of three hundred men with about two hundred 'elite archers' from Fastolf's larger body. He undertook to occupy and hold a covering position to the south of Patay, while Fastolf deployed the main body of his small army on the ridge.

This was the situation when the startled stag had burst through the line of Talbot's archers, and when their instinctive huntsmen's cries had alerted the French to their exact position. But unaware of the presence of the enemy vanguard, the English had continued the preparation of their position, hammering out their stakes in the accepted manner. Talbot had the pick of the English troops in the covering position, but Fastolf was burdened with a body of ill-trained soldiers and inexperienced officers on the ridge. Besides which, he had no heart for the fight. His was, he knew, the only English army of any strength in the area, and he realised only too clearly that this battle could be lost within hours. And the loss of such a battle could only lead to greater defeats.

However, the battle was not lost within hours, but within minutes. The French advance guard, on topping a slight rise, saw the English drawn up in a dip below them, in a vulnerable position. Inspired by the vigorous cries of the Maid (who had been exasperated at being kept back from the fray by her superiors, and was ordered to stay in the rear-guard), the French horsemen swept impetuously down the slope to cut a swathe through the English archers. These men were not ready for such a move and were consequently stupefied, finding themselves surrounded, and helpless against an attack from the flank. Exposed, most of them fell. A few managed to get away to the rear, to where Fastolf held the ridge. But their arrival only added to the confusion that was already affecting Fastolf's motley collection of men.

Military virtuoso that he was, Fastolf stood no chance. The French attack was made in such large numbers that he found himself over-whelmed before he could take any effective steps to oppose such an assault, which was, in truth, completely outside the experience of any English soldier in the field. Before this, the French had always approached a position held by them with circumspection, even a sense of trepidation. But this attack was something entirely new – the French were laying into the English in exactly the same way that the English had been assaulting them for decades. And even more strangely, the Maid of Orléans, who had spent almost the whole of this affray in the rear-guard of the action, without seeing a blow struck – except upon an English prisoner – was said to have won the battle of Patay.

But it was an undeniable defeat for the English, particularly since Lord Talbot was captured, taken ignominiously from his front line, mounted but without spurs. It was said that another horse had been brought up for him, and he was about to make a dash for it when he was seized. But his seizure was a great coup for the French, for his was a name to conjure with among them. He spent that night in a lodging-house in Patay, and the Duke of Alençon – who had earlier himself been taken prisoner at Verneuil – called in upon him to gloat over his reverse. Talbot told him with great dignity that his capture was simply 'the fortune of war', and his resolute demeanour greatly impressed his captors.[17]

Lord Scales and several other leaders had also been taken prisoner, but it was not a complete rout of the English. Fastolf managed to escape, and even to rescue something from the wreckage of English ambitions, although he lost his baggage-carts and guns. He retreated to Janville, eighteen miles away, only to find the town gates firmly closed against him. The old warrior then took his weary troops on the long march to Etampes, another twenty-four miles. He still had a body of archers, who turned to confront their attackers firmly, when the French continued to pursue them. When they had exhausted their supply of arrows, they attacked their pursuers with drawn swords. It was a long and dangerous journey, but they managed to reach safety.

On learning the news of the disaster from Fastolf, the regent sharply rebuked him, and was said to have deprived him of the Order of the Garter.[18] Fastolf had, the report went, 'lost the war in an afternoon'. It had lasted much longer than that, in fact, but it was true that the dazzling campaign was considered to have been a triumph for Jeanne d'Arc. As indeed it was, since she had inspired the French in ways unheard of before her appearance.

During the seven weeks following this calamity for the English and their allies, the Duke of Bedford acted with extraordinary judgement and energy. In Paris, once the defeat of the English became common knowledge, there was a general fear that the Armagnacs were approaching the capital, and it took much effort to calm the panicking Parisians. When they heard how their enemies were gaining ground everywhere, many citizens even abandoned their houses, taking their belongings into other towns. The outlying farmers also harvested the corn before it was ripe and brought it for sale into the city. Their alarm grew even greater when the Armagnacs unexpectedly entered Compiègne, forty-three miles to the north of Paris, taking many castles in the area without any real opposition. Several fortified towns in the vicinity of the capital also fell to them, and the Parisians now feared the worst.

The regent, although outwardly calm, took measures for strengthening the city walls. He also displaced many of the municipal officers, re-appointing others in whom he could trust more fully. He wrote to the council in England for reinforcements, and it was agreed, on 1 July, that he should have use of the troops that had been raised by the Cardinal Beaufort for his crusade against the Hussite heretics in Bohemia.[19] Ultimately several thousand men would be diverted from this crusade, and Beaufort's army comprised 250 'spears' and 2,000 archers, more men than the council had been able to muster for reinforcements at Orléans. On the same day that Beaufort was given permission to raise this force, the English met disaster at Patay. To save Beaufort from the wrath of Pope Martin V, who had ordered him to mobilise this crusading army (in return for his cardinal's hat), Bedford had 'requisitioned' the troops as they marched through northern France.

The Parisians took some comfort from the arrival in Paris of a great many archers and men-at-arms, for there were above four thousand, and Lord de L'Isle Adam recruited a further seven hundred from Picardy. All these were not counting the city troops, and the presence of these men greatly helped to boost morale in the capital.[20] But Bedford always intended to forestall any outright attack upon the city by offering battle to the dauphin before the Armagnac army could approach the walls. On 28 July orders were issued instructing various newly recruited Norman contingents to assemble as soon as possible at Lagny-sur-Marne, east of Paris. They would be under the command of Sir Ralph Butler and they were to be paid for fifteen days 'without mustering'.

It became clear that Brother Richard, the Grey Friar, who had preached at the Innocents and drawn such crowds to hear him, had been 'riding with the enemy', and as such had been sent to propagandise for the dauphin.[21] As soon as the people of Paris were certain of this, and when they heard that he was now trying to persuade other towns that had sworn faith to the regent to abandon their allegiance, they turned on his memory. In their anger and revulsion, they 'took up again in contempt of him all the games he had forbidden them'. They also left off wearing a fine medallion that he persuaded them to buy, which bore the single name of 'Jesu' (which also appeared on the banner of Jeanne d'Arc). Instead, they began to flaunt a Saint Andrew's cross, an Anglo–Burgundian symbol.[22]

Throughout the summer, people whose loyalty was open to suspicion were at first listed, then banished from Paris. As often happens in such situations, old enemies took the opportunity to inform on each other, often maliciously. Among many, Jean de Vitry complained that Macé Ogier, his chief rival, had arranged for his name to be added to this list out of pure spite. The accused managed to convince the authorities of his allegiance on this occasion, but the fact that he had numerous relatives living in the 'other realm' caused him a great deal of trouble. Michel de la Tillaye, a royal secretary, though, who was accused of favouring the 'contrary party' since as long ago as 1418, was found guilty and expelled.

But, meanwhile, Charles was daily gaining ground and many towns submitted to him, among them Troyes, the principal city in Champagne. The prospects for an immediate advance upon Paris had never been more auspicious, but the Maid's main intention had always been to have her king crowned at Rheims, and his sacred anointing must come before she could turn her attention to punishing the disloyal citizens of Paris. And by clearing the route so energetically and successfully, 'the avenging Amazon' made sure that the dauphin's coronation procession had a speedy and almost unopposed entrance into the city of Rheims. Charles de Valois was crowned on 17 July 1429, with his saviour, clad in silver armour, standing by the altar.

According to ancient custom, the new king should then have gone directly to the priory of St Marcoul, at Cornigny, to be invested with the royal power and to touch for scrofula. Charles did not fulfil this obligation because he was still negotiating with the Duke of Burgundy (who sent ambassadors to represent him at Rheims), but it was now no longer possible for the English and their allies to deny him his rightful throne. His anointing had removed all doubt of his legitimacy, as he was now a monarch sanctified. For it was only at Rheims that kings were made, since the day that St Remy had crowned Clovis King of France, using oil from the sacred ampulla. To the majority of the French, once Charles's crowning was accomplished, the Lancastrians were now no better than usurpers.

Charles's unexpected coronation had pre-empted the plans of the English council to have King Henry VI crowned in France, and it had reasserted the Valois presence in the lands east of Paris. It was obvious to people on both sides of the Channel that more assistance from England would be necessary to shore up the English position. The situation required more than bland circulars, even though another pro forma letter from King Henry had arrived on 11 July, which had been read out in public by a member of the chapter of Notre Dame. When Bedford had realised that, against all the odds, the coronation of the dauphin was inevitable, he had urged his nephew to visit his French kingdom for his own coronation. But while the military situation seemed so uncertain, the council in London was reluctant to commit itself to a royal expedition.

Since her main mission had been accomplished, Joan was now set upon attacking Paris. The regent had re-entered the capital on 24 July, and on 4 August he left the city with a force of ten thousand men, mustered from wherever he could raise them, in an effort to bar the new king's approach. Charles VII was, as always, reluctant to face an English army in force, and he had kept edging off towards his 'kingdom', even as his troops advanced into new territory. The slow movements of the French had enabled Bedford to recover some lost ground.

By 5 August the French army had approached Bray, intending to cross the south bank of the Seine there and then make their way back to Bourges. But the regent was now intent upon directly challenging King Charles – who, by accident, was a part of his army for the first time in many years, even if he was not actively leading it. A dead king would leave the crown vacant once again, and Bedford had decided to try and bring this satisfactory result about with a final encounter. His first step was to post a strong force at Bray, to head Charles off from that crossing place, whilst he himself advanced with his army to Monterau, twenty-five miles to the west. The French, seeing that they had no alternative but to face the enemy, turned and marched north to Crépy, forty miles north-east of Paris.

From his position at Monterau, the regent sent a letter to the new king by herald on 7 August. Its studied insolence was calculated to provoke the most apathetic coward into action. In it, the regent reproached Charles with deceiving the people with the help of an apostate friar (Brother Richard), and a woman of disorderly life, who clothed herself in male attire. He accused the king of having seduced the French from their allegiance to the truly legitimate king, the boy Henry, and he also taunted him with the murder of John the Fearless. While he declared himself ready to conclude a solid peace, he challenged the king, in default, to meet him in battle.

In the meantime, back in Paris, the Porte St Martin was closed, and a proclamation was made forbidding any citizen to go to the church of St Laurent for the feast and fair of 8 August, either for devotional purposes or for trade, upon pain of being hanged.[23] The church was half a mile beyond the gate, and the garrison could no longer guarantee the safety of the revellers, even at that short distance. Instead, the crowds attended a fête in the great court of St Martin-des-Champs, although there was nothing much for sale beyond eggs, cheese and fruit.

There was nothing unusual in this re-assembly, though, for in every case where a procession had been abandoned, either from danger or because the gate was closed, the organisers of the event had arranged to stop at the nearest point inside the gate, in the direction of the church. In the face of some closed gates, the faithful had often been turned off from the traditional route when only yards from their goal. Such disruptions to religious processions made the political insecurity obvious to all. The provisioning of Paris was upset by such upheavals, but the disturbance to religious life was equally troubling.

It looked for a time as though Bedford's challenge to the French would have the desired effect, for Charles advanced some twelve miles to Daumartin, bringing his troops to within twenty miles of the capital. There, the French found the English army drawn up to oppose them, and a day of skirmishing in the scorching heat followed. But in the evening, the French fell back again. Yet the march of the French towards Senlis struck Bedford as a threat to Normandy. Setting out from Paris, he took up a position at the abbey of Ste Victoire, immediately to the east of Senlis, while the French were encamped close by under Mont Piloy. On 16 August the two armies were again facing each other.[24]

The English position was well chosen, and Bedford had drawn up his men with a nice skill, and in such a way that they blocked the route to Paris, for his aim was always to defend the city. The French were also drawn up for battle, along their usual lines, and for two days the enemy hosts faced each other without engaging, except for some minor skirmishes. The men of Picardy in the regent's army so distinguished themselves in these that the duke rode down their ranks to thank them man by man. But again the French declined to attack, and once more they fell back upon Crépy.

1. Portrait of Philip the Good (1396–1467) Duke of Burgundy by Rogier Van de Weyden (Musée Communal, Bruges, Belgium/Bridgeman Art Library).

2. Portrait of Charles VII, King of France c. 1455-50 by Jean Fouquet (Giraudon/Bridgeman Art Library).

3. John of Lancaster (1389-1435) Duke of Bedford after a portrait in a prayer book, engraved by the artist George Vertue (The Stapleton Collection/Bridgeman Art Library).

4. French and English in battle
(Cotton MS Nero E © The British Library).

5. Battering rams (Pincerna).

6. Escalading and mining (Yates Thompson MS © The British Library).

7. Attack on a city (Stowe MS
© The British Library).

8. A siege
(Burney MS ©
The British
Library).

9. Medieval Hall (Pincerna).

10. A Tournament (Pincerna).

11. A Lord and his serfs (Pincerna).

12. A Knight and his family (Harley MS © The British Library).

13. An assault using a
Siege Tower (Pincerna).

14. A siege, clearly showing
defenders' and attackers'
methods (Cotton MS Nero E
© The British Library).

15. Siege with crossbow defence.

16. Joan of Arc.

17. Coronation of Henry VI (1421-71) (Giraudon/Bridgeman Art Library).

When he realised that the French had no intention of risking a battle, the regent returned with his men to Paris. For disturbing news had reached him from Normandy. The Constable de Richemont had advanced from Maine and was threatening Evreux, only twenty five-miles from Rouen. Bedford had no other choice than to take the major part of his men to that region, leaving his Burgundian allies, with a strong contingent of English troops, to hold the capital. In many respects, Rouen was as important to the English as the capital, and having taken stock of the new 'king', Bedford realised that he could expect little challenge from that quarter. In Rouen, the regent met the estates of the province in August. Reminding them of the many benefits enjoyed by them under English rule, and after making many promises of future favours, he managed to persuade them to give him a large grant for the continuation of hostilities against the French.[25]

But King Charles had, in fact, no reason to meet the English in battle, for numbers of towns were now prepared to surrender to him without a blow being struck. Château Gaillard, Torcy, Compiègne, and other such towns soon submitted to his troops. The Duke of Burgundy began to grow so fearful of French inroads into his territory, that he made secret negotiations between himself and the French, which Philippe handled very dexterously. Yet despite this, Burgundy knew that, for the time being at least, he must still cast his lot with the English, although he concluded a truce with King Charles at Compiègne on the 28th, where the two leaders entered into a pact for a definite peace. But Philippe's vacillations had greatly added to the regent's military problems and his virtual withdrawal from any further activity against the French left the English at a perceptible disadvantage, particularly when the Burgundians suddenly evacuated St Denis, which was only four miles north of Paris. This left it wide open for occupation by the French.

Part of the walls had already been thrown down and the moat filled up by them, while the more important citizens had fled to the safety of the nearby city.[26] Now, with the regent absent in Rouen, the Maid – who had never ceased to hope for the possibility of disciplining the disobedient Parisians – at last convinced her reluctant master to move forward and take this important town, the burial place of his ancestors. The Duke of Alençon was himself increasingly anxious about the king's lack of enthusiasm for an attack upon his capital city, and on 1 September he visited Charles in order to press him to make a decision. He was told that Charles would leave Senlis for the environs of Paris on the following day, but again nothing happened.

Disregarding the king's reluctance, though, other Frenchmen gathered to besiege the capital, with some of them riding boldly up to the gates, where they could see the Parisians were once again strengthening their fortifications. During the first week of September those responsible for the different quarters of the city had begun to organise the defence of their own particular section. Guns were brought up and positioned on the ramparts, and barrels full of stones were placed upon the walls. The moats were repaired and barricades were raised to divide one quarter from another, in case of insurrection from inside. The stonecutters were industriously making cannon balls. One Hilaire Caillet made no fewer than 1,176 balls, for which he charged four *livres* per hundred.[27]

No one dared to go outside the city walls to harvest the vines, or the verjuice. Many were reluctant even to go to the relatively protected area of the Marais to harvest the crop, and all prices rose immediately. There were crowds of people present at any market, but these were complete failures, for there were few goods for sale, except for cheese and eggs and some fruits of the season.

The Duke of Alençon had a letter written, and sealed with his seal, which was sent not only to the Provost of Paris but also to many merchants and aldermen, addressing them all by name. (He made it clear that he had spies within the city who had kept him informed of their 'treachery' to their anointed king by their allegiance to the invader.) The letter's tone was nevertheless conciliatory, 'with a liberal supply of fine words', and intended to rouse sympathy for the royal cause. Alençon promised that no reprisals would be taken against many who had been the king's enemies. But it was obvious to all that the letters were maliciously meant to stir the people up against each other, as well as against the English. A reply was sent to the count, which was bold enough in the circumstances. It told him not to waste any more paper on this kind of exhortation, since no one paid any attention to it![28]

By way of reply, on 5 September, Alençon set up an advance head-quarters at the village of La Chapelle. On the same day he again rode back to the king at Senlis, probably to tell him that the attack would go ahead even without the sanction of the royal presence, but that his troops expected the king to attend such a momentous action in person. He was so adamant, in fact, that Charles was forced to a decision, and he finally arrived at St Denis on the morning of 7 September, to find the town 'as if abandoned'. In the end it had been decided not to assault the capital until the king could witness its capitulation in person, along with the overdue humiliation of his recalcitrant subjects. At the king's arrival, the spirits of his army rose, and everyone was convinced that Paris would fall easily to them.

Prior to the outright assault upon Paris, there had been a number of brisk and vigorous clashes at odd points outside the city walls, many being fought at a windmill between the Porte St Denis and the village of La Chapelle, about mid-way between the capital and St Denis. Jeanne d'Arc herself decided that La Chapelle would be the best base if a serious assault were to be tried on the city – a decision that led to another immediate rise in prices, as the citizens were cut off from the little vegetable plots that many of them cultivated in this area.[29]

Paris, a city of over one hundred and fifty thousand residents, was left to be guarded by only three thousand men under the command of Louis of Luxembourg, who directed military matters with the aid of sixteen Burgundian captains and sixteen English captains.[30] This division of responsibility was meant to emphasise that the regent shared an equal concern with the Duke Philippe for the fate of the city, but it was already known that the Burgundians were now determined to play a neutral role, and a waiting game. With the royal army closer than it had been since the expulsion of the Armagnacs, the battle for Paris was initially as much about gaining the hearts and minds of its inhabitants as it was a struggle for military possession. Those who were for the dauphin had never ceased to conspire against the English, and they were greatly heartened by the proximity of the king.

Louis of Luxembourg was a deeply worried man, and with every reason to be, for it would seem that the time of retribution was at hand. On 26 August, when the main body of the French army had arrived at St Denis, he convoked an assembly in the *parlement*.[31] At it, the three chambers swore, as they had now done several times, to live in peace and union, under the obedience of King Henry of France and England, according to the peace treaty.

Bedford, however, seemed confident that Paris could not be taken easily. He, with his troops, stayed at Vernon, halfway between the capital and Rouen. He sent Sir John Radcliffe to Paris with 800 men, newly arrived from England. On 27 August they had been paid a supplementary wage to help them 'cope with the expense of living' in the capital. Despite the arrival of the English troops, the regent made a determined effort to recruit fighting men from Normandy, but this recruitment took some time to organise, as the potential soldiers were scattered all over the duchy. As it was, the English were out in their calculations by two days. They believed that the assault on Paris would take place on 10 September, and so were still at Vernon when the French fell upon the city on the 8th, the Nativity of the Virgin.

NOTES

1   The regent and his wife *had* pawned their jewels to provide funds for the siege of Orléans. Williams, *My Lord of Bedford*.
2   By what Andrew Lang called 'the dread Hurrah of the English'. Burne, *The Agincourt War*.
3   Quicherat, *Journal du siège*.
4   Ibid. The story that Suffolk surrendered to the Maid is only that, a myth.
5   The English had about 500 soldiers. Fastolf's army was estimated at 5,000

men, but the earliest French sources have it around 3,500. Burne, op. cit. (quoting Waurin).

6   Waurin, *Anchiennes Chroniques.*

7   A solution that was favoured in a more chivalrous age, for example by Edward III. Burne, op. cit.

8   Ibid.

9   Quicherat, op. cit.

10   Bourgeois de Paris.

11   Ibid.

12   That no public elections were held between 1422 and 1429 was presumably because the English feared that any sort of popular gathering could be turned against them. In view of the fact that the Parisians were always inclined towards the Burgundians, it is not particularly striking to find the same sort of men being returned to office.

13   Bourgeois de Paris.

14   Quicherat, op. cit.

15   Waurin, op. cit., who was present at the battle.

16   Quicherat, op. cit.

17   Quicherat, *Chronique de la Pucelle.* In London, a fund was immediately raised for his ransom.

18   The regent later restored the order when he realised that Fastolf's advice had been consistently sound, and that he was not really responsible for the débâcle. Lucie-Smith, *Joan of Arc.*

19   *Proceedings of the English Privy Council.*

20   Bibliothèque Nationale.

21   Brother Richard had given out badges bearing the single name 'Jesu' during his mission in Paris, which single name also appeared on the banner of Joan of Arc. Both crusades were thus seen to be not simply religious, but also political, in nature. The more sophisticated Parisians would have recognised the political message behind Brother Richard's ministry, though without necessarily associating it with the Armagnac camp.

22   *Archives Nationales.*

23   Bourgeois de Paris.

24   Quicherat, *Journal.*

25   Ibid.

26   Ibid.

27   Bourgeois de Paris.

28   Ibid.

29   Ibid.

30   Morosini, *Chronique.*

31   Quicherat, *Journal.*

CHAPTER X

1429: The Battle for Paris

As it was, the offensive began almost casually. While the Duke of Alençon and his troops kept watch on the Porte St Denis from a prudent distance, the Maid and her party assaulted the Porte St Honoré. The attack began quite late, somewhere between eleven and midday, with the royal army deploying a large number of men. As soon as they saw what was happening, the English – with their allies from Burgundy – paraded bravely above the walls, carrying standards of various colours, among them the cross of St George.[1]

An extraordinary rumour had circulated among the Parisians that Jeanne had struck a prostitute with the flat of her blade, and the supposedly magic sword – said to have been received directly from Ste Catherine-de-Fierbois – had promptly shattered. The king was reported devastated by this ill omen, and the accident had affected all those who followed her. The royal armourers had signally failed to mend the broken steel, and it was said that as a result Jeanne would no longer 'prosper in arms, to the king's benefit or otherwise'. This news greatly emboldened the Parisians, as they strutted along their walls.[2]

But the assault went ahead, and the citizens were struck by the fact that it did so on a major feast day of the church.[3] This strange decision also encouraged them, for it was felt that no good could come to the attackers, planning such a slaughter on Our Lady's most holy day. For a leader professing herself to be divinely inspired, it seemed even more sacrilegious. Later, the Maid would say that the assault had been intended to be no more than 'a skirmish or feat of arms'. Amazingly, 'there were hardly any men-at-arms in this battle, except for some forty or fifty Englishmen, who did their duty very well'. This meant that there were few trained soldiers on the defenders' side, and many of the day's successes were achieved by the efforts of ordinary citizens. Nicolas Sellier, a clerk at Notre Dame cathedral, registered the Englishmen as being among the wounded. But he saw the outcome as a triumph of the citizens, 'with divine assistance'. The Bourgeois recorded this, but Fauquembergue also congratulated the citizens 'for keeping their positions'.

At the first assault the besiegers scored an enormous success, easily taking and burning the outwork which guarded the Porte St Honoré. The French commanders, anticipating that a sally would be made against them from the neighbourhood of this gateway, then held back their main force behind the shelter of a hillock. There was heavy artillery fire from the ramparts, but the Parisians seemed to be short of powder, as their shots had little force. A number of the besieging soldiers were knocked to the ground by these shots, but they were otherwise without injury. The besiegers had brought with them large quantities of faggots, roped into huge bales, with the purpose of filling in the moats. And Jeanne now dismounted, having decided that this was the best time to test the true strength of the fortifications. Accompanied by several captains, including among them Gilles de Rais, she went down into the first ditch, which was dry.[4]

The Maid displayed her usual bravery – for not even her most dedicated enemies could question her personal courage (although she undoubtedly believed herself to be divinely protected and therefore invincible) – and the outer ditch was successfully crossed, under considerable fire. This was a signal for a general rush upon the walls, and the French surged forward to attack a stretch between the Porte St Denis and the Porte St Honoré. Their fire was so intense that the defenders were forced to retire behind the ramparts.

For a few minutes it appeared that all the assailants had to do was simply plant their ladders, scale the walls, and fire down into the unprotected defenders. As the French soldiers struggled with this task, a cry rose up within the city that all was lost, and the inhabitants came running out of the churches, where they had been attending services to celebrate the feast-day. All of them hurried home to lock their doors against the incoming troops. But, very significantly, any internal insurgence that Charles VII's advisers had banked upon failed to materialise.[5]

But the regent had made sure that these particular defences were more heavily reinforced than elsewhere, and the inner ditch proved too strong for the assailants. The Maid probed the water with her lance, trying to fathom whether it would be possible to fill up the ditch with the bundles that had been brought forward. At the same time she constantly called out to the defenders to give up their fight. 'Surrender to us quickly, in Jesus' name,' she was heard to cry. 'If you don't surrender by nightfall we shall come in by force and you will all be killed . . . Surrender to the King of France.'[6]

But even as she was uttering her threats, a crossbowman was taking aim. 'Shall we, you bloody tart?' he yelled in defiance, and he put a crossbow bolt through the fleshy part of her left thigh. Then, as she turned away in pain, her standard bearer was shot in the foot. As he lifted his visor to examine the wound, another bolt caught him full between the eyes and killed him outright. The Maid dragged herself to shelter behind the ridge that divided the two ditches, and here she remained, trying to direct the positioning of the fascines, so that ladders could be planted against the walls. But the water in the moat was too deep, making the task very difficult, and there were now not enough men left to carry out the work.

Alençon, who may or may not have been aware of what was happening, held his hand all day, and Jeanne was said to be very angry in that she was so little backed up at such a crucial time. It was the usual lack of decisive action among the French, for 'the captains did not agree among themselves about the attack on the city'. Several of the king's councillors had, in fact, withdrawn their troops throughout the day. There were between five and seven hundred French casualties, all sustained during this failed assault and the sporadic fighting that followed.[7]

When the defenders saw that 'the witch' was wounded, they were given fresh heart and their resistance became increasingly more defiant. About an hour after the bells had struck for nones, the besiegers began to withdraw. A large barn outside the walls was set on fire, and it seemed to the watching defenders that their enemies were piling their dead on the flames, 'as if at a Roman funeral',[8] although it was more likely that the French were burning the machinery they had used in the siege, lest it should fall into the hands of the besieged. It was also a plain sign of their discouragement, and it suggested to the Parisians that the Armagnacs would not be returning to the attack, at least in the immediate future. When the Parisians saw the enemy depart, they surged out of the city and captured most of the carts that had been used to bring in the faggots, carrying them into the city in triumph.

The Maid herself, although wounded, was reluctant to give up the attempt – she had, after all, promised the royal troops that Paris would fall to their assault, and had even rashly declared that she would sleep in the city that night. She had also said that the men would be made rich by the city's wealth, and that anyone who resisted would be cut down or burned in his house. She had made similar promises at Orléans, and these 'prophecies' had proved true. Now the men were disillusioned with her, for they had grown to believe that everything would happen easily under her divine guidance. So Jeanne ignored a series of messages that reached her, ordering her to abandon her position, and eventually men were sent to bring her back to company headquarters by force. As they carried her away, she still insisted that Paris could have been taken, for she was very reluctant to accept the reality of her first setback.[9]

Despite the fact that she was still suffering the effects of her wound, she rose early the next morning and went to the Duke of Alençon to plead with him to have the trumpets sounded, to muster the men for a renewed assault upon the city. The count was willing enough to try again, but he was faced with the reluctance of his captains, and even as they were arguing a message came from the king's headquarters at St Denis with orders for the army. Charles had decided that they should not make another attempt, but they were to attend upon him instead. These inexplicable orders were obeyed reluctantly, even by those who were unwilling to return immediately to the fray.

Jeanne, and many who sided with her, thought it might be possible to make an attack upon Paris from the river, by using a bridge that Alençon had ordered to be constructed across the Seine. But this idea was inexplicably abandoned, and the troops that remained behind at La Chapelle were left to their own devices. Their immediate response was to send to the city under a flag of truce to ask permission to bury their dead. It was by this request that the Parisians learned how excessive the French casualties had been, and they were greatly encouraged by such heavy losses.[10]

Charles was not in favour of Jeanne's plan to attack Paris from another flank, and he held a number of councils to discuss the position, but this was a mere subterfuge, for the king, distrusting it, in his usual manner, had already decided against the proposal. Throughout the night of 9 September, men were dismantling the bridge that Alençon had caused to be constructed, and they did this under the direct orders of the king.

King Charles had, in fact, already decided upon retreat as his best course, and he had four reasons for this. Firstly, as dauphin and now king, Charles had always preferred diplomatic negotiation to military con-frontation, and he firmly believed that his recent *rapprochement* with the Duke of Burgundy gave him the best hope of an eventual and lasting victory. Secondly, the expected revolt by his adherents in Paris had not taken place, and showed no prospect of doing so. Thirdly, as had happened in 1418, there was the terrible possibility of a massacre in the city if it was to be taken by force. But his fourth consideration was perhaps his most important one: as ever, he had not enough funds to pay his troops.[11]

So, to the relief of all Parisians, King Charles VII made his departure from St Denis on 13 September. The Maid, still hankering to overwhelm Paris, was ordered to follow him, which she did reluctantly. She blamed her removal from the war zone of Paris on the fact that the lords of her party had taken her away against her will. Had she not been wounded, she insisted, she would not have gone. Yet the wound she had received before the walls of Paris was considerably less serious than the one she had received at Orléans, and it healed within five days. Wounded or not, the Maid had no other choice than to follow her master, the man she had made king. But before she left, she dedicated a suit of armour and a sword in the church of St Denis. 'Out of devotion, as is the custom of men-at-arms when they have been wounded; and because she had been wounded before Paris, she offered them to St Denis, because this is the battle-cry of

France.' The sword she left behind, however, was not the magic sword that had been broken, but a lesser blade.[12]

Despite their considered decision to retreat from what could have been a famous victory, the French were seen to abandon the field in their habitual disorder. The march that followed was so headlong that no pattern could be kept as they retreated towards the Loire. Many territories along the route had returned to obedience to the newly crowned King of France, but these communities were not strong enough to support him financially. Yet even in the area surrounding Paris, many villages were forced to pay protection money to the king's garrisons. 'Not a man dared set foot outside the suburbs – he would be lost, killed, held to ransom higher than all he possessed, and yet dared to take no revenge.'[13]

Bedford's main army seems to have reached Paris on 15/16 September, with small groups of stragglers following on. None of the Anglo–Norman troops had arrived in time for the battle. The English, too far from Paris, had been reduced to making a military display; but if a full assault on the French had been within reach, Bedford would have brought an effective enough body of men with which to tackle them. In the event, it took him a week longer than expected to mobilise his army.

A few days later, the regent returned to St Denis, and he punished the people for having abandoned the town to the French king.[14] (Although they had, in a sense, already been punished, for the Armagnacs had gone off without paying for their lodging. They had bragged that the people of St Denis would be paid off with the loot their men would seize in Paris, after they had taken it.) But the regent was so angry with the citizens for surrendering, 'without striking a blow', that he condemned them to pay very heavy fines.

But however weak or strong was the support for Charles VII, it was clear now that the Parisians were increasingly doubtful about the merits of their English alliance. The city was in deep trouble financially, and the citizens had been constrained to improvise in order to meet the cost of defending themselves. Sanguin was one of a consortium of financiers who lent money when the authorities borrowed from the merchants. Royal finances were in a worse condition than those of the municipality, and the government had to adopt extreme measures. For example, on 31 August the *Grand Conseil* ordered that all goods confiscated from the Bishop of Troyes and other defectors should be auctioned, the proceeds being used for essential payments to the Anglo–Burgundian troops. Three days later, officials of the Châtelet were ordered to hand over the monies deposited with them by litigants with cases in progress. All the debts were incurred during the last desperate weeks before the French assault were, in fact, repaid once money from Normandy reached Paris in late September, but the Parisians were still feeling the pinch. It is noteworthy that it was

Bedford, rather than Burgundy, who raised this money. Nevertheless, confidence in the English had been severely tested.

On 18 September commissioners were appointed to look into, judge and terminate with due severity, all the cases concerned with the disobedience of those citizens who were suspected of favouring the party of Charles of Valois. Which suggests that more citizens were beginning to look to the French king as their true leader, and from now on complaints against the English would grow common, even if few Parisians wanted to hand over the city to the Armagnac murderers of John the Fearless, and it was always to be remembered that King Charles was suspicious of a city that had for so long been faithful to the Burgundians, let alone their allies.

Paris soon received a visit from Duke Philippe, who entered the city on the last day of September. He brought with him a magnificent escort, so many attendants, in fact, they had to be put up in householders' homes, and even in empty houses. The horses were stabled with pigs and cows. This company came by the Porte St Martin, which was opened for him, and ten heralds went before him, each wearing the coats of arms of his own lord, and there were also the same number of trumpeters. With great pomp they went to the church of Our Lady of St Avoyé, to make their offerings.

Philippe also brought back with him his sister, Bedford's duchess. The two dukes were seen to greet each other with every sign of affection and, as always, the regent was ready to make any sacrifice to retain the Burgundian alliance. He was conscious that all his energies would be required to keep a hold on Normandy, should the English lose their grasp on the capital. And he was deeply aware that, while the Parisians were still in fear of the Armagnacs, and were as pro-Burgundian as ever, they had never been fully reconciled to English rule.

About a week later the 'Cardinal of Winchester' arrived, even more magnificently accompanied than Duke Philippe, bringing with him a vast train of attendants, all of whom had to be accommodated. Various consultations were then held between the English, the Burgundian faction and the representatives of Paris, at which it was decided that a change should take place in the administration. At the request of the University of Paris, the *parlement*, and the townspeople, Bedford was asked to resign the regency to the Duke of Burgundy, to whom he should also grant the investiture of Champagne. The Parisians earnestly asked the Duke of Burgundy to accept their governance, as they 'loved him dearly', and they pointed out that Bedford had much to do, 'both in Normandy and elsewhere', and that these duties prevented him from dealing with them fairly. Philippe agreed to accept the regency 'with great reluctance', and he and Bedford then worked out a new campaign to be launched in the spring of 1430.[15]

But Bedford would not give up the government of Normandy,

remembering his brother's last instructions, and he remained Regent of France in general, with the Duke of Burgundy being solely responsible for the administration of Paris. This new arrangement, while mortifying to him personally, at least set him at liberty to attend to the greater affairs of Normandy, and he knew that Burgundy's regency of Paris would not be permanent. As indeed proved the case.

But, in English eyes, young Henry of England was still the King of France. A high-ranking delegation from both the councils in Paris and Rouen travelled to London in October, with the express intention of asking Henry's advisers to permit the young king to travel to France, and it seemed that the English government was now ready to act. Letters were read out at the Pillared House in Paris on 31 October, announcing that Henry's coronation in England was about to take place, and that he would set out for France immediately afterwards.

Henry's English coronation was performed at Westminster on 6 November 1429, but no sign came of the promised departure to the Continent. The young king was anointed with the holy oil of St Thomas à Becket 'with which [English] kings were accustomed to be consecrated', (or at least from the crowning of Edward II in 1307; Becket died in 1170). Significantly this rite had arisen from a desire to put the English coronation on a par with that of the 'Most Christian Kings of France'. Before this time, the French alone had possessed sacred oil, that of Clovis, and 'did not have to buy their oil at the apothecary's'.[16] The Westminster coronation was designed to show Henry VI as the first king of two realms, and the boy's imminent arrival in France was, in fact, the reason for fixing the date of his English crowning (which many of his advisers thought to be held too soon, as Henry was not quite 8 years old).[17] The Westminster service was generally regarded as the first stage of a double ceremony, even though the English king's uncle had already been crowned at Rheims, thus circumventing his claim.[18]

On 20 December a further letter was drafted by the Privy Council for dispatch to Paris and other towns, and Henry repeated his promise to travel to his other kingdom, bringing with him an army that, it was hoped, would 'push the war far away'. (Or, at least, far enough away from the walls of his capital to bring ease of mind to his subjects in that city.)

A fortnight after creating the Duke of Burgundy as the new governor of Paris, the Duke of Bedford and his forces rode out of the city on a Saturday evening. His troops went by way of St Denis, 'doing plenty of damage', as they passed through the outer suburbs, no doubt in retaliation for the sudden demotion of their leader, an insult his men felt keenly.[19] They established themselves at Rouen which, in a sense, was always the preferred centre of the English administration, and from where Bedford directed sieges in different areas with decided success. Many towns that the French had won back from the English were regained during this period, and generally with little loss of English life. Any Normans who had transferred their allegiance to Charles VII during the French king's temporary triumph were summarily put to death.

True to form, Philippe stayed for only three more weeks in his new 'capital', appointing his own captains in and around the city. (Waurin states that Philippe appointed 'suitable' captains to Vincennes and other places, but gives no names.) He then returned to his area of true interest: Flanders, after having made a truce with the Armagnacs until Christmas, although the terms of this cease-fire was for the city of Paris and its suburbs only. All the villages around the capital were forced to pay protection money to the Armagnacs. Not that the truce did much good for the Parisians, for they dared not set foot outside the suburbs for fear they would be killed or held to ransom, usually for a sum that was 'higher than all he [the victim] possessed'.[20] Nor did the citizens dare to take any revenge.

All the produce now brought into Paris was imported at even greater expense, for the carriers had to pay those Armagnacs (who were taking advantage of the English absence from the area) a fee of two or three times the true value of the goods. A hundred small faggots cost twenty-four shillings a measure, two eggs cost fourpence, a small, newly made cheese four *blancs*, and a bushel of peas from fourteen *blancs*, although the currency was very strong at this time. But, still, no provisions for All Saints or the other feast days could be bought, nor any kind of fish.

It was a period of great distress for the Parisians, because they had no visible ruler, nor enough troops to withstand the enemy. The people were impoverished to the point where even the poorest householders sought to escape from the city. The ones that managed this often joined up with others to 'commit all the crimes that Christians can',[21] roaming the country, stealing and burning, so that an expedition had to be mounted to apprehend them. On the first occasion, ninety-seven were taken.

Yet if the Parisians regretted the dismissal of Bedford as their governor, they did not show it. And, although rejected by the Parisians, the duke could not be said to have lost the regency of France, for northern France was still thought by the occupiers to be an English dominion. But to the Parisians, as arrogant then as now, France meant their city and its neighbourhood, and by making the Duke of Burgundy their governor they perhaps believed that France had symbolically passed into his control. Why the Duke of Bedford accepted this new proposal is unclear, for many saw that he was very reluctant to give up his authority. As was his wife, who was greatly treasured by the Parisians. But in the face of such opposition to their rule, 'they had to do it'.[22]

Jeanne d'Arc had failed. It was her first failure, but it would leave a lasting mark on her prestige. For almost two months she was kept by the king's side at his makeshift court while he continued to pursue his negotiations with the Duke of Burgundy, none of which were going as well as he had hoped. The main stumbling block to his ambitions was the attitude of the townspeople of Compiègne, who had declared for him, and who now resolutely refused to be handed over to Philippe, when the king tried to buy the duke's allegiance with a gift of the town. Negotiations therefore reached an impasse. Philippe wanted Compiègne, and because he could not have it, he once again strengthened his ties with the Duke of Bedford.

Alençon then began to assemble troops to make war on the English in Normandy, and he asked King Charles for permission to take the Maid with him. But this was opposed by those closest to the king, and so he refused permission. The French king's confidence in her was greatly shaken by the failure to take Paris. When she was eventually allowed into the field again, it was to carry out an assault upon the fortress of Saint-Pierre-le-Moultier, which was no more than a village, and very weakly defended. It fell to her without any noticeable resistance. To her horror, the troops began to plunder the little town, even taking the church treasures as well as the goods of the inhabitants that had been stored there for safety. It took all the Maid's persuasion to stop her men from ransacking the church.[23]

By tradition, Saint-Pierre was stormed on 2 November 1429. Seven days later, the Maid and the Constable of France, Charles d'Albret, were busily preparing for the siege of La Charité. Both wrote to the inhabitants of Riom, asking for help with the next stage of the campaign. Despite its weakness, Saint-Pierre had only been taken with a great expense of 'powder, arrows and other supplies of war' and new materials were required. Supplies came from as far afield as the town of Clermont and from Orléans, which stood to gain commercially if navigation on the upper Loire was freed for the use of the French. They sent not only supplies but also men, along with a refurbished city banner.

But Jeanne failed for a second time at La Charité. The French bombarded the town and they also delivered at least one assault, but after sitting in front of the walls for over a month, they were compelled to withdraw. When they did so, they left behind most of their artillery, perhaps because of the wintry weather that had also hampered their siege operations. Opinion laid the blame for the failure directly at the king's door. He was said to have held back money to provide victuals for the Maid's troops, and nor did he attempt to maintain her company, as a result of which she had been forced to raise her siege. Astonishingly, considering the hold that she still held over the imagination of the French soldiery, most of the Maid's troops at La Charité were common mercenaries.[24]

Winter put an end to all further operations, for the weather was bitterly cold. Jeanne d'Arc left La Charité just before Christmas, and she celebrated the Nativity at Jargeau, farther down river, having got there comparatively swiftly by boat.

The troops from Picardy left Paris just before Christmas, and the citizens heaved a universal sigh of relief. For the six thousand or so Picards were 'as thieving a set of men who ever came into Paris since the wretched war began'.[25] As soon as they were outside the gates, they beat up or robbed every man they met on their way northwards.

Yet their departure left the Parisians highly exposed, for before Christmas, long before the truce was over, the Armagnac troops were back in some force, committing atrocities against the people around Paris. 'More than ever Roman tyrants, forest brigands, or murderers forced any Christians anywhere to suffer.'[26] Not content with cruelty, they also seized everything their victims possessed. No one had the power to withstand them, and little effort was made by the authorities to subdue them. Nothing went into the city without the transporters paying two or three 'imposts' on the way. The result was that any goods brought into the city were sold at such a cost that no poor people could afford to buy anything.

Before leaving, Bedford had dismissed any further claims upon his own forces, telling the Parisians 'to put up as good a defence as they could'.[27] The citizens thought he had abandoned them simply because he had been excluded from power.

The year 1429 saw the Lancastrians suffer their first serious reverses since the start of the occupation. It was not simply that they had failed to capture Orléans or that the finest English commander, the Earl of Salisbury, had been killed in action. The French – at least temporarily – were on the offensive, showing a ferocity and sureness of purpose that had hitherto been lacking. With dramatic suddenness, the whole situation had been transformed. It has to be said that, for all her failures, this miracle was due, first and foremost, to Jeanne d'Arc. For it was she who had pointed the eyes of Frenchman to their 'true' king.

NOTES

1   Quicherat, *Journal du siège*.
2   Ibid.
3   8 September.
4   Quicherat, op. cit.
5   Bourgeois de Paris.
6   Lucie-Smith, *Joan of Arc* (quoting Ayroles).
7   Bourgeois de Paris.
8   Quicherat, op. cit.
9   Bourgeois de Paris.
10 Lucie-Smith, op. cit. (quoting Ayroles).

11 *Procès de Condamnation* (of Joan of Arc).
12 Bourgeois de Paris.
13 *Archives Nationales.*
14 Monstrelet, *Chronique.*
15 In writing about this change of rulers, the Bourgeois gives a false impression. Philippe only took over the running of Paris and its environs. There was never any question of Bedford ceasing to be the 'Regent of France', because he was always the chief representative of the dual monarchy, acting in his nephew's name. The English government would never have tolerated a Burgundian taking over this particular role.
16 Bertram Wolffe, *Henry VI* (quoting P E Schramm).
17 *Proceedings of the English Privy Council.*
18 When Bedford realised that his forces were unable to prevent the coronation of Charles VII, he had written to the English government to press for the arrival of Henry VI in his French kingdom. Rymer, *Feodora.*
19 Two days after Philippe was installed as the Ruler of Paris, Bedford sent John Salvain, the *bailli* of Rouen, to take possession of the royal books, and to discharge Charles VI's librarian. Stratford Ms (British Library).
20 Bourgeois de Paris.
21 Ibid.
22 Ibid.
23 Ayroles, quoted by Quicherat.
24 Quicherat, op. cit., quoting Percéval de Cagny.
25 Bourgeois de Paris.
26 Ibid.
27 Ibid.

CHAPTER XI

1430: The Downfall of 'The Maid'

On 2 January twelve of the ninety-seven highway robbers who had been captured at the end of 1429 were hanged on the gallows in the Place de Grève. On the 10th another eleven were taken to the market place at Les Halles where ten of them were beheaded. The eleventh, a handsome young man of 24, was stripped of his shirt and about to be blindfolded when a young girl born in that district boldly stepped forward and asked for his release. By the sheer force of her eloquence, she managed to persuade the officials to give him his life. He was taken back to the Châtelet, and some time later they were married.[1]

Most of the embassy that had left Paris for London, in October 1429, remained there until February 1430, perhaps waiting to be sure that the king really did set off for the Channel crossing. By then, the official mission had been joined by two other well-known French public figures, Rapiout, the advocate of the king at the *parlement*, and Laurent Calot, the royal secretary. They were gratified to see that preparations were at last being made for the king's departure from London, although the council had no intention of letting him leave until April. Young Henry finally began his slow progress to the coast on 24 February, and the ambassadors left on the same day. Two friars were paid on the 26th for bringing letters from Paris, and they were then able to return with the heartening news of Henry's imminent arrival in France.

An Armagnac raid on 21 March did great harm to the citizens of Paris, for the marauders stole whole herds of cattle, so that there was an even greater shortage of meat than usual. The Parisian authorities reported this raid to the Lord of Saveuses, a Burgundian commander, who had been the Captain of Amiens for many years, but who was temporarily in the capital. He armed a band of volunteers and went after the thieving Armagnacs (his party joined by three prominent businessmen). But all of the pursuers were captured by the bandits, for as soon as they got into the country they split up instead of keeping together in a solid force and, as a consequence, they were all taken in less than an hour. The Armagnacs reaped huge ransoms by capturing their pursuers in this ineffectual hunt, and they then went on to make even greater forays against the country people of the Île de France.[2]

That April was very cold, and the price of foodstuffs was artificially high, with little to eat but apples. A small bundle of logs sold for the price of two, and faggots and charcoal were as dear, if not dearer. For the lack of olive oil, the citizens were reduced to using butter, even though it was the period of fasting before Easter.

There was increasing unrest throughout the city, and in March a new plot against the English garrison came to light, though the plotters, it would seem, had very mixed motives. Jean de Montfort (who was executed for his part in this plot) had been a royal notary and secretary. He had cleverly survived the transition from the Armagnac, through the Burgundian, to the English period, but had been indicted on charges of corruption when acting as an agent for the sale of offices. He had been fined heavily for these offences, but worse was to follow. A thorough-going rogue, his practice of forging credit notes and presenting them to gullible widows and the executors of wills was also exposed. Suspended from office, he had been handed over to the Bishop of Paris, to act as his clerk, and to do penance for his crimes. Although he was still excommunicated, the bishop had released him from diocesan service, and de Montfort had then gone on to enter into the conspiracy of March 1430, in which the plotters hoped to rid the city of the English entirely, returning it to the Armagnacs. Had their plan been realised, de Montfort would have prospered under the incoming regime.

All the ringleaders of this plot had similar material motives, although each had a more compelling reason than political belief to make them take the risk of execution for their actions; all of the plotters were in financial difficulties of some kind or other. For example, Jean de la Chapelle had lost a long-running lawsuit, and Jacques Perdriel had been conducting an unsuccessful case on behalf of his wife against an Englishman, John Charlton and the Receiver of Normandy, Pierre Surreau, and this had drained him financially. All of these men in some way blamed the English authorities for their monetary predicaments, and it would appear that their main motivation arose from a long-nourished dissatisfaction with the existing state of affairs in the capital.[3]

During the early spring all military operations languished. Philippe, acting as the 'Regent of France', had arranged a further truce with Charles VII. But seeing that everything they did went well for them, the Armagnacs became much bolder and ignored this agreement. On 23 March they took ladders and went about midnight to St Denis, where they scaled the walls. They made their way into the town and killed the watchkeepers 'without mercy', and then went through the streets slaughtering everyone they saw. They plundered the town, killing many of the Picards who garrisoned it, and they took almost all their horses. When they had secured all they could manage, they rode out of town with an immense amount of loot.

Their successes inspired their admirers in Paris, long inactive, to conspire once more to admit the Armagnacs into the city, 'at no matter what cost'.[4] Even some of Paris's principal men – including members of the *parlement* and the guardians of the Châtelet – were among this number, backed up by the merchants who were suffering as a result of this new menace. It was arranged that those who were in favour of the Armagnacs retaking the city were to be marked with certain symbols, so that when the French troops entered, whoever was so marked might not be killed. A Carmelite monk, Brother Pierre d'Allée, carried letters between the two sides.

The inevitable massacre that would have resulted with the return of the Armagnacs was avoided, however, when the Carmelite was captured and confessed all under torture, accusing or implicating many others. Before Passion Week, in the days leading up to Palm Sunday, more than one hundred and fifty people were arrested. Six were beheaded on the eve of Palm Sunday, some were drowned in the Seine, and others died under torture. A fortunate few managed to buy their release, and others fled. When the Armagnac leaders realised that the venture had failed they became desperate, and their men afterwards never spared any woman or child whom they captured. And, despite this failure, they were bold enough to ride up to the gates of Paris, even though the Duke of Burgundy was daily expected to return with a substantial army.[5]

The English, too, seemed to be turning bandit. Three hundred renegade English soldiers had set off intending to capture the castle of La Chasse, and they were further prompted by greed to go by way of Chelles-Saint-Baudour, where they sacked the town and then the abbey. They arrived at La Chasse loaded down with the property of the church. But their sacking of the abbey did them no service, for the Armagnacs had meanwhile got up a force from the nearby garrisons, and they managed to pin the English deserters between themselves and the castle. Because there was so much shot being fired at them from the castle, the English did not hear them approach, and – heavily attacked from the rear – they were soon all either prisoners or dead.

The Armagnacs did very handsomely out of this skirmish, for they captured all the English horses, plus the plunder from Chelles-Saint-Baudour (which they naturally kept for themselves). There were also sizeable ransoms to be raised for the prisoners, and spoils from the dead. On the 25th they went on to take the abbey of St Maur-des-Fosses, and it now struck the Parisians that their old enemies had the upper hand at every turn. Since the Earl of Salisbury's death before Orléans, it seemed the English had been compelled to withdraw from every encounter with heavy losses 'and great disgraces'.[6]

Only the weather proved a blessing, spring was so far advanced that year there were white roses in flower on Palm Sunday. Yet the authorities were not only clearly worried by the Armagnac triumphs, small though they were, they were also concerned at the growing unrest in the capital. On 26 April they had great bonfires lit – as on St John's Day in summer – in order to calm the people, to whom these mounting successes did not appear to be so insignificant. It was given out that the bonfires had been lit for the young King Henry VI, who had landed at Boulogne with a large armed force of mercenaries to fight his French uncle's increasingly insolent army.[7]

Most Parisians regarded this as nonsense, and above all an expensive folly, but it was not exactly a bureaucratic fiction. For the young king had, indeed, arrived at Calais, having crossed the Channel on 23 April, St George's Day, a coincidence that was seen as an augury of better times to come. But Henry did not go on to Paris directly, because of the dangers of the journey at that particular period.[8] There was talk of taking him directly to Rheims to be crowned, but this idea was abandoned when it became clear that Louviers as well as Rheims would have to be retaken, and the country secured.

Having received the good news, the Parisians were then left in a state of abeyance; they did not suffer from a feeling of being abandoned, so much as from having their problems set aside.

Equally, there was no news of the Duke of Burgundy, who seemed to have reneged on his promise to defend Paris. It was constantly announced that he was on his way, but most Parisians now believed the duke to be 'like father, like son' (*Patrem sequitus sua proles*). It was known that he had sent a large force of Picards to begin the siege of Compiègne in April, but they had done nothing since, and were unlikely to do much in the immediate future. It was said that three hundred Englishmen accomplished more in matters of war than a thousand Picards, who – besides being poor soldiers – were also 'shocking thieves', stealing even from those who were supposed to be their allies.[9]

The citizens increasingly despaired of learning the true situation for themselves, although it was generally thought that the city authorities were only pretending that aid was on its way. Meanwhile, there was no sign of any present help from the nobility, and no question of any further treaties being agreed upon, to safeguard the rights of the Parisians. As a result, many prominent householders secretly left the capital, which further weakened the economy.[10]

Then, in late April, the Duke of Burgundy suddenly took up arms once more. This was very possibly influenced by the knowledge that a new English army had landed at Calais, led by Cardinal Beaufort, and with – it was rumoured – King Henry included in his train. Philippe then assembled his troops at Montdidier, thirty miles north-west of Compiègne, and he advanced to the recapture of that town. Hearing of this, the Maid Jeanne slipped away from the court, then at Sully, with a handful of followers. She made her way by stages to Compiègne, which she entered on 13 May, three weeks after the young King Henry VI had landed at Calais.

To the Parisians it seemed the worst sort of omen that on that same day there was a totally unlooked-for frost, after such clement weather. All the vines were frozen, and yet the grapes were the biggest and most promising that anyone could remember seeing for thirty years. It was, as the Bourgeois said, a question of 'God told you so'.

Jeanne d'Arc's departure from Sully may have been prompted by news of a conspiracy that was then brewing in Paris, which had been discovered by the Anglo–Burgundians during the first week of April. The plot itself was a simple act of deception: Scottish troops were to serve as decoys, dressed as drovers, taking their cattle through one of the gates of the city. When this gate was opened for them, other troops – who would be lying in ambush nearby – would rush the defences, to be assisted by sympathisers within the city. When the conspiracy was revealed, more than one hundred and fifty people were arrested.[11]

The Duke of Burgundy was nominally in charge of the siege operation against Compiègne, his army consisting of about six thousand men, divided into three groups. Included in this army was an English detachment under Sir John Montgomery. The aim of these divisions was to prevent any communication between the town and the right bank of the Oise river. During the next ten days the Maid took part in some impetuous and abortive sorties on the south bank.

On 23 April, St George's Day, celebration fires were again lit all over Paris, for it was formally announced that King Henry had finally and *definitely* crossed the Channel. The poorer people were angry at this waste of valuable firewood, as nobody believed that this was true, for there had been too many similar rumours. Again, it was thought that the authorities were simply trying to calm the citizens.

In May a male prisoner at the Porte St Anthoine, who had paid his ransom and was therefore free to go about the garrison as he wished, was responsible for a bloodbath. Finding a jailer asleep on a bench after the dinner hour – 'as people do in summer' – he took his keys from him as the man slept. He opened the cells, and unshackled three other prisoners. They went to where the jailer was still sleeping, with others, and the released men struck at them. They had killed three soldiers before the rest of the garrison had any idea of what was happening. The alarm raised, the soldiers moved to the aid of their comrades, and Lord de L'Isle Adam, who was visiting at the time, ran to them shouting orders. Hitting the nearest escapee with an axe, he felled him to the ground, killing him instantly. The rest could not break out from the confines of the fortress, and were all retaken. They swore they had not meant to kill any others, and were simply seeking to escape, but the authorities were convinced they had meant to hand the Porte over to the Armagnacs, as a prelude to the invasion of Paris. Lord de L'Isle Adam had them butchered and thrown into the Seine.[12]

Such an event could only further dismay the Parisians, but they had other news to hearten them, and news in which they could at last believe, for it came from a source much closer to them, and could be easily verified. It was said that Jeanne d'Arc had been captured. Following her decision to suddenly attack the nearest of the Burgundian posts to the north of Compiègne, she had met with disaster. Backed up by only five hundred troops, she had crossed the long causeway from the town, and by rushing headlong into the camp, where the soldiers were mostly disarmed, surprised and scattered them. But John of Luxembourg, who was reconnoitering on a hillock to the rear, had observed her bold move, and he immediately sent for reinforcements. His own harness and his troops soon came up to challenge her, yet despite this Jeanne made two further assaults at the head of her men, managing to push the enemy as far back as halfway to Margny. A hot fight then took place, in which the Maid particularly distinguished herself.[13]

But not only Luxembourg's men had been aroused, for the Duke of Burgundy's men and Montgomery's small company were also alerted. It was, in fact, the latter who cut off Jeanne's line of retreat, by attacking her party in the rear. She found herself being pushed off the causeway, whilst most of her men fled back to the safety of the city. Although she behaved with her usual superb courage, and made tremendous efforts to cover the withdrawal, the English soldiers drove her into the arms of the Burgundians. Trapped in boggy ground between the causeway and the river, a Picard archer seized her by the floating panels of her gorgeous gold and scarlet surcoat, dragging her ignominiously from her 'beautiful and fiery' dapple-grey horse. She had then been taken prisoner by Guillaume de Wandonne, a man-at-arms serving under John of Luxembourg, and it was a spirited if humiliating end to a short but dazzling, and utterly unique, military career. The Maid herself had prayed that if she were to die, she would be killed in an engagement, and it would have been better for all had this prayer been granted her, for nobody – English, French or Burgundian – would emerge with credit from the sorry aftermath of her capture.[14]

The news of 'the witch's' capture on 23 May galvanised the citizens of Paris. They were especially pleased that she had been made prisoner by the followers of John of Luxembourg, a Burgundian. A letter was sent to Philippe the Good, dated 26 May 1430, which demanded that Jeanne be sent to the city for trial, on the grounds that she was 'vehemently suspected of several crimes smacking of heresy'. The letter was written in the name of the Vicar General of the Inquisitor, who would be directly responsible for setting up such a trial, but it was clearly inspired by influential members of the university. For it openly promised that the trial would be conducted 'according to the good counsel, favour and help of the good doctors and masters of the University of Paris, and other notable councillors of this place'.[15]

Throughout her brief career, in fact, the leading members of the university had been interested in the phenomenon of the Maid, and they had long been hostile to her. A Venetian agent reported in November 1429 that leading members of the university had sent to the pope in Rome, accusing her of the same charge of heresy, on the grounds that she had sinned against the Faith 'in pretending to know and say the things that are to come'.[16] The masters of the university had kept up a continuous pressure against her since then.

Now that the Maid was a prisoner of the Burgundians, the university faculty wrote directly in their own name to the Duke Philippe and also to John of Luxembourg. In both letters the faculty expressed the fear that the prisoner might be freed by 'subtle means' and they were troubled by the talk of a ransom (to which possibility John of Luxembourg had, at first, seemed agreeable).[17] The two leaders were asked to hand Jeanne over for trial to the Bishop of Beauvais, who had a personal interest in the business, for the Maid had been largely responsible for his being turned out of his bishopric.

Both Bedford and Philippe were aware of the importance of the University of Paris, not only in the intellectual life of the nation but also throughout Europe, and both leaders were prepared to submit to its dictates. Amidst the disorders of the age it stood out for the principles of the best governmental guidance, but more importantly for intellectual rigour. Proud of its long-fought-for status, the university was now resistant to any form of outside interference. Various popes and any number of French kings had found it resistant to their control, and Philippe – as the temporary ruler of Paris – also came up against its authority, although the institution had long been sympathetic to Burgundian ambitions, seeing them as the party of reform. The Burgundian alliance with the Lancastrians had gradually forced the university to a solemn acceptance of the English demands, and they had asked Henry V to confirm their privileges after the Treaty of Troyes.[18]

The university was an exclusively masculine institution as those who governed it were men in Holy Orders, and as such they were deeply suspicious of the female sex. As academics they were equally suspicious of the supernatural, because it was beyond the scope of reason, and so they were doubly distrustful of the many visionaries who were a feature of the age, the most important of whom were women. And because the chief among these troublesome females was the Maid of Orléans, the University of Paris, as a body, was hostile towards her from her first appearance there.

That some members of the board of assessors in Poitiers, who had recommended the Maid to Charles VII, were an exiled minority of dauphinist sympathisers from among their number, only served to increase the university's detestation of her. The attack upon Paris, even though it had proved unsuccessful, was also a cause to execrate her. It had given the academics a considerable fright, even though her humiliating failure had very satisfactorily belied her prophecies, which up to that time had been dismayingly fulfilled.

The ejected Bishop of Beauvais, Pierre Cauchon, who was not of noble birth, had once been closely linked to the University of Paris, firstly as a brilliant student and then as rector. Now, either under his own authority or else as the spokesman of the dons, he travelled to the Burgundian camp outside Compiègne with a formal demand that the Maid, as a considered heretic, should be given over to him for trial. (The bishop was, in fact, acting under the instructions of Bedford and his council, who had ordered him to claim her as a sorceress taken within his diocese, and they furnished him with the six thousand *livres* for her ransom from the Burgundians.)

Cauchon's bishopric, which also made him an ecclesiastical peer of France, was generally recognised as being his reward for his long devotion to the Burgundian cause, although from 1422, he had begun to veer towards the English sphere of influence. In 1423 he had been named a councillor for the infant Henry VI, and two years later he had done an important service to Bedford when the duke was having difficulties with the Paris *parlement*. Now, in 1430, Cauchon was exactly placed to act as the intermediary between the Burgundians and the English in the matter of the transfer of Jeanne d'Arc, and the University of Paris could also feel confident that he would have their interests in mind.

On 14 July 1430 Cauchon appeared with a large retinue in the camp outside Compiègne. Backed by letters from John of Luxembourg and the Duke Philippe, he made a formal demand for the person of Jeanne d'Arc to be given over to him for trial, since she had been taken 'in his diocese and within his spiritual jurisdiction'. If the Maid – 'the witch' as the English continued to regard her – was to be tried on spiritual grounds, then Cauchon was undoubtedly the proper churchman to try her. But it soon became clear that Jeanne's transfer to his authority would only be carried out after a financial deal had been struck with her captors. It was quickly realised that the French would not ransom her, and although the English refused to recognise her as a 'prize of war', they might be prepared to pay for having her delivered into their hands.[19]

The English were disposed to come to a financial understanding with their allies, and Cauchon quickly offered terms. The 'king' – by whom he meant Bedford acting as regent for Henry VI – was prepared to give those who had captured her 6,000 *livres*, together with a pension of 200 to 300 *livres* to Guillaume de Wandonne. If this sum was still considered insufficient, the 'king' was prepared to guarantee the sum of 10,000 francs 'according to the right, usage and custom of France'. Bedford, by this time, had been reinstated as the Regent of France, and so he was now dealing with the Duke of Burgundy as a vassal of the English monarchy.[20]

Negotiations took longer than either Cauchon or the regent expected. John of Luxembourg, a bluff warrior who had lost an eye in battle, was already a pensioner of the King of England, yet he still drove an extremely hard bargain. This was largely a question of brute commerce, but there was an ambiguous quality to his negotiations, for he seems to have felt a genuine guilt at the prospect of selling this astonishing nonpareil to her outright enemies.

A more substantial obstacle to her transfer lay in the deficient state of the regent's exchequer, which at this time was greatly reduced. Luxembourg could not be paid off with promises, and he demanded hard cash from the English, to be paid up front. The English wanted to take possession of this extraordinary woman – this virgin witch, this Amazon, who, almost single-handedly, had set them back from two decades of hard fighting for their possessions in France.

The estates of Normandy were once again asked to contribute, this time a sum of 120,000 *livres tournois*, ten thousand of which was to be set aside for 'the purchase of Jeanne the Maid, who is said to be a sorcerer, a warlike person, leading the armies of the dauphin'. The money was raised very quickly, but Jeanne's price had increased by then. To meet this new demand, it was paid very largely in gold specie, which was advanced from the private purse of the King of England. Since the English dominions in France were always expected to pay their own way, the fact that this money came from England reveals how anxious the English were to have the Maid under their control.

However, with the Maid in captivity her influence over the English soldiery began to evaporate. It was clear by now that she was not infallible and, with her capture, she was dismissed by the troops as being no more than an uncommon sort of witch; a belief their leaders encouraged, both among the troops and the civilian population. For the English were far less interested in Jeanne as heretic than as a servant of Satan. This was a view they brought to bear on those who tried her, and which was confirmed the next year, when the church condemned her to be burned. It was a period of many witch-trials, and the regent may have had enough in common with his late brother, Henry V, to share the latter's extreme fear of sorcery.[21]

*

The Parisians were also heartened by the news that the English military seemed to be once again in form and had taken twelve fortresses by 2 July. On Monday the 17th a great bell at Notre Dame was cast, which was named Jacqueline, and weighed 15 tonnes. On that same day, King Henry VI and his party arrived at Rouen, the centre of the Anglo–Burgundian administration.[22] It was decided to make the city their base, and it soon became apparent that the council, having got that far into France, was little inclined to proceed any farther.

For a few weeks the city seemed completely abandoned by the military, with both 'regents' out of the capital. L'Isle Adam, too, had dispersed most of his armed retinue by this time, as it was thought that any danger of a new assault upon Paris was over. The nearest military bases were at the bridge of Charenton, to the east, and at St Cloud, to the west, but neither was at any time well armed. At Charenton, the garrison was made up of one man-at-arms and one archer. At St Cloud, there is no evidence of an armed force at this period.

But civilian life went on. On 30 July an election by the secret counting of votes was held, which was very probably the first use of a ballot in the history of Paris.[23] It is not clear why it was adopted, but the royal government was confident of reliable pro-Burgundian supporters being selected, and so it was considered to be unwise to risk a large public demonstration. Paradoxically, the secret ballot that is now seen as a guarantee of free choice was at that time introduced as a shift to control dangerous assemblies.

On 8 August the chancellor left Paris to be with the young king in Rouen, and although he returned to the capital, the king's administration in Normandy became increasingly influential over a period of weeks. This was shown by the actions of the *parlement* in its efforts to solve the perennial problem of the members' wages, which were paid from London, and which were by this time some two years behind. With the king now resident in France, it was hoped that their needs would at last be met, but it would take another two months of fruitless negotiation before the frustrated judges decided to send their own representatives to Normandy, in search of final payment. They were met with further promises that the money was on its way from England, and a series of ambassadors from Paris spent many difficult weeks trying to win the attention of King Henry's council, and more importantly the particular consideration of Cardinal Beaufort.[24]

After Jeanne d'Arc was captured, one thousand Englishmen entered Paris and then went on to besiege the Armagnacs in the abbey of St Maur-des-Fosses. The French made no resistance, but surrendered the abbey and were allowed to depart in the surety of a safe passage. There were only one hundred of them; they were not allowed to carry off their spoils, and

134

they were further disarmed, being left in possession of only one stick for their defence. The English troops then ransacked the abbey and the town with great thoroughness, 'whether their commanders liked it or not'. The place was 'stripped so clean, they did not leave a spoon standing in a saucepan!'.[25]

The Lord de Ros[26] (of Hamlake), an English baron, arrived in Paris on 16 August, 'with more ceremony than any knight ever did, who was not a king, or a duke, or an earl', with four musicians going ahead of him. Whilst the baron was in residence, a party of Armagnacs raided the Porte St Anthoine, seizing sheep, oxen and cows. Lord de Ros, 'hearing of it, took his men and rode hard after them, closely followed by another English knight'. They followed the Armagnacs as far as the Marne, to a ford beyond St Maur. But both Englishmen, missing the shallow crossing, were drowned in the deeper waters.[27]

De Ros was a harbinger, since other Englishmen would follow him, returning to Paris three or four hundred at a time. But there was now a disturbing change in their circumstances, because whenever they came into conflict with the Armagnacs, they were always – and inexplicably – trounced by inferior forces. For a time the enemy was seemingly invincible, which many believed was due to the influence of Jeanne d'Arc. But the more superstitious claimed that it was because the Earl of Salisbury had irreligiously sacked the church of Notre Dame at Cléry, and that other churches and religious places had been robbed of their most holy relics. Those who foretold the future prophesied that if God did not take pity upon Paris, she was in danger of being entirely destroyed. 'On all sides her goods were spoilt, men killed, homes set alight, and there was no one, native or stranger, to cry "Dimitte". . .'

On 28 August, St Augustine's Day, about sixty men took their carts from Paris to fetch in the corn from the surrounding fields, a crop that by long tradition belonged to the capital's citizens, and which had just been harvested near Le Bourget. Armagnacs, apprised of this by their spies – of whom they had any number in the city – came in strength to attack the loaded wagons. The men from Paris defended themselves as well as they could, but the Armagnacs overrode them without any difficulty, killing most of them and setting fire to the corn stacked in the carts. Nothing was recovered from this attack but the ironwork, for all the carts were blazing, and the wounded were thrown into the flames. Besides the dead, the Armagnacs took a score of prisoners and all the horses. They ransomed the most prosperous of their captives and killed those who were without the means to pay.

On this day, Lord Stafford, whom the English named 'Constable of France', arrived in Paris with a strong force of English troops.[28] He had passed only a league from the fighting, and yet he knew nothing about it, otherwise matters might have been very different. But, as it stood, the householders who had a commercial interest in the harvest were almost reduced to poverty by the ransoms they were forced to pay for the return of whatever was left from this disastrous foray by the Armagnacs. As a result of these depredations, it became imperative to import corn from England, but this swiftly took on more the appearance of a relief operation than a commercial venture.

On 28 August two sermons were preached in Paris, in a street outside the cathedral. Strangely, the preachers were both women, an unusual event. The elder, Pieronne, a Breton, boldly maintained that Jeanne d'Arc was a good and pious maiden, and that what she had done was by God's will.[29] Calling herself a devoted Christian, Pieronne affirmed that she herself had often spoken to God, and that He appeared to her in human form, so that He could speak with her as one friend to another. The last time He had appeared to her, He had worn a long white robe with a red tunic beneath it.

Not even the Maid had dared to claim that she spoke directly with the Almighty, and the woman was naturally taken up on a charge of blasphemy. After the briefest of trials, she was condemned to the fire, as the least prophetic could have foretold would be her fate. Before her death she confessed that she was a follower of Brother Richard, and was therefore from the enemy camp. Pieronne died on the Sunday following her remarkable sermon, maintaining to the end her belief in the goodness of the Maid's character and the righteousness of her cause. Her younger companion, who had not made the same extravagant claims, was set free.

On the day after Pieronne had been reduced to ashes, twenty-three barges filled with victuals and other merchandise were on their way to the relief of Paris. But the bargees of thirteen boats and the men-at-arms, who were there to protect them, began a fierce quarrel while the boats were in an unsafe part of the Seine. The Armagnacs took advantage of this lapse to spring a fierce attack upon them, and the quarrelling among the defenders prevented them from putting up any great fight. At least one hundred and twenty men were taken from the thirteen barges, not counting the dead. The other ten barges, in which there had been no quarrel, managed to get safely by the others and came to port. 'This shows,' the Bourgeois wrote, 'how unsafe it is for men standing in danger to quarrel with each other.'

For a time, the tide of war began to turn back in England's favour. Within weeks of Jeanne d'Arc's imprisonment, the strongly fortified castle of Gaillard had been taken, and this had been followed in the next few months by the recapture of many important towns in the region of Paris. It was only because the situation had improved so rapidly for the English that the regent considered the time had come to convey the boy-king to his capital, to show him to his more ardent French subjects.

As it was, it had taken over two years for the king to visit his French possessions, and Bedford had long urged the English council to have Henry crowned in France. The regent was, in fact deeply embittered by his failure to move the English parliament in the matter because, when he had first proposed it, it would have been relatively easy to have taken the boy to Rheims, to be crowned as the undeniable King of France. But nobody had then foreseen the arrival of Jeanne d'Arc. It had been thought enough to have Henry crowned in Westminster, on 6 November 1429, which at least put an end to the Duke of Gloucester's protectorate, although the House of Lords then left it in Bedford's power, as the senior uncle, to retain the office if he so wished.

But not only had Bedford done away with his troublesome younger brother's powers in England, he had also set aside his own in France.[30] From the time that Henry landed at Calais on 23 April 1429, it was arranged for Bedford's regency to be suspended while the boy-king was in France, although he continued to hold many important lordships, including those of Alençon, Anjou and Maine. It was also decided that if he were asked to resign them to the king, he would be handsomely recompensed for their loss. Yet it remained obvious that, despite these ordinances, the duke was still in charge, and that he was also still in league with Philippe of Burgundy.

The Burgundians, however, were as ever proving to be bad allies. At least, they were unsuccessful in their campaigns. The siege of Compiègne dragged on, with the Earl of Huntingdon replacing Sir John Montgomery on the English side, and John of Luxembourg replacing Duke Philippe, who abandoned the operation in order to take over the province of Brabant, which had fallen to him on the death of his cousin.[31] (Cardinal Beaufort was personally responsible for keeping Luxembourg in the English camp. He had persuaded him to stay loyal to Henry VI during an embassy to Burgundy, while making arrangements for the forthcoming coronation in Paris.)

In the meantime, Philippe stayed well away from Paris, leaving the city to the mercy of the Armagnacs and their accomplices. There were robbers at Lagny, yet nobody prevented them from coming up every week to the gates of the capital, where they seized men, women and children, and drove off whole herds of cattle, for which they demanded huge ransoms, to be paid always in silver or gold. Those who could not pay were bound together in couples and thrown into the Marne, or else they were hung from trees, or tied up in damp cellars and left to starve to death. Nothing 'that was in any way useful to the human body' could reach Paris without first coming into the control of the robbers; they kept all the ways covered, both by land and water. As a result, the price of wood was beyond that of most householders. 'A hundred small faggots from Brondy or Boulogne-le-Petite used to cost 6s, not 24, good coin.'[32]

But that August had been fine, and the vintage was excellent. The verjuice was 'unusually forward, the moment it was casked it began to bubble, or rather to spout'. The wines were of good quality, and 'not too expensive either'. One could buy a quart of wine, 'fit for any decent man' for six *parises*, a negligible sum. It was exactly the same price that had been set in Rouen, or 'so they said who came from there, and who could tell good wine'.[33]

Meanwhile the negotiations for handing over the Maid of Orléans, as she had come to be called, dragged on, although her purchase price had now been agreed. On 21 November the principles of the University of Paris wrote to Henry VI, expressing their communal joy at the news that the 'witch' was now in his power, and asking that she be handed over at once to ecclesiastical justice, that is, to Bishop Cauchon and the Vice-Inquisitor. On the same day they wrote to the bishop himself, rebuking him for the long delay in the case, and asking that the woman be sent at once *to Paris* for judgement, although they must have known that this second request was unlikely to be granted.[34]

Sometime around 20 December Jeanne was moved, with a strong escort, from Le Crotoy, and she was imprisoned in Rouen by the 28th of that month, incarcerated in the castle, 'in a tower towards the fields'.[35] It was here that she was kept for the duration of her trial. Despite the fact that this was an ecclesiastical matter, she was confined in a secular prison. This fortress was, in fact, very overcrowded, as it also contained King Henry VI and his entourage. However, there is no evidence that the boy-king even so much as caught a glimpse of the woman who had so singularly humiliated his army in France, and who had paved the way for his mother's unsatisfactory brother to be crowned in his stead.

His uncle the Duke of Bedford's wife, *was* said to have visited the Maid shortly after she arrived in Rouen. Or perhaps, more accurately, her women did, in the interests of the forthcoming trial, as their purpose was to examine the prisoner, to ascertain whether she was a true maid. (The examination showed that Joan was still *virgo intacta*, but that she had torn her vagina whilst riding astride.) It was later rumoured that Bedford, overcome with curiosity, had himself concealed in the room in which she was examined, although this seems unlikely in view of the regent's extremely puritanical nature.[36]

NOTES

1   Bourgeois de Paris.
2   Ibid.
3   Ibid.
4   Ibid.
5   Quicherat, *Chronique*. Not all these freebooters were allied to the Armagnacs. Franquet d'Arras was a Burgundian sympathiser, having been a captain in

the service of Jean the Fearless. He had almost 300 men under his command. Another pillager was a Scotsman, Sir Hugh Kennedy; and another was a Piedmontese mercenary, Barolommeo Barretto (who had served under Jeanne d'Arc).

6 Ibid.
7 Bourgeois de Paris.
8 Wolffe, *Henry VI.*
9 Bourgeois de Paris.
10 By 1432 there would be approximately 20,000 abandoned houses in the city, many of which were converted to be stables or pigsties. Champion, *Splendeurs et Misères de Paris.*
11 Ibid.
12 Bourgeois de Paris. There had been an earlier conspiracy in March, and a minor riot in an ecclesiastical court in May, where all present appear to have been armed, 'in the cause of the conspiracy that was discovered'.
13 Quicherat, op. cit.
14 Ibid.
15 Ibid.
16 Morosini, *Chronique.*
17 Quicherat, op. cit.
18 Ayroles, *La Vraie Jeanne d'Arc.*
19 Lucie-Smith, *Joan of Arc.*
20 Ibid.
21 Not even persons of the highest rank were immune from prosecution. Joan of Navarre, stepmother of King Henry V, was arrested on a charge of practising witchcraft. Kingsford, *Chronicles of London.*
22 The king's court had already spent three months assembling at Calais. Wolffe, *Henry VI.*
23 This seems a very English innovation, but there is no evidence of balloting between the English takeover of Paris and this date.
24 A huge amount of money had been raised for this, Henry VI's first expedition abroad, partly by loans and parliamentary grants, wool subsidies and direct taxes. It amounted to some £120,000, the highest receipts since 1418. Steel, *The Receipt of the Exchequer.*
25 Bourgeois de Paris.
26 Thomas de Ros was the eighth baron. Born in 1406, he served several times in France under Bedford. He married a daughter of the Earl of Warwick, and he died on 18 August 1430, in the king's wars in France.
27 Bourgeois de Paris.
28 Naturally, his name does not appear in the French list of Constables. The Earl of Stafford had arrived in France in the retinue of Henry VI, providing one of the largest contingents of troops. He was on his way to Brie, where he recovered several strongholds. Monstrelet, *Chronique.*
29 Bourgeois de Paris, who makes clear that he himself was unsure about his feelings with regard to the Maid of Orléans. Many Parisians seem to have been divided in their opinions of her.
30 Wolffe, op. cit. The temporary governance of France was taken into the hands of the English Council who accompanied the king, reinforced by members of the Grand Council in Paris. Bedford, during this period, was simply the Commander-in-Chief.
31 *Proceedings of the English Privy Council.*
32 Bourgeois de Paris.
33 Ibid.

34 Quicherat, *Chronique.*
35 Ibid.
36 Ibid. Such concealment was possible, as evidenced by the notaries who recorded Joan's private conversations in her cell, without her ever being aware of their hidden presence.

CHAPTER XII
1431: A Second Coronation

In January 1431 Bedford and his duchess returned to Paris from Rouen, and in that same month, on the penultimate day, the Duke of Burgundy also arrived in Paris, 'most nobly accompanied'.[1] Yet Bedford's was the most spectacular arrival, as he arrived by water, bringing with him a convoy of fifty-seven boats and twelve barges, all laden with goods. The duke and duchess had refused to leave this argosy as it proceeded up river, and Bedford had it guarded by well over four hundred men until it reached the capital, a necessary precaution.[2]

In fact it had been something of an ordeal, for the convoy was brought through the 'worst river-going weather that ever was!'. The wind had raged without stopping for three weeks, the rain had fallen almost as continuously, the river ran very high, and the convoy was working against the current. The Armagnacs had also set strong ambushes along the banks, determined to destroy the duke, his company and the abundantly laden barges. But for some reason they feared to attack him, despite having four men to his one. Some months previously, four fully laden boats had been captured on the way from Rouen, and the merchants in charge had been forced to ransom their own goods, although they did not, of course, have the personal protection of an English prince. Yet, although it remained hazardous, the river route was still the safest of all the supply routes to Paris.

The arrival of this great convoy should have brought a slight relief to the markets of Paris, and yet – soon after the arrival of the two dukes – the price of corn rose sharply. A *setier*, which cost only 40s before they came, now cost 72s, or five francs. The loaves, too, were musty and were made smaller, so that they were very dark. 'A one *blanc* loaf hardly weighed more than twelve ounces, and a working man could easily eat three or four [of these] a day.' Wine, too, despite the fine vintage of the previous year, which had heartened all, could now not easily be bought, and the poorer people had no wine and little sustenance, except for nuts, water and bread. Very few ate beans or peas 'for these cost too much to buy, and more still to cook'.[3]

As a result, there was a second great exodus of people from the capital.

On 10 February the *Chambre des Comptes* decided to order the Receiver of Paris to collect the revenues of places that lay outside the city jurisdiction, such as St Germain-en-Laye, which for some time had been 'occupied' by others. There is no record that the measure had any success.

The Duchess of Burgundy had given birth to a son, Antoine, on the last day of the previous September, and the duke was still so much taken up with her, and his sole heir, that he had little thought for his Parisian dependents. 'They do say that in the first year of marriage one must please one's wife, it is all honeymoon,' the vexed Bourgeois complained on behalf of his fellow citizens. 'That is why he could not hang about long enough to take Compiègne.'[4]

It was a time of enormous misery for the citizens. No one could make a proper living because most trade had stopped, and the poorest people were dying from hunger, and from the extreme cold. In their anguish they blamed both dukes, no longer able to believe in the promises of either man.

The Duke of Burgundy proved, as always, the least reliable, and all the more demanding. In March, as though ignorant of their existing hardship, he ordered the citizens to provide the financing for a certain number of troops needed by the English army. This was seen as another grievous burden and one hardly to be tolerated, but it was also one that could not be avoided, and so the duke's demands were met.

The augmented force, under Bedford, attacked Gournay, which was captured, and they then attacked the tower of Montjoye, which was taken by composition on 18 March. The English went on to attack Lagny, from which they 'gained no honour', as it was attacked in Holy Week, 'an evil work'. The men holed up in Lagny defended themselves very well – on one day there were four hundred and twelve cannon balls fired into the town. Yet no one was hurt, save for a solitary cock that was killed by a stray shot. Recognising failure, the English and their Parisian 'volunteers' gave up and went home.

They arrived in Paris on the eve of Easter, the first of April, and the French wits were quick to mock them, saying they had come back to their parishes to make their Paschal confessions.[5] Bedford's failure to take Lagny, a hotbed of banditry, would later come to haunt him, for it undermined the promises of the projected coronation of his nephew. The expenditure for this colossal undertaking would also leave him with little money for any further action against the marauders, who were more than ever the plague of Paris. In effect, the cost of the coming coronation would also push the war away from the forefront of English preoccupations.

The population of the city continued to decrease because of the rising price of foodstuff. In the middle of April a count was taken of all the people who had left Paris by land or water. By the 14th – the eve of Misericordia Domini – it was computed that above twelve hundred had deserted their homes, and this figure did not even include their children.[6]

But something had to be done about those who were preying upon the capital. On the following Monday, one hundred men-at-arms left for Chevreuse. They went to the old stronghold of Damiette, where some forty robbers were taking cover. All of them were captured and returned to Paris, coupled together, for punishment. They were all young men, the oldest not more than 36 years of age. On Saturday, the 13th, they were hanged on the public gallows in the Place de Grève, although nine of them were clever enough to manage their escape. On 22 April Bedford took his troop to La Motte, where he captured another one hundred brigands, whose base it was. Six were hanged on the spot and the rest bound together, two by two, and taken back to the capital to be hanged on the 26th. On the following Monday another thirty-two robbers were hanged, and on 4 May thirty others followed them.

On 25 May a general procession was made to Notre Dame and from there to the Augustins. A sermon was preached in both places, in which was declared a great spiritual gift for those who were devout enough to attain it. Pope Martin V had granted a boon at the Feast of the Holy Sacraments to all Christians who were in a position to receive it, 'truly shriven and penitent'. On the Friday before Corpus Christi a master of theology preached a further sermon, in which he related how Pope Urban IV (1261–4) had first commanded that this solemnity should always be celebrated on the first Thursday after the Octave of Pentecost, and how he had granted these pardons. The noted theologian explained the nature of these particular indulgences, and they were first published in the Church of St Augustine on 25 June.

On the eve of Holy Sacrament, 30 May, a sermon was preached in Rouen in the presence of 'my lady Jeanne'. News of it soon reached Paris. The girl was placed upon a platform, so that everyone could see her clearly, and to the horror of all present she was still dressed in men's clothing, which she would not abandon, saying it was a protection against the brutal lechery of her captors. Through the sermon, she was informed of the great and disastrous evils that had come upon Christendom, especially for the kingdom of France, through her agency.[7] Bedford fervently believed this to be true. 'The great stroke,' he said later, 'was caused in great part, as I trow, of lack of sad belief and unlawful doubt that they [the French] had in a disciple and limb of the fiend called the *Pucelle*, that used false enchantment and sorcery.'

After her death at the stake, which followed soon after, controversy raged in Paris. Whilst many people continued to think of her as a sorceress, a few others now began to believe she had been martyred, 'and for her true Lord'.[8] Most people, of course, were of the cynical opinion that whatever good or evil she had done was burned with her that day. And fortune certainly seemed to have changed sides, when – in the week of her death – the most cruel, pitiless (and successful) of all her army commanders, La Hire, was also taken. He was captured by 'other ranks' and lodged in the castle of Dourdan.

The authorities in Paris, seeking to utterly demolish the Maid's reputation, ordered a general procession to St Martin-des-Champs in thanks for their deliverance from this vile creature. There, a friar of the order of St Dominic, Inquisitor of the Faith and Master of Theology, again preached a sermon revealing all the evils this misguided woman had done to her country. He said that she had lived an unnatural life from the age of 14, when she had first put on a man's garb. He said that her pious parents had wished for her death, and would have murdered her for the good of mankind 'if they could have done so without guilt'. Since keeping the devil's company she herself had murdered Christian people. She was 'full of blood and fire' to the last. Even at her burning she had called upon Satan's henchmen, 'who appeared to her as saints', but they had deserted her in the final moments 'invoke them how she might'.[9]

It was said that she was not alone in her conspiracy against God and her country. There had been three others to aid her, though Pieronne, the Maid's companion, was now dead, and the other woman, Catherine of La Rochelle, was with the Armagnacs. All the women, including Jeanne d'Arc, were said to have been under the direction of Brother Richard the Franciscan, to whose sermons at the Innocents, and elsewhere, deluded people had flocked, 'for he was their confessor'. The preacher said that on Christmas day, in the town of Jargeau, he himself had given the holy sacrament to the 'Lady Jeanne', which had been 'very wrong of him, and for which he was now doing daily penance'.[10]

In June the English Council at last decided to pay £1,000 sterling to the *parlement* and to the *Chambre des Comptes*, with half the money being loaned by Cardinal Beaufort. But some members of the *parlement* refused the money, holding out for more. On 26 June the councillors declined a further offer of three months' arrears, insisting they be paid a full year's fees. The new principle of looking to a government beyond Paris, and for money from England, was a significant feature of the breakdown of the dual monarchy system that had been established at the Treaty of Troyes. Throughout the 1420s all official salaries had been paid with great regularity from French finances, and whatever complaints were to be made were done so to a government based in Paris. But from the time that it had been seen as possible for English money to be redirected to Paris – if there was money available for greedy lawyers, there would of a surety be money for the military – the system had become unwieldy.

In May 1431 the Duke of Bedford had received three hundred and forty-five *louis tournois* from the English Treasurer of Wars, for 310 men sent to supplement his retinue in Paris for that month. In June he obtained a further £1,253 for his wage list, and to pay those involved in the security of the capital and its nearby garrisons.[11] A further £3,555 was collected on behalf of the chancellor, Louis of Luxembourg, which may also have been intended for the Paris region.

In this year an ordinance on the subject of the ballot was issued. An election was held on 23 July. The large public elections, 'by acclamation', had been avoided since 1429, and they were replaced by the secret ballot, or else by a close discussion between a small group, meeting behind closed doors, although two months later there would be an election held by an unspecified method.

On 4 August Bedford was marching from Rouen to Paris with a slender escort, when Marshal de Boussac and Xaintraille, who were occupying Beauvais, surprised him near Mantes. The duke escaped only by taking to the water, and he made his way by boat to the capital while almost all his troops perished.

On 4 August, also, the Duke of Burgundy returned to Paris from Flanders. His journey, too, had been watched closely by the Armagnacs, who intended to capture him as he rode by the town of Mantes. But 'like a wise man', the duke's party had re-crossed the river and then ridden night and day until reaching the safety of Paris. He came through the Porte St Jacques, and his men held their own against the stray bands of Armagnacs that they did encounter.

News of this reached the English army that was besieging Louviers. A number of captains, among them the Earls of Warwick and Arundel, who were encamped before the town, withdrew from the siege, thinking the dukes had been captured. When they heard that they had both reached Paris safely, they went on to Beauvais and laid an ambush to the town. Many men of the town came rushing out to greet the besiegers 'as fast as they could',[12] in an effort to distract them. But the Duke of Burgundy, who had joined up with the English, knew what they were up to, for he had scouts in the area, and he advised his allies to ignore this bluff. He sent in one contingent, to create a diversion between the Armagnacs and the town, while the rest of the troops made a frontal attack.

It was a fierce battle. The Armagnacs fought bravely, but gave up the contest when they became aware of other troops coming up in the rear, thinking that there were more of them than were actually at hand. Their principal captains were either killed, or taken for ransom. Among those captured was a singular man, 'William the Shepherd', who was said to have 'caused the people to idolise him'. (The French High Command, first having abandoned and now lost their miraculous 'Lady Jeanne', was trying to use this poor idiot as a replacement, and they had actually attempted to pass the boy off as a woman. The Archbishop of Rheims had singled him out to be the Maid's successor. The archbishop, who had grown to know Jeanne well, was convinced the youth could take her place, since 'he talks just as well as the Maid ever did'.[13] The shepherd, clad in much the same armour as the Maid had worn, rode sidesaddle on his horse, and he used from time to time to show his hands, feet and side, which were said to bear the stigmata. 'All blotched with blood, like that of St. Francis'.[14] Not even Jeanne d'Arc had manifested the wounds of Christ, and when William was brought to Paris as a prisoner he became an object of extravagant interest.)

Another very famous man, Poton de Xantrailles, one of Jeanne's best captains, was also captured after this battle, taken prisoner by the Earl of Warwick in a brilliant enterprise. With a force of some eight hundred troops, Xantrailles had set out from Beauvais on a raid towards Rouen. Warwick got wind of it and, hastily collecting six hundred men, advanced rapidly to intercept him. The two forces met in the open at Savignies near Gournay, twenty miles south of Beauvais. It was a one-sided battle, with the French putting up a very weak opposition. They were utterly defeated and pursued all the way back to Beauvais, while Xantrailles and several other knights were taken prisoner.[15]

In mid-August a baker in the rue St Honoré baked a large batch of bread using his usual expertise and superior flour. But when it was done, it came out of the oven the colour of cinders, and tasted foul. It caused much talk among his neighbours and became a controversy among Parisians generally. Most people saw in it a dreadful omen, convinced that something even more terrible than usual was going to overtake the city. Others declared it to be a miracle because the bread had been baked on the day of Our Lord's Assumption.[16]

The baker was apprehended, along with his store of flour, and the Provost of Paris ordered some of the flour to be baked in his own oven. His own baker made up the loaves as well and carefully as he knew how to, but when it was done it looked just as unpleasant as the first batch, and tasted even worse. The authorities debated the matter, and then decided to inspect the corn from which the flour had been ground. They could see nothing wrong with the samples, and ordered some of it to be milled and baked. The loaves that came out of the official ovens had the same texture and taste as on the two previous occasions, and it was decided that the field was cursed. Some merchants, who understood the nature of corn, and who gave evidence before the provost, said that the blight came from a plant that often grows in cornfields called 'cow-wheat'. They were correct in their judgement, but their findings did not calm the people.

On 25 October the garrison of Louviers, which had held out against the English for five months, quit the town. Louviers had been surprised and captured by the famous La Hire, in 1429, and since that time his troops had used it as a base from which to make continual raids upon the countryside, plundering almost up to the walls of Rouen. Because of La Hire's depredations, Rouen had often seemed to be a city under siege. (Its citizens were, by an English law, obliged to keep the watch, and every night 240 of them manned the walls.) It is from about this time that a tale was spun about the Duke and Duchess of Bedford nearly falling into the hands of the enemy while hunting in the vicinity of Rouen.

The Armagnacs carried away whatever they could by way of spoils from Louviers, and they left with bags full of money. It was agreed that the English would not molest the city, but they did not keep to their word. With the garrison departed, the English did the opposite of what they had sworn to do, and razed the walls to the ground, after which, the more important leaders returned to Rouen to relax.

The fall of Louviers was also greeted with much relief in Paris. It was said that plenty of firewood would come into the city once Louviers was freed. But within a week, inexplicably, the price of kindling cost a *tournais* more throughout the capital.

Every day it was rumoured that the Duke of Burgundy was on his way, and that he would bring a papal legate with him to arrange a firm peace between Charles VI and his nephew Henry. But all this, it was popularly believed, was only to keep the people pacified, for most citizens were now experiencing great distress, and were now fully undeceived as to the duke's true character. In fact, as the Bourgeois wrote, 'Burgundy did not care a fig for anyone in Paris, or in the kingdom.'

But, on the other hand, Philippe was growing ever more impatient at what he saw as a needless prolongation of the war, and he complained bitterly to the English council. Bedford and his warlords answered him as well as they could, but the truth was that both England and Normandy were physically and morally exhausted. Yet they could not relinquish what they had fought so long and so hard to acquire.

Dissatisfied with their answer, Philippe again entered into negotiations with King Charles VII, and a legate of Pope Eugenius IV visited both Bedford and the English court at Rouen for the purpose of making peace. Bedford sought to keep Philippe from taking any measures for peace independently of the English council, but he was trying to manage a political horse that now yearned to break free of his rein.

Yet, conversely, all seemed to be now in order for the Duke of Bedford's long planned masterstroke, the coronation of the young Henry as King of France (having long since determined to ignore that of Charles VII at Rheims). In August, when the duke was preparing for the visit of his nephew, a solemn mass was performed, with a procession celebrating the victories most recently obtained over the young king's enemies, and the coronation programme was set in motion.[17]

147

Henry, now 9 years old, arrived in great style at the abbey of St Denis on the last day of November, nobly escorted.[18] Afterwards, he travelled on to the grim castle of Vincennes, the scene of his father's early death.[19] This fortress was now back in English hands after being in Burgundy's control since the duke was made regent. Vincennes was very important because of its proximity to the capital. In the hands of the enemy, it posed the greatest threat to the city. The 'English Nation' at the University of Paris (one of four groupings of the Faculty of Arts) feared to take the beadle's mace to King Henry when they went to pay their respects, because of the dangers of taking such a valuable object out of the city.[20]

On the next Sunday, the first day of Advent, the king entered Paris through the Porte St Denis, four days before his 10th birthday. Some of the expenses for the lavish coronation came out of the royal finances, but the spectacular entry was staged and paid for by the people of Paris. Many influential people had a share in its planning, and the arrangements were in character with the flamboyant nature of the Parisians.

Over the gate, on the side facing the countryside, were the arms of the town – a very large shield covering all the stonework of the gate, half of it painted red, with the upper part azure. It was strewn with golden fleurs-de-lys, to emphasise that the English king was now entering into his French possessions. Across the shield was a silver ship, large enough to hold three men.

Inside the town, as he rode in, were ranked the Provost of the Merchants, along with his aldermen, all wearing red, with hats upon their heads. As soon as the king entered the gate, these men erected a great azure canopy, starred with golden lilies, over his head. Four aldermen carried it over him, 'just as is done for Our Lord at Corpus Christi'. The population greeted the young king with 'Noëls' as he rode by them. Before him went the Nine Worthies – Joshua, Judas Macabeus, David, Hector, Julius Caesar, Alexander, Arthur, Charlemagne and Godfrey of Jerusalem. The Nine Worthy women followed the men, and as they mostly comprised Amazon queens, the people lining the streets must have been uncomfortably reminded of their late enemy, the Maid of Orléans. As if to further remind them of her defeat, her successor, William the Shepherd, was exhibited as a prize, tied up with strong rope like any cheap thief. He later disappeared without trace, though it was strongly rumoured that he had been thrown, bound and gagged, into the Seine. After these 'exhibits' rode a horde of knights and squires, their tabards richly emblazoned.

Not far ahead of the king went four bishops – those of Paris, Noyon and the Chancellor. The fourth was an English bishop, almost certainly that of York. After the bishops rode the Cardinal of Winchester, and next, still ahead of the king, were twenty-five heralds and the same number of trumpeters.

Bravely escorted, Henry entered his French capital. The owners of the buildings facing the route had given a festive air to their property. The *Confrérie des Pelerins de Saint-Jaques* had suspended all their wall hangings by one hundred large hooks in front of their church. The *Confrérie de la Passion de Notre Seigneur Jesus* presented a mystery play about the Nativity. The butchers' guild offered a miniature stag hunt, a great success with both the king and the bystanders, and the wine that flowed in the fountains arrived along lead-lined pipes.

Henry paused to look for some time at the mermaids at the *Ponceau Saint-Denis*, the three mermaids very ingeniously executed. In their midst was a great lily whose buds and flowers spouted out milk and wine, and all who wished could drink from this inventive fountain. Above it was an artificial wood, where 'wild men frolicked about' and 'did pretty tricks with shields'. Everyone took pleasure in this entertainment, and the young king was apparently entranced by it.

The procession reached the church of the Trinity, where actors performed a mystery play, 'The Flight into Egypt', upon a scaffold erected for that purpose. It was staged by the Queen's Fountain. From here the procession rode to St Denis, where another mystery 'The Beheading of the Glorious Martyr St Denis', was performed for the king's edification. The canopy was taken over by representatives of the goldsmiths' company, and was carried as far as St Denis-de-la-Chartre. (Henry did not enter Notre Dame on that day.) At St Denis-de-la-Chartre the mercers took over the canopy as far as the Hôtel d'Anjou, the furriers carried it to St Anthoine-le-Petit, and the butchers took it over as far as the Hôtel des Tournelles.

At the Hôtel St Pol, Queen Isabeau was at the window with her ladies. The procession stopped in front of the building, and when he saw his French grandmother – for the first time in his young life – the king took off his hood and greeted her. She immediately bowed very humbly towards him, then turned away in tears. At this time they did not speak to each other, nor was there any show of familial affection between them.

The sergeants-at-arms took over the canopy from there, as it was their right to do so by long tradition, and when the procession had reached its destination at the royal palace, the canopy was delivered to the prior of St Catherine's, to whose foundation the sergeants belonged.

The most striking tableau was that of the 'twice-crowned king', a dramatic portrayal of Henry's claim to be king both in France and England. Yet this blatant piece of propaganda was unlikely to have come from the municipality as it was not included in their accounts for the celebrations. The location of the platform immediately in front of the Châtelet suggests that the arrangements were in the hands of the provost marshal. Indeed, on a lower platform, he was depicted holding a paper and presenting it to the king by way of a request. With his other hand he was indicating the principal employees of the Châtelet, members of the college there, who had a prime position in the scene. The fact that the provost marshal and his assistants were represented as symbolising the city did not please the men of the Pillared House.

The main concern all round, though, was to bring the City of Paris to the minds of the royal party, and to stress the king's obligations to his people. 'Paris,' declared the herald, 'receives you humbly. Protect us lovingly, because this city is well famed, and most deserving of good guidance.' At the Porte St Denis the arms of Paris had adorned stonework figures, and there were slogans offering the hearts of the citizens to the king, asking him to 'receive them graciously'. All the emphasis was on Paris, and on the duties owed by the king in return for the loyalty thus symbolised in the pageantry.

Elsewhere his French ancestry was emphasised. Fleurs-de-lys decorated the canopy that was held over his head, and fleur-de-lys blazed on the escutcheons of France that featured at the Porte St Denis and at the *Ponceau* fountain. No dual monarchy symbol was seen except in the tableau at the Châtelet. Presentation of scenes from the life of St Denis, all essentially French, were accompanied by a poem reminding the immature boy of his duty to defend his faith as his predecessors had done. French traditional images were being summoned up for the edification of the 'King of France' and his advisers.[21]

The coronation itself was another matter, and the people played no part in this ceremony, either in its financing or its enactment. But because no coronation had been held within the memory of most people, the canons of Notre Dame had sent one of their number to consult the chronicles at St Denis with regard to the previous 'joyful event', that of Charles VI and his queen.[22] (The queen herself was not consulted, though it is doubtful if she would have remembered much of the proceedings after such a long span.) Parliament, too, took its time deliberating on the way the ceremony should be conducted, and what style of dress the participants should adopt. All had been agreed by the time the coronation took place on 16 December, with due ceremony, though without the presence of many notable Frenchmen.

Very early in the morning, King Henry went on foot to Notre Dame from the palace. He was accompanied by a procession of people from all classes, 'singing very tunefully'.[23] The English Exchequer had paid for the building of a great platform to be erected inside the cathedral, 'broad and long', which was approached by deep steps that were wide enough for ten or more men to walk up alongside each other. Once on the platform, they went under the crucifix, 'and as far into the choir as you had gone outside it'. The steps were all painted, and covered with azure, starred all over with fleurs-de-lys.

The king and his attendants descended into the choir. Taking his seat on a makeshift throne, he was consecrated by the Cardinal of Winchester in a ceremony similar to that in which he had been crowned in England. This was murmured against by the French who were present, and was much to the mortification of the Bishop of Paris, who was 'not at all pleased',[24] and who had already insisted that it was his prerogative. (Because it was at Rheims, and with oil from the sacred ampulla, that kings were made, it did not really matter who crowned the English boy; in the eyes of at least half of his subjects he was no proper king.)

The Bourgeois records that the coronation ceremony was more English than French in style (though it is hard to know how he could have known this). It is true that Cardinal Beaufort insisted on singing the mass in the place of the affronted Bishop of Paris, and the acclamation of the king, with its stirring shout of 'Vivat Rex!' had not been heard in France for the last 150 years. This probably struck him as very foreign.[25] (He also recorded that the large silver-gilt pot containing the wine at the offertory was seized by the king's English officers, and was not returned to its rightful owners, the canons of the cathedral, until after a long and costly law suit.)[26]

After the ceremony the whole company went to dine at the palace. Henry ate in the great hall at a huge marble table, with the rest of the royal party scattered throughout the hall. But nothing had been properly arranged or properly guarded. Much of the food (and more valuable things) had been stolen by the more light-fingered of the king's humbler subjects, who had been allowed into the hall while the king was at his coronation, in order to let them see the splendour of the display. Not only pilferers had a field day in the hall. More than forty hoods were snatched in the press of the throng, and many belt tags were cut off.

There was, in fact, such a crowd of unwanted guests at the feast that members of the University and of the *parlement* could not make their way into the hall, and the provost and his merchants did not dare to push through the crush of people. When they did attempt it, they were thrust back angrily, and many great men stumbled and fell under the pressure. Soldiers were called, and the mob was partially cleared from the room, but even the most important men of Paris could find nowhere to sit. They took their places among 'cobblers, mustard-sellers, wine-stall keepers and stonemasons' lads'. The troops tried to shift the intruders, 'but when one or two moved, a dozen more sat down in their place'.[27]

Not that they would have enjoyed the food set down before them, for it was very poorly cooked. Most of it, especially that meant for the lower orders, had been cooked the previous Thursday. All this seemed very odd to the French, but the English had been put in charge of all things culinary and they had no real taste for the work; they wished only to get the feast 'over and done with', and much of the food went uneaten. Later, even the sick in the Hospital of the Hôtel Dieu – who were used to eating food condemned as unfit – complained that they had never seen such poor 'relief' in Paris before.[28]

A small tournament was held on the day after the coronation, and on the day of St Thomas the Apostle (21 December) a solemn mass was said in the great hall of the palace. The king was present 'in royal state' and all of the *parlement* attended on him, wearing mantles and fur hoods. When the mass was ended, they made several reasonable requests of the king, which he graciously granted, and they in turn swore several oaths that were asked of them. 'Oaths that are in accordance with God and with truth, otherwise they would not have sworn them.'[29]

The lawyers of the *parlement* had been trying for some years to get their back wages paid, and the prospect of Henry's arrival had stirred them up to much discussion on the subject.[30] After agreeing on the proper way to welcome him into his second kingdom, and deciding upon the right robes to wear at the various ceremonies, they had prepared a humble speech in which they requested the arrears of wages. But they had difficulty in persuading any of their number to deliver the speech, and when it was eventually made, the king's cold demeanour and his formal assent gave those present little hope of the sums being met.[31]

The provost and his aldermen were equally poorly treated. The greatest burden had fallen upon the municipality, who had been generously funded by the citizens. Because the coronation had so swiftly followed King Henry's entry into the city, the customary offering of a substantial gift had been delayed, but after the coronation the king was presented with a handsome gold chain (of fine workmanship) which, together with a jewel-studded collar, cost a vast sum. Such generosity was traditional with the entry of kings into the city, but such largesse demanded a response from the king, and none was forthcoming.

The common people of Paris, too, had given the appealing boy-king an affectionate welcome and, if they expected some favours in return, they met with as little success as the civil servants. Henry VI offered only the most modest of celebrations in return, and he left Paris without granting any of the benefits that were expected of him, the release of prisoners, for example, and the abolition of certain taxes such as imposts, salt tax, fourths, and 'similar bad customs that are contrary to law and right'.[32] It had been an expensive move for the municipality in the campaign to persuade the English to work seriously for the betterment of the town, and the king's apparent indifference to their plight was all the more frustrating for it.

King Henry stayed in Paris until the day after Christmas, which was celebrated with great joy. But it was generally considered that he had done little in return for the loyalty shown to him. For a monarch, it was thought that he had spent less than any rich Parisian marrying off his child would have done. The tradesmen of Paris, the goldbeaters and smiths, and all those engaged in the luxury trades had received no encouragement from the king or his English courtiers. The dominant theme of his visit had been an appeal for help by the Parisians. But it would seem that their efforts had been in vain, and their prayers would go unanswered.

It was agreed that much of the problem had been caused because of the difficulty of making each side understand the other. For by this time, the English had discovered a love for their language, and had largely ceased speaking French. The weather, too, had played its part, for it was intensely cold, and so the authorities had not spent much on outdoor festivities. 'Not a soul, at home or abroad, was heard to speak a word in his favour. Yet Paris had done more to honour him than to any king [before], both when he arrived and at his consecration.'[33]

His lack of generosity was particularly resented because the Parisians had made such a great effort while enduring extreme poverty. There were fewer people left in the city, and those who remained were earning less. In the very heart of winter all provisions were desperately dear, and the price of kindling was prohibitive. One faggot of green wood still cost 4d, or six *tournois*. It was so bitterly cold that there was not one week without two or three days of hard frost, and snow fell during the day and night, and this snow was only cleared by the rain that fell at regular intervals.

NOTES

1 Bourgeois de Paris.
2 *Archives Nationales.* The rivers, the primary routes for heavy goods, were perfect targets for the bands of marauders. Merchants often had to guarantee the boatmen against losses.
3 Bourgeois de Paris.
4 Favier, *Les Contribuables parisiens.* Even though Compiègne was the key to river communications between the capital, Picardy and the Low Countries.
5 Bourgeois de Paris.
6 Ibid.
7 *Proceedings of the English Privy Council.*
8 Bourgeois de Paris.
9 Ibid.
10 Ibid.
11 Williams, *My Lord of Bedford.*
12 Bourgeois de Paris.
13 Tuetey (ed.), *Journal* of the Bourgeois de Paris.
14 Ibid.
15 Burne, *The Agincourt War.*
16 Bourgeois de Paris.
17 Ibid.
18 Wolffe, *Henry VI.* With some thousands in attendance, though they cannot all have been part of the royal entourage.
19 Bourgeois de Paris.
20 Tuetey, op. cit.
21 This description of Henry's entry into Paris is compiled from accounts by the Bourgeois, Monstrelet and from the English Public Record Office.
22 *Archives Nationales.*

23 Bourgeois de Paris.
24 Ibid.
25 Ibid. That the Bourgeois was able to describe the ceremony in such great detail supports the claim that he was employed at the cathedral.
26 Ibid.
27 Ibid.
28 The Hôtel Dieu was under the direction of the Notre Dame authorities. It had 305 beds, and it could take up to three times that number of patients (sharing a mattress) in an epidemic. Champion, *Splendeurs et misères de Paris*.
29 Bourgeois de Paris.
30 Money had been sent to France, but it was to pay off soldiers, not lawyers. In May 1431 Bedford received £345 *l.t.* from the English treasury, the wages for the 310 men who had been sent to reinforce his retinue. In June he was given £1,253 sterling to pay those involved in the security of the capital. Public Record Office.
31 Fauquembergue, *Journal*.
32 Bourgeois de Paris.
33 Monstrelet, *Chronique*.

CHAPTER XIII
1432: Alarums and Excursions

After the king had left, the Duke of Bedford discovered that he had been underpaid for the security measures that he had undertaken for the last three months of the year, although he succeeded in obtaining reimbursement from the Exchequer in London.[1] Others who had been in charge of the royal finances in Paris hoped for a furtherance of assistance from the English government coffers once the king had returned home.

In anticipation of receiving this assistance, the Treasury in Paris opened a new account on 1 January, which was devoted to the monies they expected to collect from both London and Rouen, a city that was by now seen as an intermediate capital between the two kingdoms. But this money, when it came into their hands, was earmarked to be used almost exclusively for the payment of the Lancastrian soldiery, including those who controlled the Bastille, although some of it was also allocated to the men who guarded at least two gates in Paris. Some of this funding was paid from Normandy, and none of it was ever recorded in the English accounts.[2] Those of the English council left behind when King Henry departed for his second kingdom were of the firm opinion that no extra English funds should be sent to Paris. They also expressed a desire for the number of people employed by both *parlement* and the *Chambre des Comptes* to be reduced.

On 13 January the snow froze hard for the next seventeen days. The Seine, which was already very high, reached right into the Mortellérie. The river was frozen from bank to bank, the ice reaching as far south as Corbeil. It began to thaw very gradually on St Paul's Day, at night as well as during the daylight hours, so that the river was freed little by little within six days,[3] without any bridges or buildings being damaged. Yet boatmen said that the ice was more than two feet thick. The Parisians had ineffectively tried to break up the ice by hammering stakes into it, but until the thaw it refused to give.

There was, however, considerable damage done to the cargos of wine, corn, eggs and cheese that had only reached the town of Mantes on the way to the capital. Dealers lost everything, or very nearly, as the produce had rotted due to the delay. It had also cost them as much in protection as they could have expected to receive from any sale, the bandits boldly advancing on to the ice in order to hold the dealers up to ransom.

In this month even the most wretched faggots of wood now cost five or six pence, and there was no decent firewood to be had within a thirty miles radius of the city. The Duke of Burgundy, seeing the utter misery of the citizens, allowed them the use of woods from the protected heathlands, and this helped to alleviate the general misery somewhat.[4]

On 20 February Nicholas Albergati, Cardinal of the Holy Cross in Jerusalem, and the papal legate, arrived to make peace between the two kings. Albergati (1347–1443) was a Carthusian monk, a reluctant prelate, and a reformer of both the regular and secular clergy. Much loved throughout his lifetime, at this period he was considered to be almost saintly. In France, he did his duty so 'well and thoroughly' that both monarchs promised to submit in everything that should be decided upon at the great council which was due to take place in Basle later that year. After receiving their answers, the legate left Paris and went on to visit other Christian lords elsewhere.

In March the melted river flooded. In the Place de Grève the water came up to the steps of the Pillared House, forcing the city's servants to vacate the town hall. In the Place Maubert, the water reached halfway up the bread market. The Marais, from the Porte St Martin to the Porte St Anthoine, was halfway under water until 8 April. From Christmas until Easter very few people could afford to eat fresh produce, for the average cost of any green vegetable was one *blanc* to make a single bowlful and this did not include the expense of cooking it. Good beans cost twelve *blancs* for a bushel, and peas up to fifteen.[5]

The Armagnacs attacked Rouen in the first week of March. About one hundred and sixty men managed – with assistance from inside the town – to scale the walls and capture the largest tower of the castle. But once the townspeople learned of this new assault, they defended the rest of the building so well that the Armagnacs could progress no farther. Neither could they retreat, for the citizens were massed behind them. Hard pressed, they surrendered to the townspeople's mercy. One hundred and fourteen of them were executed, others were ransomed, and many found death in the river.

In March, two months after the departure of King Henry, the Provost of Merchants of Paris wrote twice to the king, urging action against the hostile towns of Champagne. They should, he recommended, be captured and the walls demolished, so that they could no longer form a refuge for the enemy. Something, everyone agreed, must be done, for otherwise 'total perdition' seemed inevitable. Copies of this forthright letter from the

156

Paris municipality were sent to the mayor and aldermen of the City of London. And they were further requested to use what influence they possessed to assist their brother Parisians, who were still confident that with their help they could be 'relieved of the evils and sorrows they had patiently endured for so long under the lordship of their king'.[6]

Preparations were soon under way for both the royal council and the municipality of Paris to send further representatives to England. On 11 April Guillaume le Duc, a president of the council and one of Bedford's personal councillors, was ready to leave Paris with others of the council for a visit to England that was expected to last for at least eleven weeks. He was still in England on 17 July, as was Jean Milet the royal secretary.[7] Also present in London were less distinguished representatives of the city, there to put forward the views of the ordinary citizen. They had much to complain about. As a result, in May 1432 heralds shuttled between the two countries, bearing heavy messages from France, and the diplomats sought to negotiate with each other without the tedium of having to meet in person.[8]

But the English council was aware of the seriousness of the situation. During 1432 Bedford paid a total of £7,500 towards the support of troops, for six months from May to October. The siege of Lagny began on 1 May, and on 7 August the English Exchequer ordered payment for Bedford, to meet the cost of military equipment, which was to be sent with all speed, though the equipment could not have arrived before the collapse of the siege on 13 August. Both Bedford and Louis of Luxembourg were forced to contract heavy debts in order to raise a unit sufficiently strong to meet a large enemy relieving force. Again, repayment came – eventually – from the English Exchequer. King Henry's council did not entirely ignore the pleas of the hard-pressed Parisians, but to the dismay of the French, all the English efforts to help now seemed doomed to be unsuccessful.[9]

The city remained in the grip of ice and snow. On 15 April it snowed throughout the entire day, and on Palm Sunday it froze so hard between midnight and daybreak that 'every flower and bud which had come out on the trees, and all the walnut trees, were burned and blackened by frost'.[10]

Using a tactic of 'great treachery', the city of Chartres was captured by the Armagnacs on the eve of Palm Sunday. A man from Orléans, seemingly an 'honest merchant' with a safe conduct to pass between the two cities, agreed to bring in ten or a dozen carts of salt, of which there was a serious shortage. He duly arrived with the carts, each of which contained ten huge barrels. Trojan-horse-like, these contained two men, well armed. There were also two soldiers to a cart, disguised in smocks and gaiters.

Overnight, three thousand men-at-arms were billeted in the villages nearby, and guards were set along the roads so that no news could get through. When all these arrangements had been settled, the carters came to the gates of Chartres. Unsuspecting, the Captain of the Guard – who knew the merchant well – let the invaders into the city. When three of the carts were inside the gate, they halted on the drawbridge and killed the shaft horses, so putting the bridge out of action. The soldiers hidden in the barrels scrambled out and killed the gate-men with axes. The hidden reserves now raced up and forced their way into the city. The Bishop of Chartres, alerted to this penetration, armed his guards and some followers and led an attack on the Armagnacs. But his efforts were too late and in vain; he was killed outright and his men and most of the citizens who accompanied them were taken up and thrown into various prisons around the city. The merchant from Orléans was paid 4,000 gold *saluts* for his treachery.[11]

The fall of Chartres made the Parisians fearful for their safety, and made the price of bread very high. The weather was still bitterly cold and there were constant gales, so the little fruit that hung upon the trees was blown down by the fierce winds. This extreme cold lasted until after the Translation of St Nicholas in May. It was said that the husbandmen could not get fifty almonds off one hundred trees and all other fruit was either blown down or spoilt.

Again, there was a shortage of greenstuff, with only old beet tops, which had begun to sprout again available. Two or three people would try to subsist on a *blanc's* worth of this. If they were lucky they could buy cabbages that were starting to rot. Cheese was so expensive that a very small one, 'still sweating', cost three or four *blancs*. Five eggs would sell for two *blancs*.

The Provost of Paris, 'an intelligent man',[12] was put in charge of the forces heading towards the relief of Chartres. He hoped to retake it with the assistance of some of the citizens, but before they could come to his aid they were discovered and put to a terrible death. The attempt to relieve Chartres failed, and the Provost made his way back to Paris, where he was given a cool welcome. (Actually, Simon Morhier had proved no paragon over the years he had held the post of provost marshal. He was condemned in the *parlement* for imposing a levy on the sergeants of the Châtelet when they renewed their oaths to the English king, though he claimed to be following a precedent! He had also forced the tenants on his estate to mount guard on his property, and he had obtained supplies for his soldiers from the peasants without adequate repayment, contrary to English custom.)

In the first week of June Gilles de Clamécy, a knight, had been made the Keeper or Deputy Provost until the other returned. In that same week, certain men of Pontoise – along with certain English allies – planned to hand over the town to the Armagnacs. They were found out before they could take any action. Once arrested, they freely admitted that they were going to kill everyone in the town because they would not recognise their rightful lord, King Charles VII. Even the women and children were to be massacred, and so they were put to death, with all their kinfolk disgraced and their wives and children reduced to poverty. This was the first instance of Englishmen colluding with the enemy, and it affected not only the morale of the English soldiers, but created a shock wave of horror among the citizens, who saw in it, perhaps, the beginning of the end.

On St John the Baptist's Day, 24 June, a tremendous thunderstorm broke over Paris, and the lightning did much damage. The belfry at Vitry, which was made of stone, was struck and the bell cast out of the steeple. In falling, it damaged the roofing and vaulting, which fell down among the congregation, who were then at Vespers, killing five and wounding many.

On 20 July, St Peter and St Paul's Day, there was a freak hailstorm. When measured, some hailstones were found to be sixteen inches around, and many resembled billiard balls.[13] These abnormally large pellets fell in the direction of Lagny and Meaux.

On 23 July Guillaume Sanguin was dismissed from the Provostship of Merchants and a lord of *parlement*, Maître Hugues Rapiout, was appointed in his place. As the Civil Lieutenant of Paris at the time of the 1418 massacres, the latter had been rebuked for not checking them, but he had since risen to be the king's advocate at the Châtelet. Two aldermen were also changed at this time. It was widely believed that the provost of merchants had been dismissed for the provost marshal's failure to relieve the city of Chartres, as the latter could not be so easily removed.

Having lost Chartres, the Duke of Bedford made a vigorous attempt to retrieve English fortunes in Brie and the Île de France. On 10 August, St. Laurences's Day, the English launched an attack on Lagny. They took the ramparts and planted the English regent's banner upon them. But finding that the force sent out against the town made no progress he set out in person with reinforcements and cannon. Bedford pressed the siege so hotly that the garrison was on the point of capitulation, when a contingent of French troops arrived to relieve the town.

After the torrential rain and storms the weather turned unusually hot, hotter than anyone could remember. This distressed the English more than having to face their enemies. Three hundred of them were killed in one day, as many from heatstroke as from the fighting, it was said. But this catastrophe apart, there were, in any case, five Armagnacs to every two Englishmen. They were forced by circumstances to pitch their tents in the same place where they had begun the siege, and fortune was once more against them. Between Monday and Tuesday the Marne river rose four feet overnight, breaking its banks. The weather turned again, with more violent thunderstorms, and it rained for twenty-four days in a row.

Meanwhile, the spell of extraordinary heat had burned all the verjuice vines. Because of this, and because so much wine was being taken to the army, it became extremely expensive in Paris. What had cost 6d in July cost three *blancs* by mid-August. Even those with money to spare found wine hard to come by, and for the first time that even the oldest people could remember the tavern keepers closed their doors early.

The French troops sent to relieve Lagny then drew off, apparently in the direction of Paris. Bedford broke up his camp in alarm, thinking the capital would come under attack, and on St Bernard's Day, 20 August, he abandoned the siege of Lagny.[14] In his haste to leave, he was forced to abandon much of his artillery, along with cooked food, and many of the hogsheads of wine that in Paris would have fetched a high price. Valuable loaves of bread, too, were also left behind. The price of corn in Paris shot up when the news of Bedford's defection reached the city.[15]

The duke's failure to take Lagny both disgusted and dismayed the Parisians, for it badly affected their own lives. At the end of August some nuns at the convent of St Anthoine-des-Champs, along with their abbess, were imprisoned on suspicion of having plotted in the regent's absence to admit Charles's party into the capital. A nephew of the abbess, who called himself the 'true friend of Paris',[16] had planned to betray the town by secretly opening the Porte St Anthoine. The gatekeepers were to be killed first, and then everyone without exception. This became generally known after their arrest.

The nuns' involvement may have been a straightforward political gamble on their part, but it was also due to internal tensions within their order. For in the seventy years preceding the Anglo–Burgundian regime in Paris, four of the former abbesses had been related to each other, either as aunt or nieces, and all had been actively political. There had been considerable bitterness fomented inside the convent when one of their number, Pernelle le Duc, had died. Pernelle was the sister of Guillaume le Duc, who was to become Bedford's closest associate in the *parlement*, and from 1422 the nuns of St Anthoine had begun a series of actions against him. In these, they accused le Duc of manipulating his sister in order to defraud the convent, and their resentment against him – and his English allies – had simmered throughout the 20s and had now erupted. It was frustration at being unable to make their charges stick that had resulted in their involvement in the conspiracy against the English authorities.

In other parts of France also, the duke had little to encourage him, and there was increasing unrest among the people, for the two warring armies were judged to be to blame for all their miseries. This was certainly true in some instances, for while one lot destroyed the Brie country, others would be devastating Beauce and the Gatinais. Wherever they went they left the country in ruins. 'They are the enemies of God's law.' The Bourgeois spoke for his fellow citizens when he claimed the army 'loved to torment the peasantry out of sheer cruelty'.

The Armagnacs were greatly encouraged by the loss of Lagny, and their harrying of the areas around Paris became even more ferocious. Few people dared to step out of the city gates, although the vintage was just beginning. Fewer goods than ever managed to reach the city, and the citizens despaired of being able to acquire even the provisions that were necessary to sustain life. There was also a lack of armaments with which to defend themselves – much had been left before the walls of Lagny. Those 'who were in the know' said that the cost of the Lagny siege to the Parisians was more than 150,000 gold *saluts*, each worth 22s.p good currency.[17]

Then, too, there were financial problems that hit the Parisians even harder, for they were closer to their hearts. There was a gold coin then current, although it was not of the purest gold, called a *douderes*, which was worth 16s.p, but shortly after the failure at Lagny they were proclaimed to be worth no more then 14s.p. As there were many of these coins in circulation, the losses to the ordinary citizens were considerable.

On 11 September the English captured the stronghold of Maurepas, owned by the Lord of Massy, considered to be the 'cruellest shedder of blood in all France'.[18] One hundred thieves who were under his protection were captured with him. One of them, Mainguet, confessed that he had in one day thrown seven men, one after the other, down an old well and had then crushed them to death with large stones. There were other murders besides.

Because few would venture out to reap it, the corn harvest failed. The scarcity of flour now became extreme. A single *setier* of good corn cost seven *francs*, good currency, and barley went for four. There was consequently a high mortality rate among young people and children, many of whom died of an unknown epidemic.

On 2 October the English took the town and castle of Provins. Hitherto more restrained than their French rivals or their Burgundian colleagues, English discipline now seemed to have broken down, for the troops looted, stole and murdered 'as such people always do, and call it the usual custom of war'.[19]

A council was held at Auxerre to negotiate a peace between the two kings. Several lords from both sides attended it, including a number from the Duke of Burgundy. But negotiations were halted when a quarrel between the Dukes of Brittany and Alençon broke out. Bedford could not resist the opportunity of striking a blow at the French cause by sending English troops to the aid of Brittany, which was naturally seen as a provocative act by the peacemakers. This quarrel, though, was ended when the Duke of Brittany's brother, Richemont, reconciled the two dukes.

In Paris the epidemic continued unchecked, and it even attacked the Duchess of Bedford, 'the most delightful of all the great ladies then in France, for she was good and beautiful, and of a beautiful age too, being only twenty-eight when she died'. The Parisians may have respected her husband, and many feared him, but most genuinely loved his wife.[20] Her death was a real sadness for them. Several leading insitutions had stopped work in order to attend religious processions for the restoration of her health once her condition had become known. She died in the Hôtel de Bourbon on 13 November, two hours after midnight, and with her died most of the hopes of the Parisians, for she had always been seen as the strongest link between her husband and her brother, always ready to bring about conciliation. But, as ever, 'this had to be endured'.

She was buried at the Célestins, but her heart was interred at the Augustins. All the 'St Germain people' were present at her burial, along with the priests of the Fraternity of Citizens, each in a black stole and carrying a burning candle, who sang as they walked beside her corpse. As the body was being lowered into the grave, the English took up the chant, singing 'most piteously by themselves, in the fashion of their own country'.[21] Her death, which Bedford felt deeply, broke at least one of the ties that bound Philippe to him, for there were no offspring to link the two dukes by blood.

The week after her burial, the Duke of Bedford went to Mantes, where he remained three weeks in mourning before returning to the capital. The men who had gone to the conference at Auxerre also returned to Paris in that same week, having done nothing but 'spend a great deal of money and waste their time'.[22] But the public was told when they returned that they had done excellent work in bringing about a lasting peace, which was 'the reverse of true'. As people began to discover the reality of the situation, they began to protest about the failure of the negotiations, seeing that no action could be taken against their real enemies – the mercenaries turned brigands who roamed the roads, terrorising the countryside – until the warring armies laid down their weapons.

The official response to the protestors was to imprison several of them, under the pretence of avoiding a popular disturbance. When the ringleaders had paid 'and more than paid' their prison expenses, they were released.[23]

Meanwhile, when the thieves infesting the countryside heard that the negotiations had come to nothing, and that the beloved duchess was dead, 'their madness turned to frenzy'. 'No heathens, no maddened wolves, ever did worse things to Christians than these men did to honest working people and to honest merchants. Every single week they would come two or three times up to the gates of Paris. They would think nothing of kidnapping monks, nuns, priests, women, little children, old men of sixty or eighty years of age, and not one ever escaped alive out of their hands except by paying a heavy ransom. Nor was there one lord, not one, who made even the least opposition to them.'[24]

NOTES

1   Public Record Office.
2   Bibliothèque Nationale.
3   Bourgeois de Paris. There is some error here, unless there were two saints named Paul in the medieval calendar. St Paul's feast day is now recognised as 29 June.
4   Ibid.
5   Ibid.
6   Ibid.
7   Delpit, Jules, *Collection générale*.
8   Rymer, *Feodora*.
9   Public Record Office.
10   Bourgeois de Paris.
11   Monstrelet, *Chronique*.
12   Bourgeois de Paris.
13   Ibid. 'Billiard balls' is a literal translation of *billes à biller*, a game originally played in the open air. The size of the balls used then is unknown. Jusserand, *Les sports et les jeux d'exercice dans l'ancienne France*.
14   The siege had begun on 1 May. The English exchequer had been ordered to pay for the military equipment needed, which was to be sent with all speed, but it did not arrive in time to help the Duke of Bedford. Williams, *My Lord of Bedford*.
15   After the failure to capture Lagny, there was a long delay in the dispatch of further funds from England to France, although both royal councils kept in touch. Delpit, op. cit.
16   Bourgeois de Paris.
17   Ibid.
18   Ibid.
19   Fauquembergue, *Journal*.
20   Bourgeois de Paris.
21   Ibid.
22   Ibid.
23   Ibid.
24   Ibid.

CHAPTER XIV

1433: Conferences and Conspiracies

On Thursday 8 January the Duke of Bedford had his wife's obsequies celebrated at the Célestins. A donation of two *blancs* was given to all who attended these rites and some fourteen thousand people went to pay their last respects to a much-loved woman. It was a very splendid service, and four hundred pounds of wax was used for the candles that blazed throughout the church.[1]

It froze very hard in this month, and the Seine rose alarmingly, the icy conditions lasting until after St Vincent's Day. As a result, the cost of all provisions became more expensive, especially the grain used to make flour; wheat was sold for eight *francs* and barley went for five. But there was a shortage of other foodstuffs also, and small beans, 'such as was usually fed to pigs' were fetching five *francs* a *setier*. Even vetches and cockles were dear. For two weeks, no bread was eaten in Paris, 'except such as used to be made for dogs, and even that so small a man's hand would cover a 4d loaf'.[2]

Bedford returned to Normandy on 4 February. He went specifically to collect a heavy tax of 200,000 *francs*, a sum that had been granted to him when at Mantes. In that same week, the president of the *parlement*, Philippe de Morvilliers, was deprived of all royal appointments. The cause of his dismissal remained unknown, but it was a matter for some sympathy with those who knew him well. Fauquembergue, who worked in the *parlement*, greatly admired him; 'God gave him good counsel and patience,' he wrote. Morvilliers would regain his post after the English left Paris, when he was seen to have been a secret friend to the French for some time past. Indeed, the reason for his dismissal may be that, even at this time, he had 'listed towards' their side. Maître Robert Pie-de-fer, then living near the Porte St Martin, was appointed as deputy in the president's place.

A conference was held at Corbeil in the last week of March, which continued to the end of Lent. The Cardinal of Sainte-Croix presided over this consultation, which included the Bishop of Paris, several other important bishops, and many great lords. A number of high-ranking clerks were there to record the deliberations, and both the English and French parties

165

were equally represented. But it was through papal intervention that the formal representations for peace were finally initiated, based on 'Christian or moral grounds', although the rationalisation for the negotiations was the 'grievous burden' of the escalating costs.[3]

The conference sent a certain bishop to Paris, to celebrate divine office during Holy Week. He performed the acts of absolution and chrism to priests, deacons, sub-deacons and the tonsured acolytes, but he did it all so early in the morning that many members of all the orders missed it. The bishop returned to Corbeil on the same day that he had celebrated the canonical prayers.[4]

It continued exceedingly cold, with frost on almost every day until Easter. Even on St Mark's Day, 25 April, which was unbearably cold, it snowed, and there was a rattling of hailstones in the afternoon. There was a let up in this unseasonable weather shortly after the Easter celebration, but it was very cold at Pentecost, on the last day of May.

In 1433 the Duke of Bedford, as regent (for he had regained that title), left Paris for Rouen to receive the return of a heavy tax that had been laid upon the provinces. From there, he proceeded to Calais, where he punished some mutinous soldiers.[5] There, he met up with his brother Gloucester, and they stayed for a month. In anticipation of some kind of rapprochement, the Dukes of Orléans and Bourbon, prisoners in London, were moved to Dover for six weeks in order to help with the forthcoming negotiations. But when the promised French emissaries failed to appear at Calais, both dukes were returned to London.

But while Bedford was at Calais, Louis of Luxembourg, the Bishop of Therouanne and Chancellor of France, persuaded him to marry again, and to the astonishment of all, the Duke of Bedford did so, within half a year of his first wife's passing. The marriage was performed at Therouanne, on 20 April, the day after Low Sunday. This marriage was of great dynastic and political importance to the duke, for his new bride – Jacqueline or Jacquetta – was the daughter of the Count of St Pol, and the chancellor's niece. Bedford, as always, was anxious to form an alliance that would be advantageous to the English cause and the house of Luxembourg was not only rich and powerful, but they had also proved a staunch ally. His new duchess was 17, handsome and lively. Bedford, as a thank-offering, presented the cathedral with a number of fine bells, which he had cast in England for the purpose.[6]

This match may have been arranged to cement the alliance between England and Luxembourg, but it was made without the knowledge of the Duke Philippe, the feudal lord of the bride's father. It ended all friendly relations between the two rulers, as Philippe was firmly opposed to the English gaining further influence in Picardy. Cardinal Beaufort then attempted a reconciliation between the two by convening a formal meeting at St Omer, but his efforts were in vain as Philippe refused to travel there. The relationship between England and Burgundy was now deadlocked.

At midnight on 7 May the Armagnacs entered the town of St Marcel, near enough to Paris to be thought of as an outer suburb.[7] It was, in fact, taxed as part of the capital, even though it lay outside the city walls. The lack of protection in the suburbs obviously gave the encroaching forces a certain amount of cover, and the Armagnacs did much damage, taking men, women and children prisoner, and demanding huge ransoms for their release. When they abandoned the town, they left scores of hacked corpses and still burning churches behind. They also left with a 'great mass of plunder'.

This action not only increased the fears of the Parisians, for the Armagnacs had come so close, it also added to their burdens, as everything became more expensive. The Armagnacs retreated to Chartres, but they almost immediately went on the rampage again, attacking Crépy-en-Valois, a town that had been lately captured by the English. The town was soon surrendered, by an act of 'treason', to the Armagnacs. Once inside, they 'stripped their victims to the skin', and one disaster after another followed for the householders.[8]

A second conference to arrange peace talks or simply a truce between the two kings, was held at Corbeil in June. Ambassadors attended from England, France and Burgundy, and again, it was presided over by the Cardinal of Sainte-Croix. All parties were now tired of war, and for a time it seemed the conference would meet with success. Bedford himself thought it important enough to attend, and he was in personal consultation with the cardinal. But negotiations broke down when the Bishop of Therouanne took action independent of his English allies, by travelling into Normandy and gathering together an enormous number of troops, to be used as a threat against those in attendance at Corbeil.

The bishop brought his unauthorised force to Paris in the first week of July. He went from there to the conference table, where he was supposed to seal the treaty already agreed by the cardinal and King Charles's chancellor, the Archbishop of Rheims. The Bishop of Therouanne who did not want a *détente* between the two kingdoms, found unexpected allies among some other lords. Like him, they refused to sign the agreement, objecting to certain conditions.

So all who attended departed, to the extreme annoyance of those who truly wished for peace. The cardinal went on to the great council of Basle, to report on how the conference had ended.[9] When the Archbishop of Rheims left, 'his face and manner showed how angry he was at the turn that things had taken'.[10] King Henry's chancellor, when all had left, sent the troops he had collected to Milly-en-Gatenais, where they took the church and the town, burned everything to the ground, and 'did worse things than the Armagnacs ever did'. The Archbishop would show that he was no friend to Paris either.[11]

Bedford left for a visit to England before the conference ended, taking his duchess with him. They entered London on 23 June. On 13 July, in a speech to the English parliament, he defended his administration in France from some charges (for which Gloucestor was probably responsible) of neglect and carelessness. He demanded that, if any accusation were made against him, it should be made openly before the king in parliament. After some consideration, the chancellor, the Bishop of Bath and Wells, replied that neither the king, the Duke of Gloucester, nor the council had heard such charges, and that the king thanked him for his faithful service.[12]

But the fact was that the English in France were now at the end of their resources, and Bedford's decision to go to England in person was to seek supplies. A new treasurer had been appointed, and under Bedford's influence he tried to persuade parliament to invest further in the cause of France and his survey of the financial position made grim listening. Necessary expenditure exceeded revenue by nearly £30,000 without allowing a penny for active operations by sea or land, and the schedule of debts amounted to £164,000 or almost three times the normal revenue.

But the commons were weary of the chronic burden of taxes, especially for what was now seen as an unsuccessful war, in which there were no clear victories. The yield of taxation was dropping because of a decline in national prosperity; it was even considered possible that the government would be faced with declaring bankruptcy as a last expedient. But Bedford prevailed to some extent, and his cause was voted a grant, although it was quite inadequate for the changes that the regent wished to make.[13]

At this time, in Paris, rye cost £4p, or more, and other grain was almost as dear. In the last week of June, large cargoes of grain came in from Normandy. So much so that on the first Saturday of July, both wheat and rye were being hawked all over Paris at 24s p., 'a thing unheard of, that grain should be cried like charcoal'. Charcoal normally arrived in Paris by boat, and was unloaded and sold in the Place de Grève; but if brought in by road, the seller took it about the streets in an effort to sell all that he could in one day, without off-loading it from his cart. To do this, he would cry his wares about the town. On Wednesday eight-penny loaves were reduced to four-pence. Not only was there plenty of grain this year, it was also of excellent quality. There was also an abundance of fruit and vegetables, as August continued exceptionally fine, 'the finest that anyone could remember'.[14]

Yet there were many people dying, small children especially. The death rate was appalling, but no one could identify the scourge as being either a variant of the plague or the smallpox. In the popular mind, the great plague of 1348 was said to have fallen into an uneasy slumber, with now and then – as in this cloudless August – a terrible reawakening. But not since that first outbreak had it been so violent or so widespread. 'Neither by bleeding nor by clysters, nor by any precautions, could any man or woman who had fallen a victim to it, escape it.'[15] It had begun in March of 1433, and it was to continue until almost 1434. As always, public ignorance held that witches were responsible for the evil, and after them, the Jews. As a result there was some action taken against this latter community.

No help came from the authorities. The Duke of Burgundy stayed away from Paris. Nor did the Duke of Bedford come near the city after his wedding. (He was still in England, seeking to obtain adequate funding.) To the people, both dukes had left the Bishop of Therouanne and his cronies to 'regent' everything as they felt inclined.[16]

In the last week of September, certain affluent Parisians entered into a 'damnable conspiracy' together. They resolved to openly admit a large number of Scotsmen into the city, clad as English soldiers. Two hundred of these men would wear the red crosses of the 'goddams', and these same men would accompany one hundred other Scots who would masquerade as their prisoners, wearing white crosses and with their hands loosely tied, and their weapons hidden. They were to come into Paris in lots of two, one group through the Porte St Denis and the other through the Porte St Anthoine. Up to four thousand Armagnacs were to be 'set in ambush here and there in the quarries and hiding places around Paris, of which there are far too many!'[17]

The sham English soldiers were to bring in their 'prisoners' at about noon, when the gatekeepers were more occupied with eating their dinners. They would kill those in control of the gates, and everyone who happened to be entering or leaving the city. When they had captured the two fortresses they would then send for their concealed reserves, who would storm through the gates and put everyone who defied them to the sword.

'But God had pity on the town.' The conspirators were discovered and 'their deeds were turned upon themselves'.[18] Some were beheaded and others banished, after being deprived of all their possessions, their wives and children being reduced to beggary, 'bringing disgrace on themselves and their heirs'.

At roughly the same time, others were plotting to sell the town into the hands of the enemy, but now purely for financial gain. These men intended to enter Paris from the river, using small boats on St Denis's Eve (9 October), the aim being to get in by way of the moats between the gates of St Denis and St Honoré, 'as no one lives there'.[19] Like the others, they were going to kill the gatekeepers and whatever bystanders stood in their way, and then admit a larger force into the streets.

It would seem that neither of these two factions knew of the other's plots, at least according to their confessions and the public announcement made at the gallows in the Halles, where they were beheaded. To make such an entry into Paris on the eve of the feast day of the nation's greatest saint was seen to be either a profanation or a sanction, depending upon whether one was for or against the plotters, but most agreed that it was a highly unpropitious time. On the whole, the citizens were of the opinion that St Denis had protected them 'by his holy prayers'.

In England, when parliament met again in November, Bedford made – in agreement with the prayers of the commons – a promise of concord and of government according to the will of the council. On the 24th the speaker, Roger Hunt, delivered a speech before the young king in which he praised Bedford's self-denying devotion in France, but in which he conversely begged King Henry to direct the duke to remain in England. 'In order by his presence to secure the peace of the realm.'

Bedford, in reply, expressed his satisfaction at this proof of the commons' affection, and he placed himself wholly at the king's disposal. He unselfishly offered to relieve the wretched condition of the financial situation by accepting £1,500 only as his salary of chief counsellor, instead of the 8,000 marks hitherto paid to his brother Gloucester, but he would require £500 for each journey he made to and from France.[20]

He also showed his desire to act constitutionally by laying before parliament a series of articles with reference to the continual council, on 18 December 1433. In these articles, Bedford laid down his conditions for accepting his new responsibilities, 'as far as may goodly be with the weal of his [Henry VI's] lands and lordships beyond the sea'.[21] He meant that by accepting his new role in England, he would not abandon his first duty to France. Bedford was a man of the strictest honour, and he had pledged himself to his late brother.

The year was chiefly marked by successful campaigns in the eastern theatre of war, mainly undertaken by the Burgundians under the command of Philippe the Good. The duke had for some time past made short local truces with his Valois cousin whilst allowing his troops to continue fighting them under English colours, and for English pay. It was an economical method of waging warfare, but it was not entirely successful, for the French often reneged on their promises, making frequent incursions into his territory while their truces were still supposedly in operation. The duke was stung into action by these 'betrayals'. As a result of Philippe's actions against the Armagnacs, there were alternate gains made by each side, though no triumphs by the Burgundians were of any importance to the English.[22]

The failure to take Lagny was the worst blow to the English. When

Bedford visited England in June 1433, he sought not only to justify his conduct of the war but also to obtain much needed finance to continue it. The Parisians looked on anxiously while Bedford was away (he would not return for almost a year) and the council sent an appeal – this time in the form of a poem – to their colleagues in the City of London.[23] Bedford's stay in England did eventually yield a result, for money was sent to his most loyal ally, Louis of Luxembourg. But these payments were too late and too little, for they could only pay off debts or fill up shortages when they appeared, there was never any sense of a regular structure of support being created.

NOTES

1   Bourgeois de Paris.
2   Ibid.
3   Wolffe, *Henry VI*, citing the *Rotuli Parliamentorum*.
4   The Bourgeois records this with great contempt.
5   Wolffe, op. cit.
6   Bourgeois de Paris.
7   Favier, *Les contribuables parisiens*.
8   Bourgeois de Paris.
9   The cardinal would be papal representative at several sessions of the Council of Basle.
10 Monstrelet, *Chronique*.
11 Bourgeois de Paris.
12 *Proceedings of the English Privy Council.*
13 Williams, *My Lord of Bedford*.
14 Bourgeois de Paris.
15 Ibid.
16 Ibid.
17 Ibid.
18 Ibid.
19 Ibid.
20 *Rotuli Parliamentorum.*
21 Ibid.
22 Monstrelet, op. cit.
23 Delpit, *Collection générale*.

CHAPTER XV

1434: Losing Control

On 29 January 1434 a large drove of livestock, two thousand pigs, many horned cattle and flocks of sheep was on its way to Paris for the relief of the citizens. But the Armagnacs, who now had spies in every quarter of the English possessions, went out to meet this valuable herd a little beyond the town of St Denis. Their numbers being double that of the men accompanying the cattle, they soon routed them. Having killed most of the drovers, they led the animals away from the road to Paris, and the few farmers who were accompanying their livestock were seized for ransom.

A peculiar feature of this outrage, and one that particularly horrified the Parisians, was that having murdered their victims, they searched among them, and then cut the throats of each man – dead or alive – who wore an English emblem or was thought to speak English. Even to people inured to cruelty, it was inexplicable to cut the throats of those already dead. 'A dreadful inhumanity.'[1]

A week later the Armagnacs attacked Vitry by night. Having sacked it, and put most of the townspeople to the sword, they burned the town. This proved too much for the embattled Parisians. On hearing the news, some of the men volunteered to go after them the next day and they followed them for quite some distance before abandoning the chase. Thirteen poor men who followed the Parisian force decided to leave the main body in the hope of getting some of their belongings back. But when the Armagnacs saw them, they turned about and having come up to them, they rounded them up and slit their throats.[2]

About this time, the Armagnacs also captured the town and castle of Beaumont. On 27 February a levy of men and horses was taken in Paris, as many as could be raised. But on coming up to the Armagnacs, a great fear seized the men of Paris, and they beat a hasty retreat before the Armagnacs could bear down on them. 'Not hesitating, even as they fled, to steal cows, oxen, and all they could, though not everything they wanted,' the Bourgeois commented caustically. 'It is clear the best of them is worthless.'

There was no news of either duke, although Bedford was still in England, trying to obtain the funding for a new assault.[3] In July 1433

Bedford had replaced his brother's nominee, Lord Scrope, with his own man, Ralph, Lord Cromwell, as treasurer. But Cromwell had at once made it clear that this was a bad time financially to prosecute a foreign war, despite the fact that his budget had contained a memorandum 'to provide for the kingdom of France'. With Bedford obliged to remain in England, the problem was ignored until the early months of 1434, even though continuing rumours that the French were trying to raise a great army were rife, and the Norman authorities made repeated appeals for help to mount a counter-offensive.

It was said that no one truly governed in Paris for none were competent enough, and the man left in charge, the Bishop of Therouanne, was universally detested. It was said both secretly and openly, and often enough, that if it were not for him France would be at peace. He and his 'accomplices . . . were more hated and cursed than ever the Emperor Nero was.' The Bourgeois himself was not sure that the bishop entirely deserved his evil reputation, 'but God knows!'

Easter fell on 27 March, and the weather was fine for the festival, although once again the winter had been very hard, with bitter frosts. It had begun about two weeks before Christmas, and the ground had frozen hard for thirty relentless days. Some clerks of Paris, 'men swollen with learning',[4] asserted that the extreme cold would certainly last until the middle of May, or even later, and the Bourgeois wryly recorded, 'But God made other arrangements.'[5]

It turned out to be the most unusual March weather that anybody could remember, for it did not rain on any day throughout the month and it was very hot – hotter than midsummer. Fish – and herrings in particular, both kippered and white – were so plentiful during Lent that by the middle of the fasting a barrel of good white herring went for less than 26s p. Good peas were up to seven *blancs*, beans cost about four, and oil was seven *blancs* a quart – and that for the best to be had in the city.

April, too, was warm and dry, but in the last week, on the 28th, there was a hard frost. All the vines of the Marais froze that night, yet the prospects for a fine vintage had looked better than for ten years past. Together with the frost there came so many cockchafers and caterpillars that all the fruit spoiled, and apple and plum trees were 'left as leafless as at Christmas'.[6]

In an extraordinary council held in the parliament chamber at West-minster on 26 April, the Duke of Gloucester had offered to carry on the war in France. During his speech he made some observations which led Bedford to demand that his words should be set down that he might answer them before the king.[7] Gloucester was clearly put out by his brother's new pre-eminence in England, and his own consequent loss of power. For him it must have been a matter of saving face that he should put forward the idea of taking Bedford's place in France.

But when Bedford took this suggestion as a criticism of his regency and demanded the right to reply in defence of his honour, Gloucester then took his brother's challenge as a slight upon his own, and the situation grew dangerous. Cardinal Beaufort advised the young king in the matter, and his council also advised him. Their combined counsel was to have both injured parties deliver up their written 'evidences' into the king's hands, which he could then destroy. Afterwards, he would declare that the honour of neither man was in question, and would then forbid further argument. At Henry's request, the matter was dropped.

Meanwhile matters worsened rapidly for the Parisians. The soldiers 'who called themselves Frenchmen' – at Lagny and other fortresses around Paris – now came every day up to the gates. They stole and murdered with impunity, for not one of the nobility 'cared to put an end to this war', although it was truer to say that none could afford to prosecute it. Their troops had been unpaid for weeks, so the men had nothing but what they could get by adopting the very methods of those they should have been hunting down.[8]

Rumours were current in England, and inevitably reached Paris, that both the king's uncles had independently submitted plans to solve the problem of pursuing the war in France at no cost to the populace, and even without taxation. Gloucester appealed to the public with this plan, roughly estimated at some £50,000. But on examining it, the council turned it down, declaring it to be an impossible sum to raise, saying their commissioners could not collect much smaller amounts of money – even on the security of the crown jewels! When Gloucester was summoned to put his plan before parliament, no more was heard of it.

However, early in May, the Earl of Arundel[9] – whose cruelty no less than his success made him abhorrent to French patriots – recaptured Beaumont by assault, and he promptly hanged some of the robbers they took there. In this he was assisted by an English knight called Talbot. Together, they went on to besiege the castle of Creil where other bandits had taken refuge. But when it seemed the castle would not fall to them easily, they abandoned the attempt.[10]

In a meeting of the privy council on 14 June, Bedford set out the difficulties with which he had contended in France, pointing out how all things had prospered up to the unlucky siege of Orléans, 'taken in hand God knoweth by what advice'. He went on to urge the continued prosecution of the war, and he further offered to devote to it the whole of the revenues of his Norman estates.[11] He also proposed that the only item of royal revenue that was not covered by Cromwell's budget – the personal patrimony of the royal household, the Duchy of Lancaster – should be drawn upon for war expenses. (Henry V had, in fact, already arranged something similar before his death, 'in fulfilment of his will'.) This released a sum of £6,000 per annum, and Bedford suggested that it be used to provide 200 lances and 600 bowmen for duty in France.

On the 20th he took leave of the English council, exhorting them to observe the articles which he had proposed. It was not an entirely altruistic gesture, for as collateral he asked for certain castles in Medoc. But the council considered they had no right to alienate this property from the crown. They promised, however, that when the king had reached adulthood, he should be advised to reward his uncle for his exceptional services.

A few days later, the duke was recalled to France by a general uprising against the English garrisons in Normandy, although he was still at Gravesend on 6 July.[12] His return to France was financed by Beaufort, who furnished a loan of 10,000 marks for the 'safeguard of King Henry's realm of France', plus another 3,000 marks to provide Bedford's escort of only 100 lances and 300 bowmen, half the number the regent had called for. (The council, preferring to hang on to the Lancaster revenue, apparently could not find the money.) The whole sum was due to be repaid to Beaufort in 1434–5, and the cardinal attached stringent conditions to his loan, as he was still owed money for his coronation expenses in Paris. Among other provisos, 7,000 marks worth of crown jewels were among the securities he demanded, and it would appear that more than one third of the 1433 lay taxation was mortgaged to Beaufort in advance of payment.

During his stay in England, two embassies had arrived from Philippe of Burgundy, each time suggesting proposals for a peace treaty.[13] To the first Bedford had spoken of Philippe in conciliatory terms, but when the second embassy arrived – shortly before his own departure for France – the duke was not so accommodating. The embassy stated that Philippe desired King Henry either to agree to terms or to be more active in prosecuting the war. The council, no doubt acting on Bedford's advice, answered that the war was being carried on with vigour. This was very true, for a dangerous insurrection in Normandy was then in the course of being repressed by the Earl of Arundel.[14]

The Paris administration was insecure, and the chancellor revealed this when, on 17 May 1434, he wrote to Lord Cromwell, the Treasurer of England.[15] In his letter he described the great difficulty his governing body was experiencing in trying to maintain both the captaincies and the common soldiery of Paris and the outlying fortresses. It was creating even greater hardship for the people of Paris, and he himself had been forced to borrow money from an influential Genoese banker, Jean Sec. He asked Cromwell to ensure that this debt was repaid through Anferon Spinola, a Genoese merchant based in London.

In a warrant of 18 February, it had been agreed by the king's council in

London that funds for the defence of Paris should be sent to Louis of Luxembourg for a full year from 29 September 1434 to 1435. For the first time in a decade, it would seem that at last a regular issue of money would be paid to the army in the region of the French capital. Yet, by the time of the first warrant, the soldiers' wages were already in arrears. The limited cash for immediate use was diminishing even as expenditure increased.

On 28 June the municipality gave leave of absence to three of its officers who wished to go on a pilgrimage to Santiago de Compostela. They received permission only after swearing on holy relics that they would do nothing to assist King Henry's enemies while passing through the lands to the south. Although the pilgrimage was taken on personal grounds, they were also visiting the shrine in order to claim the saint's aid for the better ordering of affairs in Paris.[16]

Their prayers apparently went unanswered, for in July the Maître Hugues Rapiout was deposed from the merchant provostship, and two other aldermen were changed.

There was no news of either of the two regents. 'They might have been dead.'[17] The people were told constantly that they were coming very soon, 'now this one, now that'. Meanwhile the enemy came every day to plunder the outskirts of Paris, up to the city walls. No one, neither English knight nor Anglo–Burgundian lord, had the means to stop them. The great council was still sitting in Basle. No news came from them, either.

On 20 August the English in Normandy attacked the militia of some small towns, and killed at least 1,200 of them at St Sauveur-Dive. The Norman peasants had organised themselves to deal with the bandits who were then preying on them, having given up hope of receiving aid from the English command. Their attempts to come to grips with this new menace were countered by the bandits, one gang of which, headed by an Englishman, Richard Venables, ambushed and massacred some thirteen thousand peasants at St-Sauveur-Dive. When the bandits were in turn captured by an Anglo–Norman troop, Bedford had Venables and his second-in-command executed publicly at Rouen. The situation remained unchanged, however, for the bandits who had escaped from Bedford's men simply regrouped and again targeted the peasants. Local people were thus incited to rebellion, and they were then 'legitimately crushed'.[18]

In the late autumn, to the further consternation of the English, there was a surprising development when Duke Philippe concluded one of his local truces with Charles VII, and negotiations for a possible peace treaty appeared likely. With even the normally docile citizens of Normandy rising up against them, the Engish needed the Burgundians more than ever to maintain an increasingly fragile position.

On 7 October a terrible gale blew up. It began at two in the afternoon and it continued until between ten and eleven at night. In this space of time it demolished innumerable chimneys and even a few houses in Paris.

In the country it beat down walnut and apple trees 'past reckoning'. So fierce was this gale in the forest of Vincennes that in less than five hours it had flattened more than three hundred and sixty of the largest trees, 'their roots are all in the air', not counting hundreds of smaller trees that were 'not worth mentioning.'[19] The damage was colossal.

Wine grew very scarce and correspondingly dearer. None was drinkable at less than three *blancs*. There was very good wheat, though at St Andrew's Tide, in late November, it sold for 22s.p, and other grain was similarly cheap.

Bedford returned to Paris from Normandy on 18 December, bringing with him his young wife. Processions were organised to go out into the country to meet the couple. Mendicant friars and the representatives of parishes, 'vested and carrying crosses and censers, as one would do for God' formed the bulk of the column.[20] The children and choir of Notre Dame were at the St Denis gatehouse, and they sang 'very sweetly' as the duke's cavalcade entered the city. 'Deluded people' greeted the duke with a great show of respect, and the Bourgeois felt they had done him 'too much honour.'

Nothing more was said about the Norman militiamen who had been killed near St-Sauveur-Dive, except that they had possibly 'deserved it'. Some English aristocrats were certainly of the opinion that there had been good cause in killing them, for 'the rabble had tried to stop gentlemen going about their affairs'. That the 'gentlemen' had taken to banditry was a fact that was largely ignored.

The duke and duchess stayed in Paris to celebrate Christmas, although it was not kept with the same splendour as on former occasions. It was apparent to all that the English had lost control of the situation, although the English and Burgundian forces had gained much ground on the borders of Valois and Picardy, and Talbot, at the head of reinforcements from England, was successful in the county of Beauvais. On the other hand, the constable was on the edge of making peace with Charles VII, and Duke Philippe was being strongly pressed by the pope, the Holy Roman Emperor, and the council still sitting at Basle, to come to terms with the king. But by the end of the year, there was no news in Paris of the council at Basle. Not 'in sermons or in any other way. They might [as well] all have been at Jerusalem!'[21]

The weather was very mild until St Andrew's Day,[22] when it began to freeze until the ground was iron-hard.

NOTES

1 Bourgeois de Paris.
2 Ibid.
3 Wolffe, *Henry VI*.
4 Bourgeois de Paris.
5 Ibid.
6 Ibid.
7 Wolffe, op. cit., quoting PPC.
8 Ibid.
9 Bourgeois de Paris. John Fitzalan, Earl of Arundel (1408–35).
10 He did, however, conduct a fairly successful campaign in Maine and Anjou, even extending his operations to the Loire. Burne, *The Agincourt War*.
11 Wolffe, op. cit., quoting PPC.
12 Ibid.
13 Williams, *My Lord of Bedford*.
14 Louis of Luxembourg.
15 Public Record Office.
16 Bourgeois de Paris.
17 Ibid.
18 Ibid. The Bourgeois thought that nothing was done about this atrocity, though by this time he was too accustomed to such horrors to raise anything but a feeble protest.
19 Ibid.
20 Ibid.
21 Ibid.
22 30 November.

CHAPTER XVI
1435: Betrayal

In mid-August 1433, over lunch in a tavern, a number of drunken diners had come to the conclusion that matters would never improve in France until there was a 'peaceful king'. By 1435 this opinion had been incorporated into a fifteen-verse poem, 'A complaint on the Miseries of Paris', in which it was said that such miseries could not be ended without the 'blessing of peace'.[1]

Others were thinking along the same lines. Duke Philippe met the chief ministers of Charles VII at Nevers in January 1435. In the next month the preliminaries for a peace treaty were signed. But Philippe made it clear to the French that this peace was not to be regarded as an offensive alliance against the English. And because the duke still felt that he could not ratify any proper terms without the consent of his ally, the English were invited to be present at the second meeting between the Valois and Burgundian governments.

It was arranged that the peace conference should take place in Arras in July. The English consented to appear, although they did so without any enthusiasm. It seemed to them to be the worst time to treat for peace, because although they themselves were weary, the French seemed to be at the end of their strength.[2] It was felt that with a little more perseverance the long wars of attrition could be finally brought to an end, and to the English advantage. But the alliance with Burgundy must be retained at all costs, and so it was as much to humour Philippe as for any other reason that Bedford consented to allow his emissaries to attend the conference within the appointed time.

The frost lasted for almost the first quarter of the year, 'less nine days'. There were no periods of thaw, and it snowed for well over forty days without cease. It was decided that the streets should be cleared and the snow shovelled into carts, to be dumped in the Place de Grève, where no other activity could take place because of the severity of the weather. But as fast as the householders cleared their allotted patches, they were blocked up again. Snow was piled up 'like haycocks' in the middle of the streets from one end of Paris to the other. The ice did not begin to melt until the Annunciation of Our Lady in March, a week from the end of the month.[3]

The Bedfords left Paris on 10 February, the duke in bad humour, for he had been forced to assent to the attendance of English ambassadors at the new congress to be held in Arras. This conference of sovereign states would once again attempt to find a solution to the ending of the war.

Wine continued to be scarce, and even the thinnest went for three *blancs* a quart, and even then it could only be obtained through the black market. As a consequence of this, beer was so heavily taxed that it, too, was beyond the pocket of most drinkers. Every person who sold beer was forced by law to pay seven *blancs* every week over and above the fourth and the impost. Fruit also became very expensive, good largish Capendu apples selling for 16s.p a hundred.

It froze again at the end of March, and there was not a day without rime until after Easter, which fell on 17 April. All the low-lying vines were frozen in the Marais along with all the trellised *bourdelays* (a vine for producing verjuice) in the little market gardens. All the fig trees and the laurels, large and small, died, as did the beautiful pine tree at the abbey of St Victor, a famous centre of learning outside the city walls on the south bank of the Seine. It was considered to be the loveliest tree in France. Most of the cherry trees, too, were affected because of the intense cold. More than one hundred and forty birds were found dead, having sheltered together for warmth in a hollow tree. The almond trees bore hardly any bloom.

The Duke of Burgundy finally arrived on Maundy Thursday, 14 April, 'when they sell salt pork'. He brought with him a dazzling company of lords and ladies, along with his duchess and a 'fine son'.[4] He also brought with him three very good-looking youngsters, his bastards, and a beautiful little girl, who was also his and not born in marriage. The oldest of these children was not more than 10.

Philippe also brought with him three heavy wagons covered with cloth of gold and silver, and a litter for his legitimate son. (The others could ride extremely well.) There were at least one hundred wagons to carry supplies for himself and his people, as well as twenty carts. These were loaded with arms, artillery, salt meat, salt fish, cheese and Burgundy wine. He was 'equipped for everything one could or should have for peace or war'.[5] He also brought a great number of tents in case his company was forced to camp out in open country, although the inclement weather had largely dissuaded them from doing so. Each waggoner was paid 40s.p daily, and each carter received two *francs*.

The duke's company kept Easter in Paris, and he held a plenary court that was open to all comers. On the day after the festival, the doctors of the university spoke to him on the subject of peace, and on the Tuesday the duke had obsequies celebrated for his late sister, the Duchess of Bedford. It matched that of her husband in every way, with Philippe making a rich offering of money and lights, with every priest who cared to attend holding a separate mass.

On the Wednesday women of noble birth or citizen rank went before the Duchess of Burgundy and begged her 'very movingly' to take the matter of the kingdom's peace under her own protection. She answered them kindly, 'My dear friends, it is one of the things I most long for in this world, and that I beg my lord both night and day, because I see how greatly it is needed. And I know for certain that my lord is more than willing to risk both his goods and his body for it.'[6] The ladies thanked her and took their leave. On the following day the duke's party left Paris, in order to attend the conference at Arras, although this was not due to take place until 1 July.

While he was at Rouen, in the first week of May, the Duke of Bedford heard that some French companies had seized Rhue and were desolating Ponthieu and Artois. He ordered the Earl of Arundel to march from Mantes to Ponthieu, but the earl was defeated and captured by Armagnacs before Gerberoy. Most of his men were killed, and he himself was wounded. The Armagnacs had trapped his men between an attack from the castle and another, made unexpectedly and simultaneously by La Hire and Xantrailles, from outside. (La Hire had been exchanged for Lord Talbot, as each man was considered the equal of the other.) Arundel and a remnant of his vanguard had taken up a defensive point, protected by hedges and stakes, but cannon were brought from the castle, which finished them off. Arundel's ankle was shattered by a shot from a culverin, and his foot was later amputated. But despite this, or perhaps because of the shock involved in its removal, he died soon afterwards.[7]

With Arundel dead, a still more notable commander was on hand to step into his shoes, for tremendous efforts had been made in England to raise the enormous ransom demanded for the release of Lord Talbot. When the English captured Xantrailles it could not have come at a more opportune moment, and all question of a ransom was dropped on either side, with an exchange between these two important warriors quickly arranged. Talbot swiftly replaced the dead earl.

In the spring of 1435 he was given only eight hundred men, yet he soon made his presence felt. He carried out extensive operations in the area north of Paris, in which he recaptured many important towns, some of which abjectly surrendered on the mere news that the great 'and terrible' Talbot was approaching. Gisors on the eastern border of Normandy soon fell, and Creil, Clermont and Crépy in the Oise watershed followed in turn.[8]

Philippe of Burgundy, too, was also having successes within his own borders to the south, and throughout this time the French reaction was distinctly and increasingly weak. The Maid of Orléans might never have lived. Charles VII had not the financial means to raise a field army with which to attack the allies, and his cause – once again – was in a poor way.[9]

Despite this, on 13 May the Duke of Burgundy wrote to the Parisians, telling them of his plans for a general peace, in which he would arbitrate between the warring parties. By 27 May Brother Jerome, an Austin friar, was sent to London with various letters relating to this matter. The Parisians, delighted at the prospect of a cessation of hostilities, sent an envoy to stress their support for Philippe's policy. The English council, in response to this enthusiasm, wrote to Paris and adjacent towns, asking them to send representatives to the forthcoming peace conference at Arras, but reminding the citizens to remain on guard against the Armagnacs. The council promised that if the negotiations at Arras came to nothing, a powerful army would be sent for their defence.[10] To the Parisians, this was a mixed blessing, as they would undoubtedly be charged for the upkeep of this protective force.[11]

Yet throughout the area of the war all outward appearance of law and order was swiftly vanishing, and brigandage, reminiscent of the Free Companies of the previous century, was springing up, so that it became increasingly difficult to get food into Paris. The citizens sent a despairing appeal to London for reinforcements, at least, with which to drive the enemy from their gates. For in the small hours of the night between the last day of May and the first day of June, the Armagnacs had retaken St Denis, and Paris was now blockaded on all sides.

The citizens were also aware that their physical defences were no longer as sound as they had been, particularly in the area of Ste Geneviève on the left bank, as the church was built at the top of the hill, which rose above the outside wall. There was a similar problem on the right bank, where a rubbish tip, some 500 years old, and therefore overtopping the wall, commanded the fortifications of Charles V. The village of Montmartre, on its hill, also formed an observation post for the enemy (it would do so until the 19th century), but it was too far away to be any real danger in the medieval period. But closer in, the city was overlooked by gentle slopes to the east that could give an advantage to the enemy, the present day heights of Belleville. In the west, the Champs-Elysées – then indeed Elysian pasturage – was another dangerous area, rising rapidly from the flat terrain of the city proper.

The city itself remained impregnable, but no one could enter or leave without risking their lives. Women and girls were taken by force from the villages in the countryside around the capital, and for want of manpower the fields lay untouched. To emphasise their hold upon the city, the Armagnacs cut all the corn around Paris and sent it to be milled for their own use. Not for the first time, the citizens were faced with famine.

As before, the Armagnacs cut the throats of all the men they captured, of whatever class, and they left their bodies lying in the middle of the road, a feast for flies and rodents. Women, too, once they had served the men's lusts, were treated as callously.

Hearing that the Parisians were now in the greatest alarm, the Duke of Bedford despatched a force sufficient to clear the neighbourhood of the French marauders, but they did not arrive in Paris until towards the end of August. They were under the command of the Lords Willoughby, Scales and Stafford. Stafford's nephew, the Bastard of St Pol, was also of the company along with minor peers.[12] This nephew could have been one of a great tribe, for Stafford's wife, Anne Neville, was one of twenty-three children. Robert, Lord Willoughby, who had had a long and active career in France, was eventually put in sole command of Paris.

From the start of the peace conference at Arras, negotiations were protracted and the bargains to be struck were multifold. Not even the presence of the pope's legate, Cardinal Albergati, who presided throughout, could keep the representatives in line, and at times it seemed that this peace conference was merely a continuation of the war between four walls.

Indeed, the proceedings had hardly commenced before they were interrupted by an occurrence that could well have wrecked the entire event before it was fully under way. The French generals La Hire and Xantrailles chose this critical moment to make a raid into Burgundian territory. This disturbing news reached Arras, only thirty miles north of where the French were plundering the area, even as Duke Philippe was entertaining King Charles's envoys. The duke instantly turned out a force, to which the English and even some Valois knights attached themselves, to repel these 'disturbers of the peace'.[13] Any real fighting was avoided, however (much to the chagrin of the English) and the raiders were allowed to return to their own territory, minus their booty. The others returned to Arras, and the peace conference then proceeded.

Each side then opened up with proposals that were widely divided. But the wily cardinal gradually whittled down their national differences, with concessions of territory being made by all sides, but especially by the French party. It soon, however, became apparent that negotiations would split irrevocably on the question of King Henry's right to the French throne. To the French, the English king's title had been pre-empted by their master's coronation in the sacred cathedral of Rheims. But the English envoys were equally adamant in their condemnation of this ceremony, stating baldly that Charles VII had been crowned by the intervention of a witch, since acknowledged as such, who had been publicly burned after a rigorous trial conducted by the highest representatives of the church.

The Duke of Burgundy now found himself to be the chief mediator between these two opposing forces, and he exhausted all his powers of persuasion on the issue. Cardinal Beaufort, the leading English delegate, became so worked up on the question that the 'sweat ran down his face.'[14]

Nothing could convince the English that the true king had been crowned at Rheims, and negotiations were soon heading for a stalemate.

In the last week of August, the English attacked the Armagnacs at St Denis, and they took from them control of the Croult river. But their coming was hardly a relief for the villagers in the area, as in order to build huts for themselves, the soldiers took material from all the houses in St Ouen, Aubervilliers and La Chapelle. They did this so ruthlessly that little was left to the unfortunate householders – no doors, windows or ironwork, in fact nothing that could be moved.[15]

The Armagnacs had already cut the corn around Paris, but the English went on to ravage the fields. After they had set up camp, all vegetables were taken for their use. There were still crops standing, but the English wreaked havoc on them. They even cut down vines, with grapes still on them, and used them to thatch their huts. When they had made themselves comfortable, they began to casually loot the villages they had left untouched.

The Armagnacs, seeing that they were now surrounded, made frequent sorties, attacking and killing as many of the English as they could, and they also killed from inside the town using both large and small guns, especially the 'little long guns' known as 'snakes'. A wound from one of these was always fatal.

But the English and Burgundians, under their leaders Talbot and L'Isle Adam, carried out many successful operations in the area around Paris, retaking many minor strongholds that had fallen into French hands, and which invariably sheltered brigands and freebooters.

The day after Our Lady's Nativity (8 September), an army of six thousand Englishmen mounted an assault upon St Denis, the attack conducted with all the old vigour shown throughout decades of fighting.[16] There was a heavy bombardment of the walls, followed by an assault with scaling ladders, with the troops being forced to wade breast-high through the moat.

But the attempt was repulsed, with the defenders fighting back fiercely, and killing many of the raiders, including some important knights. Fastolf's nephew, Sir Robert Harling, fell during this attack and his body was afterwards cut up and boiled in a cauldron at the St Nicolas cemetery until the flesh came away from his bones. These were then carefully cleaned and packed into a chest, to be taken for burial in his ancestral lands in England. His flesh and entrails were buried in a large grave at the French cemetery.

That August remained very fine. The corn was good and plentiful away from the wasted fields around Paris. Because the English were now present in that area, the marauders stayed away and so flour began to reappear in the city's markets. The mulberries did not bear, but peaches were more plentiful than ever. Good ones sold for only 2d to the hundred. Besides a lack of mulberries, though, there were no almonds.

The conference was still in session at Arras, but no news of it reached Paris. Had it done so, there would have been little to cheer the citizens. The English were clinging obstinately to unrealistic demands, refusing to give up Paris or to renounce King Henry's claim to the French throne. On 31 August the English ambassadors declared themselves unable to assent to the French conditions, and on 6 September they withdrew from Arras, walking out on the negotiations.

The French delegates were so alarmed by this departure they sent messengers after the English envoys with a startling new proposal. This suggestion was extraordinary in its implications, as the French seemed to be denying their sovereign's claim to his throne. For the proposal was that King Henry should renounce his title until he came of age, at which time he could reassert his claim. This would, of course, have meant a new outbreak of hostilities, for Charles VII would not willingly renounce a throne he had occupied for four years, and neither would he deny his heirs their royal inheritance. But a postponement would, of course, allow the French to regroup and greatly strengthen their military power.

The English government summarily rejected this desperate compromise. Feeling in London ran high against such an accommodation, with the mob attacking French settlers. The unfortunate messenger who brought this unwelcome message was lucky to escape with his life.[17] The Lord Chancellor answered for the English: 'The King of England and France, my master, has seen the letters and offers that you have brought to him, which have much displeased him, and not without reason. For which thing he has assembled those of his blood and lineage for advice on the subject. And you can now return across the sea.'[18]

The advice given to the young king, now growing up to be a gentle and saintly scholar, was a continuation of the war by any means. He was the son of Henry V, who had been promised the French crown in perpetuity for his heirs. The English military still believed that they were destined to be the true masters in France. Thereupon Duke Philippe abandoned his former allies and made a separate and highly profitable peace with King Charles VII, unilaterally breaking his alliance, sworn at the Treaty of Troyes.[19]

With Burgundy now a declared enemy of the English presence in France, Bedford saw that the cause for which he struggled so long faced ruin. Without the aid of the Burgundians, the dual monarchy had no future, and its demise was imminent. But the duke, already a sick man, was spared the pain of seeing this, for he himself died at Rouen on 14 September, Holy Cross Day. He had last taken up arms only a week before at the siege of St Denis, but now, broken in health and spirit he literally turned his face to the wall and breathed his last.[20]

Having spent most of his adult life in the conquest of Normandy, it was thought proper that he should be buried in its chief city, Rouen. He was given a princely funeral as befitted his great station, and he was 'honourably' buried in the choir of the cathedral church of Notre Dame. He left no children by either of his wives. By his will, made four days before his death, he left all his possessions to his wife except one castle, which was to go to his bastard son. His nephew, King Henry, was to have all in remainder.

This 'splendid English prince' was a man much in advance of his age. Even his enemies conceded that – however mistakenly on occasion – he had nursed far-seeing projects for the unification and betterment of the two kingdoms. The Bourgeois of Paris, who had criticised him often in the privacy of his journals, described him as 'noble in birth and worth: wise, liberal, feared and loved.' He was remembered by at least one Parisian as being quite unlike his fellow Englishmen, 'for he was always building, and never wanted to make war on any one'.

Above all the men of his time, Bedford was conspicuous for his fidelity and unselfishness, and he stands in marked contrast to his brother, the Duke of Gloucester, in that he rarely allowed his own interests to hinder the performance of his duty. Bedford's motto '*A vous entière*', expresses the character of his life. He had supported a long and disheartening conflict with great courage, and at times had shown real flair. The ultimate failure of the cause to which he devoted himself, and which he must have accepted in his final hours, was due to no fault of his, although he had made many mistakes.[21]

Humphrey, the Duke of Gloucester, took his place as the heir to the throne of England. He immediately proclaimed it to be his duty to carry on the struggle for the throne of France, and this view was popular, for it was easy to persuade the English at home that the failure in France had been due to mismanagement and treachery. His policy also appealed to those who had profited from the war, either by adding to their reputation or else by gaining from it financially, and so money was found to continue hostilities.

For a time, events in France tended to work in Gloucester's favour, for the English had some minor successes. At the beginning of September L'Isle Adam was hard at work on the siege of St Denis, although when, on the 20th, the peace of Arras was sealed, the English could no longer count on the services of the 'Marshal of France'. On the contrary, having explained his position to members of the Duke of Burgundy's Chivalric Order of the Golden Fleece, he returned to Philippe's service.[22]

The Armagnacs at St Denis, however, agreed to a truce – 'at discretion' – on 24 September, having despaired of being relieved by their, as ever, procrastinating comrades. It was true that on that same night some men of

188

their party captured the bridge at Meulan, so that negotiations that were supposed to have begun at St Denis were thrown into disarray, yet it was concluded that agreement had to be reached, and some concessions made. The Armagnacs were told that they could depart with everything that they could personally carry away, without let or hindrance. Having agreed to this, they went out of the town on 4 October. Although defeated, the Armagnacs still managed to jeer at the English, asking to be remembered to the kings who were interred in the abbey. More sincerely, they asked the English to pay tribute to their comrades who had met an honourable death and were also buried there.[23]

There were some 15,000 Armagnacs, 'well clad and mounted'. About four hundred had been killed in skirmishes and assaults, but the reason for their submission was not lack of troops, but an acute shortage of fresh water as their river had been captured. They also lacked wine and salt and, as they had brought no doctors with them, many of their wounded had died for lack of attention. But for these factors they would not have surrendered so 'cheaply'.

St Denis was one thing, Paris was another. When the bridge at Meulan fell into enemy hands, all prices in Paris had risen except that of wine. Corn went from 20s p to two francs. Cheese, butter, oil and bread were dearer by a third to a half. Meat, too, was hard to come by, and lard sold for four *blancs* a pint.

Two days after the Armagnacs had abandoned St Denis, they were galloping up to the walls of the city, pillaging and looting with all their old savagery. The Parisians were once again confined to their streets, for few dared to venture out of the gates. They could not rely upon the English to come to their defence, for they were also busily pillaging and looting, sacking St Denis and leaving nothing behind that could be moved. Then, when the English had stolen all they could, they had the gates and walls knocked down, making St Denis an open town.

They were inexplicably encouraged in this by the Bishop of Therouanne, the chancellor. Every single week, for as long as the siege had lasted, he had spent one or two nights with the army, having had a little fortress made for him in the Ile St Denis, protected all round by very broad and deep trenches.[24]

Queen Isabeau died in the Hôtel St Pol on Saturday 24 September. For three days all who wanted to could go to see her grossly deformed body lying in state, after which it was laid out in her bedroom, where it remained neglected, as that of her dead husband's had been. It was then taken to Notre Dame on 14 October at four in the afternoon. Fourteen bellmen and one hundred torches accompanied it. No women of great rank were present except for the Duchess of Brabant, 'the lady of Bavaria', who was the queen's niece, and she alone followed the body on its last journey.[25]

Sixteen men, attired in black, were required to bear the overweight coffin on their shoulders. As was usual, an effigy of the queen was carried above her body, and it was generally considered to be very realistic, looking 'as if she slept'. It carried the royal sceptre in her right hand.

Vigils were said for her very solemnly at the great cathedral. The Abbot of Ste Geneviève officiated, and the Processions of Paris attended. On the day after the mass was said for her, the body was put aboard a boat on the Seine, and then taken by water to be buried at St Denis-en-France. It was not thought safe to carry her overland because the Armagnacs were still roaming the countryside. The late queen had been an object of great hatred to them, and it was possible that had her corpse fallen into their hands, it might have been violated in the same way that the Armagnacs treated all their dead enemies. No word of mourning came from her son in his capital of Bourges.

The city administration was worried that the defection of the Duke of Burgundy would influence his men still present in Paris. As the English were still at war with Charles VII, it was open to their Burgundian supporters who remained faithful to their cause to maintain their old hostilities to the Armagnacs, despite the fact that their master had finally shown his hand. When Jean de Rinel, the most high-ranking anglophile among the royal secretaries, returned from the conference at Arras, he produced some letters of Charles VI, dated 23 September 1420, whereby the murderers of Duke John the Fearless were held guilty of *lèse-majesté*. In an effort to set the Burgundians in Paris against their duke, he registered these letters at *parlement* on 14 October, the day on which the queen's body was ceremoniously taken to lie in state at Notre Dame. It was remembered by many that she and the murdered duke had once ruled Paris, and to the city's benefit.

The Provost of Paris, Simon Morhier, issued a *vidimus* of these letters, so that they could be brought to the public notice. It was hoped that because the Burgundian faction in Paris were already well used to the lengthy absences of their duke, they would also continue to serve the citizens regardless of his new policies.

But this was not to be, nor could it have been possible. The last collaboration between the English and their Burgundian allies was at the siege of St Denis. A few weeks later these same Burgundian troops were to be found fighting on the side of the Valois. Philippe had, in all conscience, offered to remain neutral after the signing of the Treaty of Arras, but the English, infuriated with the 'false, forsworn Duke', contemptuously rejected his offer. Henry VI would never forgive his 'good uncle', whose treachery still rankled after twenty years.[26]

190

From this time onward they bravely set about the formidable task of opposing both their old enemies and their former allies, but theirs was a lost cause. The defection of the Burgundians dealt a deathblow to English ambitions. Even Cardinal Beaufort was converted to the wise but unpopular view that England must at last come to terms with France. His nephews John and Edmund Beaufort, and also William de la Pole, the Earl of Suffolk, supported him in this view. Most of the royal household officials were on the same side, for they saw the administrative difficulties in continuing the struggle in France. Greatly aided by the young king's inherently peaceful nature, they helped to influence him to the same view.

The situation in Paris grew ever more precarious. The city was more isolated than ever as supplies grew daily more erratic when the new military successes of the French cut off the major commercial roads. The Seine, once the most vital mercantile artery, was now irretrievably clogged as the Armagnacs mobilised their troops along its banks and tributaries, effectively denying commercial lifeblood to the aorta of Paris. Supplies from Normandy were almost completely cut off.[27]

The mood of despondency was so intense that when the city's councillors met on 8 November, to decide upon whether or not to open the next session of the council on the 12th of the month as usual, there was a motion against it. Even so, older counsel prevailed, and it was decided that the session should be convened, despite the external upheavals and the internal difficulties within the city. Notwithstanding this decision some members refused to appear, and a number actually took the opportunity to leave the city. (Clément de Fauquembergue, a clerk of the court, who had admittedly never been a committed Lancastrian supporter, went off to visit his family in northern France and did not return.) Even the chancellor, Louis of Luxembourg, was not present at the opening of *parlement*.[28]

But the councillors who did attend decided that their duty still lay with the English, and this was an unfortunate resolution. Their great protector Bedford was dead, and the chancellor was making extended visits to Normandy, leaving a considerable gap in the leadership of Paris. As the weeks passed this breach was seen as being even more menacing. Branlart, a councillor at the *Chambre des Enquêtes*, reported considerable popular unrest among the populace arising from the perceived dangers to the city and the manifest inability of the authorities to act in their defence. Branlart used very strong language in his dispatch (which was considerably watered down for the final report).[29]

On 10 November it was decided that a full assembly of notables should be held soon. But the growing threat to the citizens was made apparent the very next day when news came that the bridge at Charenton, less then four miles from the centre of Paris, had been captured by the Armagnacs. At the first of the two large meetings held on the 12th, there was plenty to discuss, and the discussions were held amid a mounting sense of panic. Conspicuously, Lord Willoughby was the only Englishman present at these meetings.

A decision was made for new measures to be taken to guard against incursions along the river, and – calling upon God to preserve them – it was arranged for the parishes to take part in religious processions. This, it was thought, would boost the flagging morale of the citizens. It was also decided to send more letters to the King of England, begging for a new relief force. Letters were also sent to the Chancellor of Normandy and to the Duke of Burgundy, along with those of his councillors who were judged most likely to be sympathetic to the plight of the Parisians.

Paris, then, at the end of 1435, was truly isolated. She was, however, not forgotten, although there was a considerable delay on the part of the English in sending aid. Louis Galet and his fellow ambassadors were paid at Westminster on 16 December for their mission to England, in which the fears of the Parisians were fully reported. Accounts of 'troubles, piteous and lamentable' were also related by Morice and Jan Perier, envoys from Rouen, and these prompted King Henry and his council to write to his French subjects, promising a great army in the new year.

But this promise would be fulfilled too slowly and inadequately. Some weeks were to pass before Sir Thomas Beaumont and between six and eight hundred men were ready for embarkation as the first part of a new task force, a 'grand army'. In the coming months, the French ambassadors were forced to complain repeatedly that only six ships had been assembled, which was clearly not enough to transport an army of the size required to face the rumoured forces of King Charles VII. The English army was, in case, reported to be disbanding even as it mobilised.

NOTES

1 Longnon, *Documents parisiens*.
2 Perroy, *The Hundred Years War*.
3 Bourgeois de Paris
4 This son, Charles, was born in 1433. The duke's earlier, legitimate sons had died in infancy.
5 Bourgeois de Paris.
6 Ibid.
7 Burne, *The Agincourt War*.
8 Ibid.
9 'The Valois kingdom was not merely out of breath, it was at the end of its strength.' Burne, op. cit., quoting Perroy.
10 British Library, *Cotton Caligula*. Cited by Thomson in *Paris and its People*.
11 This letter was received in Paris on 25 June. General processions were ordered 'to thank God for the good intentions of the [English] king'. *Archives Nationales*.
12 Ibid.

13 Monstrelet, *Chronique*.
14 Ibid.
15 Bourgeois de Paris.
16 Ibid.
17 The man was Le Fèvre, a famous chronicler of the time, who was present at many of the events he described. Burne, op. cit.
18 Ferguson, *English Diplomacy*.
19 Bourgeois de Paris.
20 *Dictionary of National Biography*.
21 Vale, *War and Chivalry*.
22 Bourgeois de Paris.
23 Ibid.
24 Ibid.
25 Ibid.
26 Monstrelet, op. cit. Philippe's first wife had been Henry's mother's sister.
27 *Archives Nationales*.
28 Fauquembergue, *Journal*.
29 *Archives Nationales*. Chamollion-Figeac, *Lettres des rois*.

CHAPTER XVII

1436: Closing Stages

The military situation did not deteriorate greatly throughout January 1436, but the regime in Paris was almost bankrupt, and assistance from England had virtually ceased by the end of 1435. On 10 February Jacques du Châtillier, the Bishop of Paris, who was the highest-ranking man in the council during the absence of the chancellor, lent the city two hundred gold *saluts*. For this considerable loan he was to be given a handsome security in the shape of a richly ornamented gold representation of the Trinity, which would be handed over to him by the *Changeur du Trésor* if it were beyond the council to repay him.[1]

In that same month, fresh discontent broke out in Paris in a new and unexpected way. Guillaume de la Haye, a knight who had been captured on an earlier exploit in Champagne, had since been transferred – after prolonged litigation – from the secure confinement of the Bastille to the less restricted royal prison of the Concièrgerie. Here he was at liberty to speak with anyone who wished to see him and who could bribe the warders for that purpose, and from his cell de la Haye was actively encouraging support not only for his release but also for the recognition of Charles VII.

On 11 February a report reached *parlement* that certain 'people of low standing' wanted to go and fetch him out of the prison in order to make him their 'chief and captain'.[2] The authorities acted promptly, putting the agitator into solitary confinement, but this threat had scarcely been countered before they were faced with another coup. A Scotsman, who had infiltrated the guard at the castle of Vincennes, had secretly admitted Armagnac troops into an essential outpost of security, which the enemy had swiftly overcome. (In this, the Scotsman seems to have been aided by the Abbess of St Anthoine-des-Champs.)[3] It was becoming apparent that isolated units of the Armagnac forces were steadily gaining control of the city's outer defences.

The French, in fact, now having only one enemy to engage with, were encouraged to make war more determinedly than ever. They entered Normandy in some force and captured some of its best seaports. Montvilliers, Dieppe, Honfleur surrendered to them, along with a number of 'good towns and castelries'.[4] Their army was then emboldened to draw nearer Paris, and they took Corbeil, Blois de Vincennes, Beauté, Pontoise and St Germain-en-Laye, along with other towns and castles that were almost as important. The French armies thus effectively encircled the city, and no goods could come into Paris from any direction 'neither upstream nor downstream'[5] without their permission, and this was grudgingly given.

Louis of Luxembourg returned from Normandy in March, and a final effort was made to restore order. The chancellor made no attempt to disguise the problems that were facing them – it would have been impossible in any case – and he addressed a public assembly of leading officers and citizens on 15 March. At this meeting he announced that anyone who wished to leave the city would be allowed to depart, but those who elected to stay must once again renew their oath of loyalty to King Henry, 'on pain of their soul's damnation'.[6] This oath did not exclude priests or the religious orders, and anyone who refused to take it would lose all their possessions, be banished, 'or worse'.

The next day he extended the Grand Conseil, which included Lord Willoughby, the Captain of the Bastille and the Bishops of Paris and Lisieux[7]. (It also included Jean le Clerk, a former chancellor, and Jean de Courcelles, who had formally replaced L'Isle Adam as Captain of the Louvre on 17 March. Others present were Gilles de Clamécy, the heads of the department of the exchequer, the provost marshal, the Provost of Merchants, all the aldermen, and other dignitaries responsible for the issuing of ordnance or maintaining loyalty in the capital.)

It was ordered that any appearance of the enemy before the city walls should be ignored, except by the guards, and that Parisians should go about their business as usual. Finally, instructions were issued forbidding ordinary citizens and the common soldiery from going on to the walls, except under the orders of the captains (for the soldiers) or the municipality (for the civilian watch).

The council was particularly anxious about the buildings that were seen to be vulnerable to enemy attack. On 20 March special orders were given to the chapter of Notre Dame, and those canons whose houses opened on to the river that they should have their doors sealed.[8]

By the end of March it was realised that it was impossible to repay Jacques du Châtillier, and the authorities were forced to seek help from another prominent member of the council, Jean Jamés, the city's Master of the Works. He lent them a considerable sum in *francs*, and his security was even more extravagant than Châtillier's: a gilded image of the Mary Magdalen, two cups and five jewelled goblets, and a gold salt-cellar ornamented with stones and pearls.[9] All these treasures were to be returned if he was repaid within two months, otherwise they could be sold. As with the earlier loan there was little chance of them being redeemed, and there was every possibility that the regime would have collapsed by then. In April Christopher des Moulins made a further loan to the hard-pressed *Changeur du Trésor*, for which he received a silver ewer and an ornate statue of the Virgin in a gold casket, to be redeemed within a month.[10]

Not only the prospect of receiving money from England was out of the question, it was also impossible to get advice from the government in London. On 15 March Gervaise le Vulre, a royal secretary, travelled secretly from Paris in order to get a positive answer from the English council. He spent two fruitless months applying to the government, and Jacot le Hern, a domestic servant of Louis of Luxembourg, who arrived in London at Easter, was equally unsuccessful. Such response as both men did obtain was, in any case, too late to have any serious effect. It was increasingly obvious that despite the most strenuous efforts of the council and its financial officers, Paris could no longer be effectively defended. A concerted attack by the Armagnacs would leave the city wide open to a full invasion.

John Talbot, the commander of the English forces in the area between the Seine, the Somme and the sea, undoubtedly realised this in the winter of 1435/36, when he moved his command from Paris, where he had been the captain of the Bastille. He removed his troops to Rouen, settling them in by 5 January. Pontoise, its garrison weakened by Talbot's defection, was lost around 20 February. It was said that the Parisians sent a deputation to Pontoise, before its fall, to ask Lord Willoughby to return to Paris and take command there.[11]

Whether this is true or not, Willoughby certainly returned to Paris, where he was left to bear the brunt of the inevitable assault, although Talbot did leave behind a portion of his mobile retinue, to be used as Lord Willoughby thought fit.[12] Talbot and Willoughby had a personal escort of twenty men-at-arms and sixty archers.[13] Talbot also had an additional retinue of twenty mounted men-at-arms and another sixty archers. Of these, he left nine lances and twelve archers 'for the safekeeping, as agreed, with those of the highest rank in Paris', keeping the rest 'around our person.' A muster was taken in Paris on 8 February, and another muster was taken in Rouen on the 29th. The Parisian muster reveals that Willoughby had about fifteen thousand men with him at the end, and although he played his part in council meetings, it was obvious that he was now powerless to put up any strong resistance to the strengthening legions of the French king's forces.

Both the French and the Burgundians were now anxious to see an end of the English regime in the capital. Early in March Charles VII sent the Constable de Richemont from Poitiers to the Paris region. First though, he ensured that Duke Philippe was firmly on his side. Since the previous

December the duke had been engaged in negotiations that were so secret their purpose could not even be committed to his account book.[14] In particular there was the secret journey of Jean de Belloy, a former alderman in Paris, L'Isle Adam and the Franche-Comté Herald, in February to March of 1436. Philippe was certainly planning to provoke the fall of Paris, but he continued to maintain his contacts with the regime there.[15] It was only from the middle of March that decisive moves were finally made. This followed the final effort at a conciliation involving the brothers Jean and Louis of Luxembourg, whose dual cooperation was considered utterly necessary for victory.

From 18 March Philippe de Ternant was in command of a body of troops to be used solely for the reduction of the capital.[16] Within a few days he was joined by L'Isle Adam, who brought with him another force supplied by the Duke of Burgundy. At Pontoise, on 3 April, they met up with Richemont, who had transferred his force from Corbeil by way of Lagny-sur-Marne, summoning troops from French garrisons in Champagne and Brie as he rode on.[17] All of these massed troops made camp around Pontoise.

The period of Lent in this year was a particularly rigorous time of fasting and penance, for all the Lenten fare was very expensive, and food got no cheaper as the forty days from Ash Wednesday advanced. By Easter, pickled herring was selling for fourteen *francs*, and corn fetched four *francs*, whereas it had been only 20s.p for the best quality at Candlemas. The returns on wages were so poor that many a woman who had earned six *blancs* a day was forced to give her body in prostitution, and was glad to be given two *blancs* for the sacrifice. 'They learned to live upon it, too.'[18]

On the Friday of the third week of Lent, the English troops were sent to all the villages in the area of Pontoise, where they were ordered to set fire to corn and oats, and to destroy any vegetables stored within the houses. Apart from this act of official terrorism, acting of their own free will, they stole everything they could find, and took prisoners for ransom, in the manner of the Armagnacs. Trustworthy reports in Paris stated that good corn, ready for milling had been burned, in amounts enough to feed six thousand people for half a year. This when neither corn nor flour could be brought into the city.[19]

What was most remarkable about the continuation of the 'wicked, devilish' war was that it was prolonged by the will of only three men, and they not great soldiers but men of the cloth, all three of them bishops. Therouanne, the chancellor, 'a very cruel man'; the Bishop of Lisieux, formerly of Beauvais; and the Bishop of Paris – all of them unshakeable supporters of the English party. 'No doubt it was through their madness that many people were pitilessly killed, secretly and openly, by drowning and other means, not counting those who died without honour in battle.'[20]

As food-stocks decreased, new measures were introduced to ration provisions. A tally was ordered, and in the week before Palm Sunday officials were sent all over Paris to make a reckoning of how much corn or flour, oats, beans and peas the householders stored in their larders.

On top of this, the supply of fish ran out two weeks before Easter, and onions became scarce. Since nothing could even be *smuggled* into the city, the Parisians now ran the very real risk of being starved into submission. Because it now seemed inevitable that the French would break into Paris and it would be therefore necessary to identify friend from foe, the bishops compelled everyone to wear a cross of red linen pinned to their clothing, on pain of death and loss of goods. The rulers all wore broad white sashes that were covered with small crosses of red.

Wearing such a distinctive battle dress was a long practice that had military origins. The French troops had always worn an upright white cross on their clothing, for identification in battle, while the English had favoured a cross of red. From 1411 the Armagnacs had begun to wear a characteristic sash, the *bende*. All this made perfect sense on the battlefield, but the decision to force civilians to openly show their allegiance seemed to be further evidence of the increasing madness and desperation of the authorities.

On the Wednesday of Holy Week four hundred English troops deserted their posts in Paris because they had not been paid in months. By Maundy Thursday they were still at Notre-Dame-des-Champs, where they inflicted great damage. On that one day they ate up all the eggs and cheeses they could find, before scavenging other fare. They plundered the church, stealing crosses, chalices and cloths. They then turned their attention to the houses, and 'left no more behind them than a fire does'.[21] Although within three days they would meet their match when Armagnac troops sought them out, when almost all of them were killed.

On Easter Tuesday, about midnight, the rulers of Paris again sent between six and eight hundred English men out of Paris, with instructions to set fire to all the villages, however small, on the Seine between the capital and Pontoise. At St Denis, the English decided to sack the abbey, even to breaking up even the most venerated relics to get at the gold and silver that ornamented their containers. One ruffian, watching a priest saying mass, 'and thinking that it went on too long'[22] leapt forward as the priest held up the sacrament, grabbed the chalice from his hands, and bolted from the church. His comrades then took the cloths off altars along with whatever jewels they could find.

They then rode off to create the desolation ordered by the bishops. But the Lord de L'Isle Adam, who had come out from Pontoise and taken the field, attacked and killed nearly all of these desecrators. L'Isle Adam, once Philippe of Burgundy finally broke his trust with the Lancastrians, also changed sides along with his master, and now chased the English as diligently as he once put the Armagnacs to flight, slaughtering as he followed, from beyond Epinay up to the walls of Paris, even to the St Denis entrance.

As a result of the Burgundian sortie, two hundred English troops, who had been scattered among the villages and had seen what transpired, took refuge in a tower in St Denis, which was called the Velin tower. Hearing that they were holed up there, L'Isle Adam declared that he would not leave until he had them. He detached some of his men for the task of forcing them into the open and then rounding them up, and when they were captured they were killed at once, without any possibility of ransom.

Sir Thomas Beaumont also met his end at this overwhelming rout. He and his troop had been forced to abandon the supplies they were bringing to the relief of Paris, but they had managed to evade the constable's forces on the way. But, now, making a sortie to pillage St Denis and the neighbouring villages, they also came up against L'Isle Adam and were cut to pieces, with the majority of them killed, along with their leader. Only a few remained on the retreat to the capital.[23]

If confirmation was needed that the English cause in their city was doomed, the sight of Beaumont's relief force straggling back to the safety of their walls must have been conclusive evidence for the Parisians. 'Those whose opinions carried weight in Paris were well aware of what had to be done.'[24]

With the final desertion of the Burgundians, the Parisians quickly followed their example. Michel de Laillier, for example, quickly took steps to preserve himself and his family. Careful of his own interests, on Good Friday, 6 April, he found a tenant for his house in Rouen, and in the week after Easter he began to gather the backing of a small group of Burgundian adherents in the Les Halles district, and at the university. Finally, when, on the Friday after Easter, the Lords of the Confederacy appeared before the gates of Paris, he and his fellow conspirators managed to convince a number of other citizens that their best interests lay in submitting to the enemy forces. Many of these citizens then declared that the gates should be opened to the French king's soldiers.[25]

Among the French noblemen leading the massed troops outside the walls of Paris were Arthur of Brittany, the Constable of France, the Bastard of Orléans, and the Lord de L'Isle Adam.[26] At the Porte St Jacques, they sent in a herald with a demand to be let into the city peacefully, threatening that otherwise 'you will all die of famine, of scarcity, or some other death'.[27] The gatekeepers, looking over the wall, saw so many armed men they formed the opinion that they were looking at the whole might of King Charles's army. Frightened by the sight, and fearing an outburst of violence from the citizens now mustering behind them, clamouring for some agreement to be reached, the porters agreed to open the gates.

But even then Paris only surrendered when their fears of a French revenge were declared – and thought – to be groundless. L'Isle Adam declared that the city would remain under the authority of the Duke of Burgundy, whose party they had followed so well over the years, while Richemont had come prepared to quell the fears of the citizens with King Charles's letters of amnesty, sealed with the king's great seal. There were to be none of the repercussions that had followed other surrenders.

The Lord de L'Isle Adam, no stranger to the city under English rule, went in to Paris first, climbing up a long ladder that was let down for him so that he could plant the royal banner of France above the gate. When this was done, he shouted, 'The town is ours!'[28] which seemed a signal for the porters to do the bidding of those massing behind them, and once the gate was opened, the French army swept down through the university district and across the *cité*. The three English-led batallions that had been formed to resist were powerless, reduced as much by the readiness of the Parisians to welcome the conquerors as by the military might that now surged throughout the city's streets.

The news of the admittance of the French spread quickly from one end of Paris to the other and many people very sensibly at once replaced their red crosses with a white upright cross or failing that the one of St Andrew. (Over the past few days any number of entrepreneurial tailors had been busily stitching these new badges of loyalty. Yet even after Richemont unfurled a Burgundian standard upon entering the city, many Parisians were still undecided as to whether they should respond by wearing a Burgundian badge or the upright cross of the French.)

Within a day or so, however, fewer and fewer people appeared with the red cross emblazoned on their clothing, and the English and their supporters became hourly more conspicuous. The Parisian desertion was blatant. When the chancellor was told of how things had turned so drastically against the English cause, he sent word at once to the provost and to Lord Willoughby. But all he could advise was that the few English troops left for the defence of the city, and what remained of their adherents, were to arm themselves as best they could.

On the other hand, the people of Paris took fresh heart, for nothing could be worse than what they had recently endured. Had not the French constable promised amnesty, and would not the Duke of Burgundy help to protect them against unfair reprisals? Michel de Laillier, a financier, who had once underwritten Bedford's campaigns, now played a leading part in opening all the gates of Paris to the former enemy. He and several others armed the people and made for the Porte St Denis. There, they found that some four thousand men had gathered together from the outlying villages and were waiting for admittance to the capital, for the news had quickly spread.

These were men who had long hated the English and their rulers, and they longed to destroy them. Some of them guarded the gate of St Denis,

201

while most of their number went in search of the English and their allies. Meanwhile, the rulers had assembled these troops and formed them into three companies. The first was commanded by Lord Willoughby, the second was under the chancellor and the provost, and the third was led by Jean l'Archier, the provost's lieutenant, 'one of the cruellest Christians in the world . . . a fat villain, round as a barrel'.[29]

The English authorities particularly feared that trouble would start in the area of the Halles so they sent to the provost marshal's contingent there. On the way he met a friend, the merchant Le Vavaseur, who advised him to make his peace with the French, who had by this time advanced some way into the city. It was clear that this was *his* intention, 'Or we shall all be finished.'[30] The provost hit him across the face with the flat of his sword, so that Le Vavaseur fell to his knees, and he was then killed by the other men.

The chancellor and his forces went along the Grande Rue St Denis, and Jean l'Archier took the route along the rue St Martin with his men. None of the three companies had more than two or three hundred armed men or archers, a pitiful number considering the forces that were massed against them, and this not counting the now disillusioned citizens. Nonetheless, they seemed in good spirit. 'St George! St George!' they cried. 'French traitors! We'll kill the lot of you!'[31]

They were, indeed, prepared to kill anyone they met, but they found no one in the streets, except for two luckless householders 'who were killed several times over.'[32]

Their archers shot arrows into windows, in order to dislodge snipers, or just discourage them, but the chains that had been stretched across the streets to bring down horses hampered their movements. Nevertheless they managed to reach the Porte St Denis where they received a warm welcome, 'though not one to their liking.'[33] Seeing the crowds assembled with four cannon placed 'to blow them to hell', the troops fled as fast as they could to the Porte St Anthoine, where they took refuge in the fortress. Others fell back to the Porte Baudoyer in the rue St Anthoine, which was held by the butcher-captain, Jean le Gois. The final retreat for the English was the fortress-prison of the Bastille.[34]

(Simon Morhier alone did not enter the Bastille, but instead managed to escape from Paris. He was, however, turned upon by his followers, who handed him over to a French captain who then exacted a crippling ransom before allowing the former provost marshal to join his fellow exiles in Normandy.)

The constable and his attendants made their way through the streets as calmly as though they had never been out of the city. They had decided against an earlier decision to sack the city and to murder all those who disputed their right to be in command. (Even then Paris was too great and beautiful a metropolis to be despoiled.)

Instead, the newcomers set about providing for the near-starving inhabitants, although those who drove the carts had plans of their own. A hundred and more wagons brought much needed corn and other commodities into the city, and it was agreed among the benefactors that they would first sell off the contents of the carts to the wretched citizens and then fill up the empty space with loot.

But the Parisians were flocking into the churches, to give thanks to God for their 'deliverance', and when it was realised that it had been the decision of the people to let them in without further conflict, the constable decided against punishing the majority, as had been planned. Instead, he thanked them in the name of their 'true' king, Charles VII, for having returned the 'chief of the kingdom's cities' so peacefully to him. He forgave anyone of any rank, 'present or absent', who had done any wrong to 'our lord the King'.[35]

He had trumpets sounded, and a proclamation was read out forbidding his troops 'on pain of hanging by the neck' to take lodging in any citizen's house against that householder's will. Hanging would also be the penalty for insulting or robbing any person of any rank, 'except the natives of England and their mercenaries'.[36]

The Parisians reacted to this with great relief and before the day was out they were happily rooting out their former occupiers. All who were found were held to ransom and their property seized. Certain householders who had fled with the chancellor into the Porte St Anthoine were also stripped of their belongings. But there was an astonishing lack of reprisals against the occupying force. Nobody of any rank, or whatever his native language, or his known crimes against King Charles, was killed for it.

On the day after the entry, such a quantity of goods came into Paris that corn was selling for half the price that had formerly been asked for it. The old market in front of the Madeleine church, shut for twenty years, was now re-opened, and the corn was sold from there. The price of all food-stuffs dropped as dramatically.[37]

The men who had taken refuge in the Porte St Anthoine now found themselves on the edge of starvation, and so they negotiated with the constable, making a bargain with him that, for a sizeable sum, they would be granted a safe conduct out of Paris into English-held territory. Because of an acute shortage of money, Richemont decided to avoid a siege, and as he wished to make a clean break between the old order and the new, he also allowed those inside the Bastille to buy their way out.

Their safe conducts guaranteed, they made their exodus on Tuesday 17 April 1436, pursued by the taunts of the Parisians. 'No one was ever jeered or booed as they were, especially the chancellor, the provost's lieutenant, and the master of the Butchers, who had been King Henry's treasurer.[38] Most Parisians recognised that, for an occupying power, the English had been relatively amiable, and their garrison was allowed to depart with no great molestation, although their departure was described as being 'amid the [catcalls] of the burgesses who had once hailed it with delight'. The most notable of the deportees was Louis of Luxembourg, the chancellor, accompanied by Jean de Saint-Yon and Jean L'Archier, the Lieutenant of Criminal Affairs.[39]

Another solemn procession was made on the following Sunday. It rained very hard that day, throughout the whole time the ceremony lasted, for over four hours there and back. The Lords of Ste Geneviève went barefoot, carrying the effigies of their patron saint and also that of St Marcel, and they found it hard to keep their footing on the slippery paving stones. All who took part were soaked to the skin, looking as though 'they had been thrown into the Seine'.[40] The rain mingled with sweat on their faces, and everybody who took part was worn out and exhausted. Yet not one of them seemed disheartened, but rather exhilarated. For Paris was free of the English, whom the citizens had grown to fear and hate as much as once they had feared and hated their new occupiers – the tools of King Charles VII, the Armagnacs. But it was also recalled – too late – that Charles himself had no reason to love them.

NOTES

1   Bibliothèque Nationale.
2   Fauquembergue, *Journal*.
3   Bourgeois de Paris. In 1432 Vincennes had been occupied briefly by the Armagnacs before being taken back into English control.
4   Ibid.
5   Ibid.
6   Ibid.
7   *Archives Nationales*.
8   Bourgeois de Paris.
9   Bibliothèque Nationale.
10 Ibid.
11 Chartier, *Chronique de Charles VII*.
12 Pontoise was lost to the English on 20 February. Beaucourt, *Histoire de Charles VI*.
13 *Archives Nationales*.
14 Ibid.
15 Beaucourt, op. cit.
16 *Archives Nationales*.
17 Guillaume Gruel, scribe to the Constable of France. He also campaigned under him.
18 Bourgeois de Paris.
19 Ibid.
20 Ibid.
21 Ibid.
22 Ibid.
23 Monstrelet, *Chronique*.
24 Bourgeois de Paris.

25 Monstrelet, op. cit.
26 On 13 April 1436.
27 Bourgeois de Paris.
28 Ibid.
29 Monstrelet, op. cit.
30 Bourgeois de Paris.
31 Ibid.
32 Ibid.
33 Ibid.
34 Monstrelet, op. cit.
35 Ibid.
36 Ibid.
37 Bourgeois de Paris.
38 Monstrelet, op. cit.
39 He had held the post from 1418.
40 Bourgeois de Paris.

Epilogue

The English cause in Paris now seemed lost, but they continued to fight in France, in a strong bid to retain Normandy at least. But they would make one more attempt to retake their most fabulous possession, and within a year of their quitting the capital they were back at its gates, after they had unexpectedly recovered Pontoise.

Pontoise is on the direct road from Rouen to Paris from the north, and it was a military fortress of the first order. Its castle dominated the bridge over the Oise river, and this was a formidable obstacle, well stocked with military stores and well garrisoned. Yet on 12 February 1437 Lord Talbot made a sudden attack upon this citadel. The weather was so hard that the river was frozen over, and it was later said that Talbot crossed over the ice, disguising an advance force as villagers from the outlying countryside, carrying hampers and baskets of produce, as if on their way to market. He also camouflaged his scaling party in white, in order to conceal them as they approached the town walls at daybreak, a stratagem that proved completely successful, for the men were able to scale the walls and enter the town without attracting attention. There they were met by their comrades who had quietly taken up their positions during the night, after first disarming the guards. Now, they opened the gates to the remainder of the English troops.

The first the sleeping French knew that their town had been taken from them within the space of an hour was the great shout raised by the storming troops, 'The town is ours! Saint George! Talbot!'[1] With the result that L'Isle Adam and his men fled from the town without striking a blow, leaving all their belongings and an immense quantity of military stores behind. And in this way the gateway to Paris was captured with no real losses.

Encouraged by this triumph, Talbot – 'this valiant English chevalier' – at once decided upon making use of the 'gateway'.[2] Despite having only a minimal force under his command, he resolved upon attacking Paris, arguing that the city could be retaken by using the same elements of daring and surprise. Later, this would seem to many to have been a mere act of bravado, or even desperation; the English fighting men had been

207

deeply mortified by the surrender of Paris to soldiers whom they considered to be their inferiors.

Who can divine Lord John's motives in attacking Paris? He was a man more proficient with the sword than the pen, and he left no record of his thoughts at the outset of his campaign.[3] His intentions, perhaps, can only be understood by his actions. But whatever his object, his splendidly audacious move had an astonishing initial success. With only a handful of men he penetrated right up to the walls of the capital, crossing the frozen moat, and setting up the machinery to climb the walls. But the task proved to be beyond their limited powers. Their efforts were met by a powerful response from the Armagnac defenders. Assailed by powerful artillery, backed up by a flurry of arrows from crossbow shafts, they were forced away from the walls, and were compelled to abandon the enterprise.

The English troops fell back in good order to their bastion of Pontoise, and they were also surprisingly in good heart. It must have seemed to them, after such a near success, whilst using such a small force, that all it would take to re-conquer Paris would be a larger army. But this army never materialised, and Paris remained under the control of the much-feared Armagnacs.[4]

Yet it was not until eighteen months after the English had abandoned Paris that King Charles VII considered it safe to travel to his capital. On 12 November 1437 he entered the city, to the acclamation of his new subjects. But three weeks later he left it again for the safety of his beloved Loire country. Even so Paris had reclaimed its position, after sixteen years of occupation, as the capital of France.

The English continued the struggle until 1444, when they sought a truce with France. Henry's government was so desperate for peace they arranged to marry him off to a French princess, Margaret of Anjou, in hope of a two-year moratorium. But even this marriage, and the surrender of Maine did not secure peace, and mile by mile the English were forced to relinquish the last of their continental provinces. The French had tasted success and wished for a 'final' and crushing victory, but the English still displaying an astonishing arrogance, refused to make reparation during a short treaty, with the result that, after a crushing defeat at Formigny they lost their greatest possession, Normandy.[5] Beaten at Castillon they surrendered Guyenne. In time, they were 'driven from the whole of France', with the exception of Calais. The Lilies of France at last claimed victory over the Red Roses of England.

Much of the credit must go to Charles VII, who at last faced up to his rights and duties; the lethargic dauphin becoming a vigorous king. He unified his realm without upsetting the privileges of his nobles or unsettling the bourgeoisie, and he reformed his finances by establishing a single annual budget and a permanent system of taxation. Strengthened by these regular reserves, he recruited and maintained a standing army, and with such an army the monarchy at last had a weapon which could be relied upon to bring it victory. Under Charles and his successors, English claims to the throne of France would remain vainglorious posturing. The Kings of France would remain purely French, and the city of Paris – so highly prized by the English – would once again become their sole capital.

NOTES

1   Monstrelet, *Chronique*.
2   De Maupoint, *Journal*.
3   There are, surprisingly, no contemporary English accounts of these events.
4   In an uneasy liaison with the Burgundians.
5   Burne, *The Agincourt War*.

Bibliography

Allmand, C T, *100 Years War*, Cambridge, 1988
____ *Lancastrian Normandy*, Oxford BLitt thesis, 1958, unpublished
Archives Nationales
Armstrong, C A J, *La Double Monarchie*, Studies in Medieval History, Oxford, 1948
Autrand, F, *Charles VI*, Paris, 1986
Ayroles, J B J, *La Vraie Jeanne d'Arc*, 5 vols, Paris, 1890–1902
Basin, Thomas, *Histoire du Règne de Charles VII* (ed. J Quicherat), Société de l'Histoire de France, Paris, 1855
Beaucourt, Gaston, *Histoire de Charles VI*, Paris, 1881–9
Bourgeois de Paris, *Journal* (ed. J Quicherat), Société de l'Histoire de France, Paris, 1841–9
Bournon, *Chroniques* (ed. F D de Mory d'Elvange), Nancy, 1838
Brie, E W D (ed.), *The Brut, or the Chronicles of England*, London, 1906
Burne, A H, *The Agincourt War*, London, 1956
Burney, E M, *The English Rule in Normandy*, Oxford BLitt thesis, 1958, unpublished
Cambridge Economic History
Champion, Pierre, *Splendeurs et Misères de Paris*, Paris, 1906
____ *Jeanne d'Arc*, Paris, 1933
Champollion-Figeac, *Lettres des Rois*, 12 vols, Paris, 1839–47
Chartier, Jean, *Les Chroniques de Charles VII*, 3 vols, Paris, 1858
Chastellain, Georges, *Oeuvres* (ed. K de Lettenhove), Académie royale de Belge, 1863–6
Cousinot, Guillaume, *Chronique de la Pucelle* (ed. Vallet de Viriville), Paris, 1859
Delisle, L P, *Le Cabinet de Manuscripts de la Bibliothèque Nationale*, 4 vols, Paris, 1866
Delpit, Jules, *Collection générale des documents français*, Paris, 1867
de Maupoint, *Journal parisien (1437–1469)*, Bibliothèque Nationale College Garnier, 1878
Dickinson, J G, *The Congress of Arras,1435*, Oxford, 1955
Dictionary of National Biography, Oxford, 1917

Fauquembergue, C, *Journal 1417–30* (ed. Tuetey), 3 vols, Paris, 1903–15

Favier, J, *Les contribuables parisiens*, Geneva, 1970

Ferguson, J, *English Diplomacy, 1442–1446*, Oxford, 1972

Garsonnin, M, *Le Guet et les Compagnies*, Orléans, 1898

Glasson, *Châtelet: Abuses of Procedure*, Paris, 1893

Gregory, William, *Chronicle 1189–1467* (ed. James Gairdner), Historical Collections of a Citizen of London, Camden Society, 1879

Griffiths, R A, *The Reign of Henry VI*, London, 1981

Gruel, G, *Chronique d'Arthur de Richemont* (ed. A le Vasseur), Paris, 1890

Holland-Smith, John, *Joan of Arc*, London, 1973

Holmes, G A, 'Cardinal Beaufort', *English Historical Review*, 1973

Hutchinson, H F, *Henry V*, London, 1967

Juvenal des Ursins, *Histoire de Charles VII*, Paris, 1653

Kingsford, C L, *Chronicles of London*, Oxford, 1905

Lang, A, *The Maid of France* (4th edn), London, 1922

le Fèvre, Jean, *Chronique*, Paris, 1876

Lewis, P S, 'Later Medieval France', *The Historical Journal*, 1958

Longnon, Auguste, *Documents parisiens*, Paris, 1978

Lot, Ferdinand, *L'Art Militaire et les armées au moyen age*, Paris, 1946

Lucie-Smith, Edward, *Joan of Arc*, London, 1976

McKenna, J W, 'Henry VI of England', *Journal of the Warburg and Courtauld Institute*, XXVIII, 1965

Metz, Guilbert de, *Description de Paris*, Paris, 1867

Molandon, *L'Armée anglaise*, Orléans, 1867

Monstrelet, Enguerrand de, *La Cronique de Monstrelet* (trans. Thomas Johne), London, 1840

Morosini, Antoine, *Chronique* (trans. & ed. L Dorez), Paris 1898–1902

Newhall, R A, *The English Conquest of Normandy*, Newhaven, CT, 1924

Perroy, Eduard, *The Hundred Years War* (trans. W B Wells), New York, 1951

Quicherat, Jules, *Chronique*, Société de l'Histoire de France, Paris, 1841–9

Rowe, B J H, *The Grand Conseil*, Oxford Essays in Medieval History, Oxford, 1934

Rymer, T (ed.), *Feodora Concentiones Litterae . . . et Acta Publica*, 20 vols, London, 1704–35

Sauval, H, *Histoire et recherches*, 3 vols, Paris, 1724

Shirley, Janet, *A Parisian Journal*, Oxford, 1968

Steel, A B, *The Receipt of the Exchequer*, Cambridge, 1954

Stevenson, J (ed.), *Wars of the English during the reign of Henry VI. Letters and Papers*, Royal Society, London, 1861–4

Strachey, J et al, *Rotuli Parliamentorum*, 1767–7

Stratford Ms, British Library

Thompson, G Ll, *Paris and its People under English Rule*, Oxford, 1991

Tuetey (ed.), *Bourgeois de Paris; his Journal*, Paris, 1881

Vale, M G A, *Charles VII*, Berkeley CA, 1974

____ *War and Chivalry*, London, 1981

Vaughan, Richard, *Philip the Good*, London, 1970

Vidier, *Comptes du domain de la ville de Paris*, 1948

Waurin, Jean de, *Anchiennes Chroniques d'Angleterre* (ed. E Dupont), Paris, 1858–63

Williams, E C, *My Lord of Bedford*, London, 1963

Wolffe, B P, *Henry VI*, Newhaven CT, 2001

Wyllie, J H and Waugh, W T, *The Reign of Henry V*, Cambridge, 1929

Index

215